BRINGING WORDS TO LIFE

Also from Isabel L. Beck, Margaret G. McKeown, and Linda Kucan

Creating Robust Vocabulary:
Frequently Asked Questions and Extended Examples
Isabel L. Beck, Margaret G. McKeown, and Linda Kucan

Making Sense of Phonics:
The Hows and Whys
Isabel L. Beck

Bringing Reading Research to Life
Edited by Margaret G. McKeown and Linda Kucan

Bringing Words to Life

Robust Vocabulary Instruction

SECOND EDITION

Isabel L. Beck
Margaret G. McKeown
Linda Kucan

THE GUILFORD PRESS
New York   London

© 2013 The Guilford Press
A Division of Guilford Publications, Inc.
370 Seventh Avenue, Suite 1200, New York, NY 10001
www.guilford.com

Printed in the United States of America

This book is printed on acid-free paper.

Last digit is print number: 9   8   7   6   5   4

Library of Congress Cataloging-in-Publication Data

Beck, Isabel L.
    Bringing words to life : robust vocabulary instruction / Isabel L. Beck,
Margaret G. McKeown, Linda Kucan.—2nd ed.
        p. cm.
    Includes bibliographical references and index.
    ISBN 978-1-4625-0816-7 (pbk.)—ISBN 978-1-4625-0824-2 (hardcover)
    1. Vocabulary—Study and teaching.   I. McKeown, Margaret G.
II. Kucan, Linda.   III. Title.
    LB1574.5.B43 2013
    372.44—dc23

                                                                2012030160

About the Authors

Isabel L. Beck, PhD, is Professor Emerita of Education in the School of Education at the University of Pittsburgh. She has conducted research and published widely in the areas of decoding, vocabulary, and comprehension. Her contributions have been acknowledged by awards from the International Reading Association, the National Reading Conference. and the American Federation of Teachers. Most recently she was elected to the National Academy of Education.

Margaret G. McKeown, PhD, is Clinical Professor of Education in the School of Education and a Senior Scientist at the Learning Research and Development Center, both at the University of Pittsburgh. Her research on reading comprehension and vocabulary has been published extensively in outlets for both researcher and practitioner audiences. Dr. McKeown is a recipient of the Dissertation of the Year Award from the International Reading Association and a National Academy of Education Spencer Fellowship. Before her career in research, she taught elementary school.

Linda Kucan, PhD, is Associate Professor in the Department of Instruction and Learning at the University of Pittsburgh School of Education. In addition to vocabulary instruction, her research includes work related to classroom talk about texts and motivating tasks to support comprehension of text. Dr. Kucan has published her work in both scholarly and practitioner-oriented outlets. She is coauthor with Annemarie Palincsar of *Comprehension Instruction Through Text-Based Discussion*, a book and DVD set.

Preface

Our editor called us more than a year ago to point out that *Bringing Words to Life* (BWTL) would soon be 10 years old. We suspected that he was telling us this because on several occasions he had hinted that it would soon be time for a second edition. Each of us had different thoughts about the potential request.

Isabel Beck mused that when her 9-year-old grandchild turned 10, the family "wouldn't be thinking of a second edition." Linda Kucan's thoughts left no question of where she stood: "My students love the book. Why mess around with something that's working?" Margaret McKeown's reaction was: "Ten years old? I have cheese in my refrigerator older than that!"

Another phone call from our editor confirmed what we had suspected. He wanted a second edition. This time, our thoughts were virtually identical. No. Of course we were more considerate than that, and voiced our hesitations: no time, not on any of our agendas, and mostly we didn't know why a second edition was needed. Our editor astutely told us that a second edition wasn't like writing a whole new book. Moreover, he made the point that he was not in any hurry and just hoped we would take some time to think about it.

For a while, none of us gave our editor's request any thought. However, eventually one of us pointed out to the others that it really wasn't fair. After all, we had said we would think about it. So we met as a group and decided to go through several chapters in order to evaluate them, that is, think about what we might change, eliminate, or add in the future to a new edition that we *might* want to do at the right time, but not now.

So we started with Chapter 1 and did a kind of two-step: skim a chapter and talk about it, skim a chapter and talk about it; more talking than skimming. And as we went along we found things that we might change, *if* we were doing a new edition of the book, which, of course, we were not. One of us mentioned that we were making some important points and offering some good ideas, and another said she would take good notes for a future edition.

In Chapter 1, we were concerned that we had not offered more about learning words from context, especially when the Common Core State Standards have emphasized that. We thought that the nature of robust vocabulary instruction should be elaborated, since it was the keystone of the first BWTL and remains the keystone of our continuing research. As such, we wanted readers who were not familiar with robust vocabulary instruction to leave Chapter 1 knowing a little more about it than we had originally offered. Moreover, we talked about theory that was not available at the time of the first edition and that we certainly would want to include in a second edition. We also saw that too little information had been given directly about our three-tier framework and, were we planning a new edition, which we were not, we would make the discussion of tiers more prominent.

Our summary of Chapter 1 was that the topics we had covered were appropriate, a few needed to be elaborated, and there was a better way to organize it. And with that each one of us would have been happy to get our hands into Chapter 1, but our lives were such that we just could not.

We sampled several other chapters and saw lesser or greater things that should be included, elaborated, better explained, and the like. All of our discussion interested us; we were getting tempted, but we didn't want to act too rashly—that is, call our editor and say "yes." When, however, we began talking about what topics were missing—vocabulary and writing, struggling readers, English learners—that was it. We knew that we *had* to write a second edition. And so we called our editor and said "yes!" This second edition is the consequence of that "yes."

Let us tell you concretely, albeit briefly, about what you will find in the new BWTL. Returning to Chapter 1, we fixed what we indicated above needed to be fixed. How much did we fix? One way to respond is to note that Chapter 1 in the first BWTL was 5,775 words. In the new edition, it is 7,481 words. What those numbers don't address is the rewriting or editing of portions of the first BWTL that we kept, and the reorganization of the chapter. Based on these developments, we can say that substantial changes were made to Chapter 1.

Now to what you will find in Chapter 2 of this edition of BWTL. Chapter 2 in the first edition began with a fundamental question: What words, or what kinds of words, are important to teach? In the first BWTL we provided criteria for selecting Tier Two words for instruction and illustrated the criteria through a number of examples. That content remains. In this new edition, however, a great deal more was added. First, since the earlier edition of BWTL, other scholars have provided input, in addition to our tiered framework, on the kinds of words best targeted for instruction. We include discussion of those approaches. Additionally, we take on the predicament that teachers of intermediate grades face when their curricular resources include vocabulary for science, social studies, math, spelling, and reading by discussing the role each set of words plays in the specific subject matter. The new version of Chapter 2 is almost twice as long as the first version: 4,732 to 8,391 words.

In Chapter 3 of the first BWTL, we dealt with introducing the meaning of new words. We raised issues about relying on dictionary definitions and proposed that a better way to introduce words is to think about explaining a word's meaning rather than providing a definition. All that remains, albeit with some rewriting. Additionally, we introduce two important matters associated with word meaning: multiple meanings and core meaning. We suggest when it is appropriate to include multiple meanings with the introduction of a new word, and when it would be best not to include multiple meanings yet. We also bring up the idea of multiple senses of a word, for example, a *distinction* between two things, in contrast to doing something with *distinction*. The new Chapter 3 is about 1,000 words longer than the earlier one: 4,894 to 5,750.

The current Chapter 4, which deals with robust instruction for young children, starts with a new section that was not available at the time of BWTL's first publication—several empirical research studies that looked at the effects of robust instruction on young students' knowledge and use of Tier Two words. The rest of the chapter deals with the details of robust instruction: introducing target words and following up with those words for several days beyond their introduction for young learners. After the publication of BWTL, we heard from teachers that they loved the examples, but wanted more. Thus, this chapter is now rich with examples. The chapter is more than 2,000 words longer than the earlier version: 7,219 to 9,298.

Chapter 5 is parallel to Chapter 4 in that it's about developing activities for students, but the focus is on students from the intermediate grades through high school. The main new material in this chapter deals more extensively with how vocabulary work can derive from novels. Toward that end, we include examples from a new novel targeted to intermediate-grade students, *Dead End in Norvelt* by Jack Gantos (2011), the 2012 Newbery Award Winner. The new Chapter 5 is the only chapter that is shorter than the original: reduced to 6,953 from 8,888 words.

The reason for this is that we did some reorganization of Chapters 4 and 5, which involved developing a new Chapter 6, "Assessing and

Maintaining New Vocabulary." In our evaluations of the original book, we recognized that there were just a few mentions of assessment. We realized that because assessment is the final part of an instructional sequence, more material and greater organization of material needed to be provided. Thus, the new Chapter 6 starts with a section on assessment.

We view the umbrella structure of robust instruction as comprising four sections: introduction, follow-up, assessment, and maintenance. The first three sections, for the most part, occur in the classroom, but the maintenance section is mostly targeted at ways to move new words into life beyond school—home, sports, neighborhood, even TV and the like. Thus, the second section of Chapter 6 is about maintaining words. We have devoted 5,062 words to the new Chapter 6.

With the addition of Chapter 6, chapter numbers no longer have a one-to-one correspondence between the two BWTL editions. The original Chapter 6, "Making the Most of Natural Contexts" is now Chapter 7, under the new title "Working with Instructional and Natural Contexts." A major new section in our context chapter is the introduction and discussion of Robust Academic Vocabulary Encounters (RAVE). RAVE is an ongoing research and development project in which we attempt to teach vocabulary from Coxhead's (1998) *Academic Word List* (AWL) in the context of short informational pieces, which we drew from Internet-based resources such as journals, national newspapers, and professional blogs. These authentic contexts serve as a starting point for discussing what a word means and how it is used within different contexts. Chapter 7 in this second edition of BWTL is 7,710 words, compared to 4,284 in the first edition.

Chapter 8, "Vocabulary and Writing," is new. The chapter points to the similarity of the mental processes in reading and writing. Concern about the lack of research on the impact of vocabulary knowledge on writing is put forth. Two projects that bear on the relationship of vocabulary to writing are presented. One incorporates some unique ways of targeting vocabulary toward improving writing. The other is a research study that compares the writing of one group of students who were taught words through robust vocabulary instruction with the writing of another group who were taught through traditional approaches. Chapter 8 has 5,228 new words.

Chapter 9, "Differentiating Vocabulary Instruction," tackles topics that did not appear in the original BWTL: response to intervention (RTI) and English learners (ELs). RTI is a model for supporting struggling readers beyond their core reading instruction. Students who are having difficulty are provided with small-group instruction, and those who are seriously at risk are provided with one-on-one instruction. We chose this model for supporting those in need because RTI has been implemented in many areas and there are some empirical data that suggest positive findings. Toward providing as practical suggestions as possible, we use the standard RAVE lesson (see Chapter 7) and adapt and enhance it for use with RTI students. The other half of Chapter 9 is targeted to ELs. Providing effective English instruction for ELs is enormously important as more and more EL children enroll in school. Again, toward providing concrete instructional help to teachers, we further adapt the RTI RAVE lesson for EL students. This new chapter is 7,140 words.

Chapter 10, " Energizing the Verbal Environment," is our final chapter and covers the same topics as Chapter 7 in the first edition. Although the focus is the same—creating conditions in which students become interested in and aware of words—we have included many new books and poems as classroom resources. The word count for each chapter is virtually the same: 3,667 for the original chapter and 3,392 for the current chapter.

Writing this book has been an adventure we didn't originally want to take, but an adventure we *had* to take. We started planning the words in this book the day after we said "yes" to our editor. It is our fervent hope that this second edition enriches our original readers' views of vocabulary instruction, and presents to our new readers a fuller understanding of the importance and joyfulness of interest in words.

Contents

CHAPTER 1

Rationale for
Robust Vocabulary Instruction

As we start this book, we reflect for a moment on the roles vocabulary plays in people's lives. A rich vocabulary supports learning about the world, encountering new ideas, enjoying the beauty of language. A rich vocabulary enhances an interview, allows one to see the humor in wordplay, shores up what an individual wants to say, and, especially, wants to write. It is clear that a large and rich vocabulary is the hallmark of an educated individual. Indeed, a large vocabulary repertoire facilitates becoming an educated person to the extent that vocabulary knowledge is strongly related to reading proficiency in particular and school achievement in general.

There is much evidence—strong correlations, several causal studies, as well as rich theoretical orientations—that shows that vocabulary is tightly related to reading comprehension across the age span: in primary grades (Baker, Simmons, & Kame'enui, 1998), in the intermediate grades (Beck, Perfetti, & McKeown, 1982), in high school (Cunningham & Stanovich, 1997), and with adults (Smith, 1941). According to Perfetti and Adolf (2012), " . . . for any encounter with a given test, it is the quality of the reader's word knowledge (form as well as meaning) for the words in that text that is crucial to comprehension" (p. 14).

The practical problem is that there are profound differences in vocabulary knowledge among learners from different ability or socioeconomic (SES) groups from toddlers to adults. Consider that:

- By age 3, there is strong evidence of a gap in vocabulary knowledge for children of different SES groups (Hart & Risley, 1995).

1

When children enter school the gap continues:

- In kindergarten, sizable differences are found between students (of varying SES) in the number of words known (Baker et al., 1998).
- First-grade children from higher SES groups know about twice as many words as children from lower SES groups (Graves, Brunetti, & Slater, 1982; Graves & Slater, 1987).
- First-grade vocabulary predicted students' reading achievement in their junior year in high school (Cunningham & Stanovich, 1997).
- High-knowledge third graders had vocabularies about equal to lowest-performing 12th graders (Smith, 1941).
- Once established, differences in vocabulary knowledge remain (Biemiller, 2001; Hart & Risley, 1995; Juel, Biancarosa, Coker, & Deffes, 2003).

Evidence of how strongly students' word trajectories are set early in their school careers is bad news indeed! But a hopeful spin can be put on the bad news by considering the status of vocabulary instruction in the schools. The fact that early differences in vocabulary remain through the school years is understandable if little has been done to change that situation during the school years. So perhaps it is not so much the case that those differences cannot be changed but rather that little has been done to focus on making them change.

A decade ago the available evidence indicated that there was little emphasis on the acquisition of vocabulary in school curricula (Biemiller, 2001; Scott, Jamieson, & Asselin, 1998; Watts, 1995). So, given the evidence, in the first edition of *Bringing Words to Life: Robust Vocabulary Instruction* (Beck, McKeown, & Kucan, 2002), we summed up vocabulary instruction in the schools as "there isn't much." As to nature of the instruction, at the time of the first edition, our review of the early commercial basal readers in the early 2000s, revealed approaches to vocabulary instruction in the form of traditional dictionary definitions and short exercises, such as a cloze paragraph or matching words with definitions or synonyms. Those of us who taught inservice teachers saw that those were exactly the approaches that teachers initially took when asked to develop vocabulary lessons for class assignments.

Now, a decade later, we need to ask whether those characterizations of classroom vocabulary instruction still hold. Two sources can shed some light on the issue: first, descriptions of vocabulary instruction presented in commercial basal materials published after 2008/2009, and second, studies that describe current classroom vocabulary instruction.

As to the nature of vocabulary instruction in current basals, we have seen a little change in how several of the newer basals provide vocabulary instruction. In some basals, we saw more thoughtful selection of sets of words targeted for instruction. One basal, for sure, and at least one other basal, kind of, provided student-friendly definitions. Occasionally, we saw some follow-up activities that seemed to have a little verve. In one basal we saw a week's words maintained across the week's lessons and brought up in subsequent lessons, neither of which was found in earlier basals. But in other basals we did not find such features, let alone anything that suggested that vocabulary research had undergirded instruction.

Turning to the second source of information about classroom instruction, over the 10 years since *Bringing Words to Life* was first published, several investigators have dealt with research about what classroom vocabulary instruction is like, and each has concluded that instruction was wanting (Blachowicz & Fisher, 2006; Walsh, 2003). Blachowicz, Fisher, Ogle, and Watts-Taffe's (2006) summary about classroom vocabulary practices documents "less-than-robust classroom practice" (p. 524).

In contrast, it was—and is—our position that the operative principle for vocabulary instruction is that it be robust: vigorous, strong, and powerful in effect. A robust approach to vocabulary involves directly explaining the meanings of words along with thought-provoking, playful, and interactive follow-up.* The findings of studies that examined robust instruction has shown it to be effective, not only for learning the meanings of words but also for affecting reading comprehension (Beck et al., 1982; McKeown, Beck, Omanson, & Perfetti, 1983; McKeown, Beck, Omanson, & Pople, 1985).

When *Bringing Words to Life* was first published, virtually all the research that was available was directed toward older students, including the studies we had conducted. Nevertheless, even with the absence of empirical research about the effects of robust instruction on young children's knowledge of sophisticated words, it was with some confidence that we passed along the details of robust instruction to teachers in the primary grades.

Where did that confidence come from? We were able to include in the first edition of *Bringing Words to Life* some discussion of vocabulary instruction for young children, as we were in the midst of a set of studies involving kindergarten and first-grade children in robust vocabulary. We have now completed three studies, all of which confirmed the viability and potential for teaching young students sophisticated words. We discuss this work in

---

*We initially called our vocabulary instruction "rich"; we changed the label to "robust" with the publication in 2002 of the first edition of *Bringing Words to Life*. In articles and chapters published before 2002, the original works use the "rich" label. However, in this book we will use the newer label "robust" throughout, since it is the more recent label. No matter the label, the kind of instruction is the same.

Chapter 4, but to offer an appetizer of sorts—we provide some examples of kindergartners using sophisticated words in the classroom.

These examples from kindergartners, brought to us at a national meeting by an excited director of literacy, were taught the words *nuisance, concentrate, reluctant, intimidated, drenched,* and *glanced* through robust instruction. Teachers reported comments such as "He's being a nuisance" and "I can't concentrate." And when several target words were posted, children wrote sentences such as "I was reluctant to ride my bike," "I was intimidated win I went to a new school," "I was drenched becuz I got vre wet," and "I glanced at a car It is pnk an blu."

Our research with implementing robust vocabulary instruction in a variety of classrooms supports our emphasis on the importance of instruction. This is in contrast to an approach to vocabulary development that focuses on learning words from context, which we address in the following sections.

THE ROLE OF CONTEXT IN THE ACQUISITION
OF VOCABULARY KNOWLEDGE

The word *context* is prevalent in both research and practice. In the vocabulary instructional world, context can mean one of two conditions. There are **instructional contexts**, which are intentionally written to support figuring out an unfamiliar word's likely meaning. The other notion of context is connected to learning new words in the course of reading **naturally occurring text**. From at least the beginning of the 20th century, educational researchers no less prominent than Thorndike associated learning from context via "wide reading" as *the* way that vocabulary was learned. The importance of wide reading to vocabulary development is supported by more current researchers (Anderson, Wilson, & Fielding, 1988; Nagy & Herman, 1985) with the logical follow-up that vocabulary instruction should focus on students learning words from context. Few would disagree that wide reading is a major way people learn words, nor would they argue against the need for schools to support wide reading.

To understand the requirements and limitations of learning words from context in the course of independent reading, we consider several assumptions that underlie this view of vocabulary acquisition. First, it is the case that words *are* learned from context. Second, instruction must focus on learning vocabulary from context because there are just too many words to teach to get the job done through direct instruction. Closely related is the question of how and why certain words are targeted for instruction. Let us examine these issues.

Words *Are* Learned from Context, but . . .

It is indeed true that words are learned from context, but in the course of an individual's development the type of context changes. Early word learning takes place through oral contexts, and oral environments play a role forever, but under most conditions they begin to play a lesser role. Most of the words children customarily encounter in oral language beyond their earliest years, both at home and in school, are words that they already know. Thus, the source of later vocabulary learning shifts to written contexts—what children read. The problem is that it is not so easy to learn word meanings from written context. Written context lacks many of the features of oral language that support learning new word meanings, such as intonation, body language, and shared physical surroundings. As such, written language is a far less effective vehicle for learning new words than oral language.

In terms of learning new words in the course of reading, research shows that it does occur, but in small increments. That is, by no means will all the unfamiliar words encountered in reading be learned, and those that are learned will require multiple encounters with them before learning is accomplished. Studies estimate that of 100 unfamiliar words met in reading, between 5 and 15 of them will be learned (Nagy, Herman, & Anderson, 1985; Swanborn & de Glopper, 1999). However, in order for any word learning to occur from reading, two conditions need to be met. First, students must read widely enough to encounter a substantial number of unfamiliar words; that means they must read enough text to encounter lots of words and they must read text of sufficient difficulty to include words that are not already familiar. Second, students must have the skills to infer word meaning information from the contexts they read. The problem is that many students in need of vocabulary development do not engage in wide reading, especially of the kinds of books that contain unfamiliar vocabulary, and these students are less able to derive meaningful information from the context (McKeown, 1985). Thus, calculations of how many words are learned from reading overestimate what occurs for many students.

The Nature of Naturally Occurring Text

Another problematic issue about relying on contexts is that many natural contexts are not all that informative for deriving word meanings. This is because an author's purpose is to tell a story or explain a phenomenon, not to convey the meaning of a set of words. Toward getting a handle on the kinds of contexts found in natural texts, a number of years ago we examined the story contexts for several sets of target words (i.e., words that were targeted to be learned from context) in two basal reading programs (Beck,

McKeown, & McCaslin, 1983). From our examination of the contexts from which the target words were to be learned, we speculated that their effectiveness in determining word meaning would fall along a continuum. Along the continuum, we identified four kinds of categories of natural contexts. Below is a description of the four categories, including an example of each that was created to typify those found in the basal programs we examined.

At one end of our continuum are **misdirective contexts**, those contexts that rather than revealing the meaning of the target word, seem to direct the student to an incorrect meaning. For example:

> Gregory had done all he could to complete the task. When Horace approached his cousin he could see that Gregory was exhausted. Smiling broadly, Horace said, "You know there are *dire* results for your attempt."

Here the context would likely lead a reader to ascribe a positive connotation to *dire*. The description of Horace as "smiling broadly" might encourage one to believe that Gregory was going to receive good things. And the statement, "You know there are dire results for your attempt" does not preclude thinking that dire refers to something desirable. But such contexts do not make word meaning transparent.

Problems dealing with misdirective contexts are not confined to written contexts nor are they confined to children. Elizabeth Fasulo, a literacy coach from Montgomery County, Maryland, upon rereading *Charlotte's Web* (White, 1952, p. 162) e-mailed us an "enchanting example of a misdirective context." It's from the following dialogue between Wilbur and Charlotte:

> "It's time I made an egg sac and filled it with eggs."
> "I didn't know you could lay eggs," said Wilbur in amazement.
> "Oh sure," said the spider, "I'm versatile."
> "What does versatile mean? Full of eggs?" asked Wilbur.
> "Certainly not," said Charlotte.

This example represents the problematic nature of initial encounters with words for young students (and little pigs). Thus, incorrect conclusions about word meaning are likely to be drawn. We hasten to point out that contexts such as the one above are not in themselves wrong, or a misuse of language. The words used communicate the ideas well—if one knows the meanings of the words. But such contexts do not make word meaning transparent. Thus, it is easy to draw incorrect conclusions about word meaning.

Next along the continuum of contexts are **nondirective contexts**, which seem to be of no assistance in directing the reader toward any particular meaning for a word. For example:

Dan heard the door open and wondered who had arrived. He couldn't make out the voices. Then he recognized the lumbering footsteps on the stairs and knew it was Aunt Grace.

In this example, *lumbering* has any number of inferrable associations: *light, lively, familiar,* and *heavy* would all fit the context, but each would communicate a different meaning.

Further along the continuum we find **general contexts**, which seem to provide enough information for the reader to place the word in a general category. Consider this example:

Joe and Stan arrived at the party at 7 o'clock. By 9:30, the evening seemed to drag for Stan. But Joe really seemed to be having a good time at the party. "I wish I could be as gregarious as he is," thought Stan.

In this passage, it is easy to infer that *gregarious* describes someone who enjoys parties. As such, the passage provides clues to the meaning, although the specific characteristics of the word remain unclear.

Finally, we reach **directive contexts**, which seem likely to lead the student to a specific, correct meaning for a word. For example:

When the cat pounced on the dog, he leapt up, yelping, and knocked down a shelf of books. The animals ran past Wendy, tripping her. She cried out and fell to the floor. As the noise and confusion mounted, Mother hollered upstairs, "What's all that commotion?"

In this example, the reader is led to the meaning of *commotion* through clues from the description of the scene and by a definitional phrase, "noise and confusion."

Directive contexts are similar to instructional contexts as they both provide information around the target word that supports a reader to infer the meaning. The difference is that instructional contexts do so intentionally and directive contexts are unintentional. That is, an author might use an unfamiliar word in a sentence that happened to have clues to the word's meaning, but there was no intention to provide the clues. (Further discussion of instructional contexts appears in Chapter 7.)

To test the validity of our context categories, we selected two stories from basal programs and categorized the contexts surrounding target words according to our scheme. We then obscured the target words and presented the stories to 13 adults. We chose to use adult subjects because the target words were already part of their vocabulary repertoires and as such would provide a rigorous test for our categories.

The data clearly supported the categorization system. The adults were able to supply an average of 11 out of 13 words we categorized as having directive contexts. Correct identification dropped sharply for the general context category, and it dropped even further for the nondirective category. Only one subject could identify any word in the misdirective category.

This demonstration suggests that it is precarious to believe that naturally occurring contexts are sufficient, or even generally helpful, in providing clues to promote initial acquisition of a word's meaning. Again, it is important to point out that textual materials are written by professional authors who are conscious of their word choices to communicate events and ideas. The stories were not developed to provide contexts to help readers figure out the meaning of words.

Given the issues discussed above, it must be acknowledged that relying on wide reading for vocabulary growth adds to the inequities in individual differences in vocabulary knowledge. Struggling readers do not read well enough to make wide reading an option. To acquire word knowledge from reading requires adequate decoding skills, the ability to recognize that a word is unknown, and the competency to extract meaningful information about the word from the context. Readers cannot be engaging with the latter two if they are struggling with decoding. Thus, depending on wide reading as a source of vocabulary growth leaves those children and young people who are most in need of enhancing their vocabulary repertoires with a very serious deficit. In summary, written context is clearly an important source of new vocabulary for any reader. But relying on learning word meanings from independent reading is not an adequate way to deal with students' vocabulary development.

There *Are* Too Many Words to Teach, but . . .

The major argument for emphasizing learning from context comes from those who have examined the number of words that students will encounter during their school years and pronounced the task of directly teaching vocabulary simply too large. The logic that follows is that there is virtually no choice but to emphasize learning from context. A key point, however, is that many words in the language do not call for attention. It is this situation that makes direct instruction in word meanings feasible, for if most words in the language required instruction equally, clearly there would be too many words to cover in school. This notion of differential attention to words influenced our construct of words in tiers.

The Three-Tiers Framework

To get a perspective on the kinds of words that need instructional attention, consider a mature literate individual's vocabulary as comprising three tiers (Beck, McKeown, & Omanson, 1987). The first tier consists of the most basic words: *warm, dog, tired, run, talk, party, swim, look*, and so on. These are the words that typically appear in oral conversations, and so children are exposed to them at high frequency from a very early age. This high exposure means that children become familiar with this set of words pretty readily, and so these Tier One words rarely require instructional attention to their meanings in school. Moving to the third tier—this set of words has a frequency of use that is quite low and often limited to specific topics and domains. Some examples of Tier Three words might be *filibuster, pantheon*, and *epidermis*. In general, a rich understanding of these words would not be of high utility for most learners. These words are probably best learned when a specific need arises, such as introducing *filibuster* during a unit about the U.S. Congress. The content words of science and social studies reside in this tier.

The second tier contains words that are of high utility for mature language users and are found across a variety of domains. Examples include *contradict, circumstances, precede, auspicious, fervent*, and *retrospect*. These words are characteristic of written text and are found only infrequently in conversation, which means that students are less likely to learn these words independently, compared with Tier One words. Because of the large role Tier Two words play in a language user's repertoire, rich knowledge of words in the second tier can have a powerful impact on verbal functioning. Thus, instruction directed toward Tier Two words can be most productive.

How large is the task of teaching Tier Two words? We can get a handle on the size of the effort by extrapolating from Nagy and Anderson's (1984) analysis of words in printed school English for third through ninth grade. Nagy and Anderson estimate that:

- Good readers in this age range read approximately one million words of text per year.
- There are 88,500 words (actually word families—groups of related words such as *introduce, introduction, reintroduce*, and *introducing*) in printed school English, and half of these are so rare that even avid readers may encounter them only once in their lifetime of reading.
- There are about 15,000 word families that would be encountered at least once every 10 years.

Using these figures, it seems reasonable to consider these 15,000 word families as comprising Tiers One and Two. Interestingly, Nation (2001) has posed a similar number as a reasonable vocabulary, saying that "To read with minimal disturbance from unknown vocabulary, language users probably need a vocabulary of 15,000 to 20,000 words" (p. 20). These 15,000 word families represent words that occur once or more in 10 million running words of text. Our best estimate of Tier One, the most familiar words that need little or no instruction, is 8,000 word families. We base this number on Nagy and Anderson's statement that a typical third grader likely knows about 8,000 words. That leaves about 7,000 word families for Tier Two.

Seven thousand words may still seem like quite a large number for instruction to undertake over the course of, say, kindergarten through ninth grade. That would amount to an average of 700 words per year. So, would a reasonable goal be to teach them all? Or teach half of them? There is no way to answer that question with certainty. But we assert that attention to a substantial portion of those words, say, an average of 400 per year, would make a significant contribution to an individual's verbal functioning. Aiming for this number of words would allow the depth of instruction needed to affect students' text comprehension ability. We believe this to be the case because about 400 words per year conforms to the rate at which we taught words in some of our previous research, which resulted in improvements in word knowledge and in comprehension of texts containing the instructed words (Beck et al., 1982).

KNOWING A WORD IS NOT
AN ALL-OR-NOTHING PROPOSITION

It is not the case that one either knows or does not know a word. In fact, word knowledge is a rather complex concept. We focus on two of the issues involved in word knowledge. The first is that the extent of knowledge one may have about individual words can range from a little to a lot, and the second is that there are qualitatively different kinds of knowledge about words.

That there are differences in extent and kind of word knowledge is not a new idea. Almost 50 years ago, Dale (1965) offered a description of the extent of word knowledge in terms of four stages. More recently, Beck and colleagues (1987) suggested that an individual's knowledge about a word can be described as falling along a continuum. As the table below indicates, there are several differences between the two classification schemes, but there are more similarities.

Dale (1965)	Beck, McKeown, & Omanson (1987)
Stage 1: Never saw it before.	No knowledge
Stage 2: Heard it, but don't know what it means.	General sense; for example, *mendacious* has a negative connotation
Stage 3: Recognizes it in context as having something to do with _____.	Narrow, context-bound knowledge
	Has knowledge of a word but not able to recall it readily enough to use in appropriate situation
Stage 4: Knows it well.	Rich, decontextualized knowledge of a word's meaning, its relationship to other words, and its extension to metaphorical uses

On the first row, both classification schemes start exactly the same by noting the absence of knowledge. One difference is in the second row. Dale (1965) describes an individual who is aware that a particular word exists but does not know what it means, such as a young child who knows that there is a word *liberty*—presumably from the pledge of allegiance—but doesn't know what it means. In contrast, Beck and colleagues' (1987) second row describes an individual who knows that liberty is a good thing, but not what it means. Both descriptions on the third row are illustrations of needing a context to recall a word. On the fourth row, Beck and colleagues include what might be called fluency or facility, whereas Dale does not attend to that feature. And on the last row, Dale simply states that the most advanced stage of word knowledge is "knows it well," while Beck and colleagues include examples of what the most advanced kind of knowledge involves, such as understanding what someone is doing when he or she is *devouring* a book. The details of the classifications are not nearly as important as the overall concept—word knowledge is not an all-or-nothing proposition.

Other researchers offer additional dimensions of word knowledge. Kame'enui, Dixon, and Carnine (1987) add an interesting facet that they labeled "derived knowledge." That is, an individual may derive enough information about a word to understand it in the context being read or heard, but then not remember the information, and thus does not "learn" the word.

Miller's (1978) description of dimensions of word knowledge includes the important consideration of the relationship of a word to other concepts, such as topics to which the word can apply and the kinds of discourse in which the word is typically found. The importance of the relationship to other words is illustrated well in two examples described by Nagy and Scott (2000): "How well a person knows the meaning of *whale* depends in part on their understanding of *mammal*. A person who already knows the words *hot, cold,* and *cool* has already acquired some of the components of the word *warm*, even if the word *warm* has not yet been encountered" (p. 272; original emphasis).

Further dimensions of word knowledge include its register, that is, whether a word is used in formal or less formal contexts, its grammatical form, and its affective connotations (Nagy & Scott, 2000). And, as if all of the above were not complicated enough, Nagy and Scott (2000) point out that different facets of word knowledge are relatively independent. Thus, a learner might know the definition of a word but be unable to produce a context for it, or be able to use it in seemingly appropriate ways but actually have a misunderstanding of its meaning.

Perfetti (2007), in his recent model of word knowledge, the lexical quality hypothesis (LQH), discusses word knowledge by specifying the word features that characterize high-quality entries in a reader's mental dictionary, or lexicon. Just as is the case of an entry in a dictionary, several features of a word are available in a high-quality mental representation. One of course is its meaning, or *semantic representation*, for example, knowing that a *serendipitous* event is a good thing that happens accidentally. Another feature is its pronunciation (ser-uhn-**dip**-i-tous), or *phonological representation*. An additional feature is its spelling, or *orthographic representation*. Linking the spelling of a word to its pronunciation is what happens during reading.

Other important attributes of a word relate to its morphology and syntax. The word *serendipitous* has recognizable morphemes, or units of meaning, including the suffix *-ous*, which means "full of" or "having." A serendipitous event has or is full of good fortune. The word *serendipitous* also has a specific syntax, or role in a sentence, and that function is related to its form. For example, serendipitous is the adjective form of the word *serendipity*, which is a noun. According to Perfetti (2007), it is the interconnectedness of semantics, phonology, orthography, morphology, and syntax that constitute a high-quality representation.

When a learner acquires information about a word's meaning, connections form in the brain to other words and to experiences that are related to what has been learned (Perfetti, 2007; Reichle & Perfetti, 2003; Wolf, 2007). So if you were to think about the word *dance* . . . what comes to mind? . . . probably not "rhythmic body movements to music" but more likely you will think about dances you have gone to; kinds of dances— modern, waltz, hip hop; ballet lessons you took as a child; and so on. All the contexts in which you have encountered the word *dance* or experienced such an event lead to the building of an abstract representation of the word's meaning.

The abstract nature of the representation means that when you read the word in a new context, you are not dependent on specific information from a particular context that you have met before, which could limit your understanding of that new context. Rather, the representation you have created has many associated concepts and can bring the most relevant ones to the surface to help make the new context meaningful. Representations of word meaning, if they are of high quality, are flexible and allow rapid retrieval of meaning when we meet the word in text (Perfetti, 2007).

Based on the notion that rich word knowledge is built through multiple encounters with words, the LQH holds that what seems like a deficit in ability for less able comprehenders is more likely the result of knowledge differences—knowledge that has not been acquired or not practiced to a high enough level. When we consider what that means for instruction, this is good news, as it implies that we can help students to become good comprehenders by providing the experiences to build the knowledge they are lacking and support their practice of it.

What it means to know a word is clearly a complicated, multifaceted matter, and one that has serious implications for how words are taught. Most importantly, how do you decide what kind and how much instruction is adequate for students to learn words? That depends on what kind of learning is desired. We think that most often the goals that teachers have are like those specified in the fourth and fifth rows in Dale's (1965) and Beck and colleagues' (1987) classification schemes, shown earlier—that is, for the students to be able to use the instructed words in comprehension of text containing those words and to recall the words well enough to use them in writing. That calls for a deep kind of knowledge, which requires robust instruction. We consider robust instruction in the section that follows.

MAKING WORDS COME TO LIFE THROUGH ROBUST INSTRUCTION

People who have large vocabularies tend to be intrigued with words. As such, a major impetus for writing this book is our concern that school vocabulary instruction tends to be dull, rather than of the sort that might instigate student's interest and awareness of words. Becoming interested and aware of words is not a likely outcome of the way instruction is typically handled, which is to have students look up definitions in a dictionary or glossary (Scott et al., 2003; Watts, 1995). Indeed, asking students to look up words in the dictionary and use them in a sentence is a stereotypic example of what students find uninteresting in school.

Less than interesting instruction is not a concern of merely wanting students to enjoy classroom activities. Rather, students need to develop an interest in and awareness of words in order to adequately build their vocabulary repertoires. Among what needs to occur is that students keep using new words so they come to "own" the words. Students need to notice words in their environments whose meanings they do not know. They need to become aware of and explore relationships among words in order to refine and fully develop word meanings. Indeed, being curious about the meaning of an unknown word that one encounters and intrigued by how it relates to other words is a hallmark of those who develop large vocabularies.

Development of these facets of word knowledge must be the direct focus of instructional conditions. It has been our experience that students become interested and enthusiastic about words when instruction is rich and lively. We developed a variety of instructional activities for use in all the grade levels in which we worked. As we developed these activities we attempted to articulate what a particular activity did for students and we kept in mind that the materials needed to have some verve. There will be many, many examples of these throughout this book and in the Appendix. Here we provide some general ideas of several of the kind of activities that comprise what we call robust vocabulary instruction. We start out with some enhancements we made to traditional activities—matching and writing sentences in which new words are incorporated.

We included tasks that required students to quickly match a known word with a new word. For example, to elicit *accomplice*, the teacher presents the clue word *thief* and students respond with *accomplice*. Here the intent was that students expand their mental networks of related words, which in the case of *accomplice* likely includes *thief, bank, police, robber*. The teacher might offer *scoundrel, bandit, illegal*—all toward the principle that the greater the amount of semantic connections in a person's network, the more rich and flexible their understanding of words.

Matching exercises have probably been used for decades. What is important is that teachers and developers know the purpose of a given matching exercise. If the exercise were matching new words with definitions, it presumably enhances word/definition associations, not known/new word associations.

Another mainstay of traditional instruction is asking students to write a sentence that incorporates a target word. Before students face a blank sheet of paper and the direction to write sentences that makes sense for, say, five new words, we put sentence stems on the paper and ask students to complete them. For example, the stem, "The *accomplice* swore he would never break the law again because _____" is presented. The value of stems is that they provide a direction that scaffold students' thinking. In contrast, in traditional vocabulary instruction asking students to write sentences with target words usually occurs right after the only instruction received was a definition. The inadequacies of the results are well known— for example, "I saw a philanthropist."

When a set of words allowed it, we attempted to tap affective associations. For example, when the teacher said "philanthropist," students were to say "yay" or "boo" depending on how they felt about someone who could be called a philanthropist. The value of this is that if everything else fails, we assert that the learner would keep the idea that a philanthropist and virtuoso were positive, and miser and accomplice had negative connotations, as described on both the Dale (1965) and Beck and colleagues (1987) classification schemes. Knowing a domain in which a word fits can be useful. When encountering *virtuoso*, the reader likely has a memory trace and when the word appears in subsequent text another facet might be added. That sequence was actually the way one of us remembers learning the full meaning of *bucolic*. When encountering *bucolic*, she processed it as quiet peaceful, and that was sufficient to understand what was being said. That *bucolic* also has rural and pastorial features was not processed until she was reading a travel book.

We have developed game-like tasks that had to be completed under timed conditions, and tasks that took advantage of semantic or affective relationships between the target words and previously acquired vocabulary. There were several variations of how two words might be related. For example, how could *gregarious* and *hermit* go together? "A hermit doesn't want to be with people; someone who is gregarious wants to be with people." Another relationship task was one in which 12 previously learned words were displayed on cards and students were asked to sort them into piles of words that could go together. The rules were that a pile had to have at least two words, and the student had to tell how the words went together. Asking students why they responded the ways they did is very characteristic of robust instruction. In the sorting activity, one student perplexed us with his choice of *eavesdrop* and *gregarious*. When asked why they went together, he responded, "If someone reports you to the teacher for talking to a friend, they are eavesdropping, and you're being gregarious." This kind of ability to make an unusual but very fitting relationship illustrates the depth of understanding that had developed from the kind of instruction he had experienced.

We also took advantage of popular games, in particular, Jeopardy. The teacher said "virtuoso" and a student would need to respond with something like, "What is someone who plays the violin exceptionally well called?" The teacher said "boisterous" and a student responded, "What could you call a class of students talking loudly and shouting across the room?"

Extension of word use beyond the classroom was one of the important aspects of our vocabulary research, so we arranged conditions that encouraged students to notice words in environments beyond school. Toward that end we included a motivational device to increase the chances that this would occur. The device we used in our vocabulary studies was Word Wizard. Students could earn points toward becoming a word wizard by reporting the circumstances of having seen, heard, or used target words outside of class. Points were tallied every few weeks, and students received certificates based on their totals. (Further discussion of Word Wizard is found in Chapter 6.)

We relished the many anecdotes that Word Wizard provided. A long-time favorite was a boy who quietly told his teacher that he had heard a word on TV, but that it was a bad word. (Note: The week's words included *frank*—to be honest.) The teacher told him, that if he wanted to, he could whisper what he had heard to her. With the boy's lips close to the teacher's ear, the boy said, "I heard a man on TV say 'Frankly, my dear, I don't give a damn.'"

Since using the Word Wizard in our studies and describing it to teachers, we have seen teachers develop a host of variations that are useful for similar purposes and across various grade levels. In one teacher's classroom, the Word Wizard device she created allowed first-grade children to "show off" their new vocabulary expertise. At any time that a child could explain the meaning of three of the words under the display, he or she received each of those words on cards, as well as a Word Wizard hat. Then, with the Word Wizard hat and the three cards, the child could go through the school and any adult could read the word on one of the cards and ask the child to explain its meaning. The other teachers, and in particular the principal, got into it, and there were many oohs and aahs heard when a Word Wizard was in the hall!

Older students could earn extra credit by finding words and uses for words outside of class or a free pass for a night's homework or a quiz and the like. The discovery of examples of target words in various environments can be left up to the students' motivation, as in the case of doing so for extra credit and, indeed, for Word Wizard points. However, looking for examples of words in various environments can be primed somewhat. For example, the teacher can assign a word or several words for students to find or to invent an example or application for. The teacher might ask students to find the words *reasonable, inexpensive,* or *competitive* in newspaper or TV advertisements.

Over the years as robust vocabulary was implemented, we virtually always received reports from teachers about what a difference it made in students' interest in vocabulary. And from different places in the country we heard about similar responses. During school assemblies, a rumble would go through the place in the auditorium where the class in which we had implemented our vocabulary approach was sitting when a speaker mentioned one of the words they had learned—for instance, when a newspaper reporter was introduced as a *journalist*, when the principal asked particular students to stand to be *commended* for some *accomplishment*, in a safety discussion when the crossing guard told the students they shouldn't be *meandering* across the street. The rumble of recognition had an unintended consequence when a substitute librarian made a fourth-grade class go back to their homeroom because the whole class had misbehaved. It seems that when the librarian had mentioned the publisher, Harcourt Brace, the students had misheard it as "embrace," and shouted "*embrace, embrace* that's a word, that's a word." One might wonder whether prior to the incident there had been any other student acting up!

After the publication of the first edition of *Bringing Words to Life*, we turned our attention to developing systematic instruction for children in the primary grades and engaging in empirical work with the young children. We drew on our earlier experiences with vocabulary instruction for students in the intermediate grades to develop instruction for children in the earliest grades. The teachers who implemented the materials reported the children's excitement with vocabulary. And we saw it again for ourselves in our new work. A favorite anecdote is about the first grader who reported to his teacher, "I told my mother that I was going to act more *mature*, and she took me to Toys R Us."

SUMMARY

In this chapter, we emphasized the disparity in vocabulary knowledge for children from diverse SES groups, which is among the reasons we call for starting vocabulary instruction in kindergarten. A three-tiers framework was presented that classifies words as those that are learned in everyday common language (Tier One), those that are more prevalent in written language (Tier Two), and those that are tightly associated with a content area (Tier Three). Two classifications of what it means to know a word showed that knowing a word is not an all-or-nothing proposition.

We explained difficulty of deriving meanings from unfamiliar words in naturally occurring contexts. And, we presented a continuum of four kinds of contexts from misdirective to directive as a means of highlighting some of the textual situations that occur in naturally occurring contexts that can make it difficult or not so difficult to derive meaning. Several examples in the chapter described young children taught using a Tier Two word and enjoying it. A key notion in the chapter is that robust instruction is needed in order to mediate comprehending and composing.

YOUR TURN

1. Completing the accompanying chart should provide some evidence for the notion that word knowledge is indeed multifaceted. Put a check under the appropriate category to show your knowledge of each word.

Word	Know it well, can explain it, use it	Know something about it, can relate it to a situation	Have seen or heard the word	Do not know the word
palpable				
admonish				
sagacious				
ameliorate				
pneumonia				
heredity				

2. Choose an excerpt from a magazine article, newspaper, or novel. Select 10 target words and categorize them as having one of the following contexts: **misdirective**, **nondirective**, **general**, or **directive**. Make a photocopy of the excerpt and block out the 10 target words. Ask a few adults to try to figure out what the missing words are. Words in what kinds of contexts were most difficult for readers to figure out? Which were easiest? Do your results agree with ours?

3. Sort the following words into which of the three tiers each belongs: *child, forlorn, exquisite, oboe, birthday, stethoscope, break, colonial, cherish, repeal.*

CHAPTER 2

Choosing Words to Teach

Consider the following list of words whose meanings were to be introduced in conjunction with a reading selection in a third-grade basal: *gym, recite, prefer, perform, enjoying, billions* (Farr et al., 2000). Think about the difference in the utility and familiarity of the words. For example, not only is *gym* most likely known by third graders, it also has a much more limited role in a literate repertoire relative to *prefer* and *perform*.

Why do you think these words were selected? One obvious reason for selecting words to teach is that students do not know the words. Although *recite, prefer, perform*, and *billions* may be unfamiliar to many third graders, *gym* and *enjoying* are likely known by most third graders. Familiarity does not seem to be the principle used to make the selection. What about importance or usefulness? Are the selected words useful for reading and writing? Would the words be important to know because they appear in other texts with a high degree of frequency? Some—but not all—of the words might be considered useful or important. So, the question remains: Why were the words selected? The purpose of this chapter is to consider what principles might be used for selecting words to teach.

WHICH WORDS TO TEACH?

The earliest attention to the kinds of words to be taught was Beck and McKeown's concept of word tiers, initially introduced in Beck and colleagues (1987), which became more prominent in Beck, McKeown, and Kucan's books, *Bringing Words to Life* (2002) and *Creating Robust Vocabulary* (2008). As we just described in Chapter 1, we conceptualized a three-tier heuristic by considering that different words have different utility and roles in the language (Beck et al., 1987). Recall that we designated Tier One as words typically found in oral language and Tier Three consists of words that tend to be limited to specific domains (e.g., *enzyme*) or so rare that an avid reader would likely not encounter them in a lifetime (e.g., *abecedarian*). Tier Two comprises wide-ranging words of high utility for literate language users. These are words that are more characteristic of written language (e.g., *emerge*), and not so common in conversation (Hayes & Ahrens, 1988).

In this recent period of vocabulary research, other vocabulary scholars have provided input on the kinds of words best targeted for instruction. The approaches can be roughly divided into those researchers who, like Beck and McKeown, describe criteria for choosing words (Nation, 2001; Stahl & Nagy, 2006), and those who have developed procedures for identifying specific words (Biemiller, 2001, 2005; Hiebert, 2005).

First, let us consider those methods focused on objective procedures for identifying words. Biemiller (2005) developed a system for selecting words based on testing words from several levels of the living word vocabulary (LWV). The LWV was developed by Dale and O'Rourke (1979) to investigate students' actual word knowledge. The researchers did this by testing students through multiple-choice items at grades 4, 6, 8, 10, 12, and early college. In contrast, frequency counts are based on how often a word appears in a database, such as words in printed school materials. There are several problems with LWV: it is dated, and its methodology has been called into question (Hiebert, 2005; Nagy & Hiebert, 2011). But it is the only source available based on students' knowledge of words.

Biemiller and Slonim's (2001) methods involved testing words from the LWV's fourth-grade level and found that most of the words known by 80% of fourth graders were actually already known by children at the end of second grade. Then after more testing, the researchers identified optimal candidates for instruction as those words that 30–70% of children knew when tested and which thus seemed likely to be learned next. Biemiller and Slonim noted that their results indicated that words were learned in a roughly sequential order and interpreted this finding as offering a developmental view of the acquisition of vocabulary. Thus, given their view that word learning was a developmental matter, they suggested that teaching words in the order that they seemed to be acquired would be beneficial.

But the order of word learning is not developmental. Something that is developmental means that an individual must go through specific sequenced stages, such as the common example of walking before running. The sequence of learning the meanings of words does not reside in innate human development; that is, our brains are not wired to acquire words in any given sequence. The order of learning words resides in children's environments and experiences: what they hear, see, are told, read, and the like.

Beyond the fact that there is no innate sequence, adhering to any sequence for learning words is not necessary because words are not related in a hierarchical way; that is, many words that support general language and literacy do not comprise an organized system in which certain words precede others conceptually. For example, if a child understands the concept of *stubborn*, he or she could learn *obstinate* before *headstrong* or *defiant* before *obstinate* and the like. (We note that a number of words in the content areas do have hierarchical relations, which as we already asserted should be dealt with in the course of dealing with the content in which they appear.)

Hiebert's (2005) approach for selecting words for instruction was based on frequency counts. So, as a reminder, let us talk briefly about what word frequencies are. Usually when people talk about word frequency, they are referring to a listing of words by their frequency of appearance in written language. The standard example for a long time was Carroll, Davies, and Richman's *Word Frequency Book*. Published in 1971, it was produced by examining a large collection of texts used in school through grade 12. Other similar resources exist, such as the more recent *Educator's Word Frequency Guide* (Zeno, Ivens, Millard, & Duvvuri, 1995). These resources list all the words from the texts they include in their corpus by the number of times they appear (their frequency) as well as at what grade levels.

We acknowledge that frequencies can provide some information, but some problems are inevitable when word frequency is the primary source for identifying words. For example, the words *work, works, worked*, and *working* are all separate entries, yet the meaning of those words is virtually the same. In contrast, a word that has different meanings is listed only once. For example, whether *bank* means financial institution, edge of a river, or angle of an airplane is not taken into account. *B-a-n-k* appears one time on the list, and its associated frequency represents all the different meanings. In other words, there is no way to get the frequency of the word *bank* meaning a financial institution. Moreover, the boundary between high and low frequency is an arbitrary one so that the low-frequency category includes both words that almost got into the high-frequency category as well as words that are truly rare (Nation, 2001).

Hiebert's (2005) goal was to identify words that are unknown to students in first through fourth grades, but that also appear in a significant portion of texts in grades five and above so that those words could be the targets of instruction. The goal to do that is certainly admirable. Hiebert selected the words in the texts used in the fourth-grade versions of three prominent standards-based tests and the National Assessment of Educational Progress on which to establish frequency counts. Specifically, she categorized the words from her frequency data according to zones that correspond to bands of frequency. Zones 1 through 4 contain 5,586 words that Hiebert has designated for teaching in grades one through four. With instruction directed to Zones 1 through 4, students would have been taught about 92% of the words on the prominent tests.

An example of a difference between tiers and frequencies illustrates another problem of relying on frequencies. Most would agree that *breaking* is simply a form of *break*—a word that even toddlers are likely familiar with, and thus we would put it in Tier One. *Complicated*, on the other hand, is a rather sophisticated word, less common to children's oral language, and needs some explanation to communicate. Yet it is a useful word as it is likely to appear in many domains and circumstances—from describing television plots to theories of the galaxy! All this makes it a prototypical Tier Two word. Yet according to Carroll and colleagues' *Word Frequency Book* (1971), *break* and *complicated* have the same frequency count.

As the above example suggests, we would not recommend relying on frequency lists as the primary resource for selecting words to teach, although frequency can be one useful resource. Frequency lists can seem very tempting, because they are objective—gathered from actual data on use of words in the language. But this very fact is also why they should not be relied on. Frequency merely indicates how often a word appears in print compared to other words in the language. That fact does not exactly translate into how difficult a word is or even how useful it is to a user's repertoire.

Other scholars have taken an approach more similar to Beck and McKeown's, categorizing words as to their role and utility in the language and laying out guidelines for selecting words to teach. Stahl and Nagy (2006) approach the issue of which words and what kind of attention to devote to different words by using characteristics such as frequency, utility, and requirements for learning to create descriptive categories of word types. Two key categories that Stahl and Nagy assert merit significant attention are "high-frequency words" and "high-utility general vocabulary." Stahl and Nagy characterize high-frequency words as those that make up the bulk of words in any genre, spoken or written. This category is similar to our Tier One words. Stahl and Nagy suggest that many if not most students will be familiar with these words early in their school careers. However, given the importance of these words, Stahl and Nagy suggest providing many opportunities for students to deal with these words in context.

Stahl and Nagy's (2006) high-utility general vocabulary words, similar to our Tier Two words, are described as those that "may be uncommon in conversation but are part of the core of written language that students encounter in their texts . . . words you'd expect to be part of a literate person's vocabulary" (p. 61). They offer examples for the first nine letters of the alphabet: *abolish, banish, chamber, deliberate, exceed, frequent, genuine, hospitable, initiative.*

Nation (2001) provides similar considerations about which words merit instruction, and, although his discussion is targeted to learning English as a second language, the constructs he presents are relevant for first-language learning as well. Nation identifies four kinds of vocabulary to consider when designing instruction: high frequency, academic, technical, and low frequency and points out that almost 80% of the running words in any text are high frequency. It is easy to see why high-frequency words constitute such a high percentage of running words in any text by considering the table below in which we list every 10th word of the highest 300 words in the language. It is also easy to see why these are not the words that differentiate students with high and low vocabulary knowledge or good and poor comprehenders (Cunningham & Stanovich, 1998; Hayes & Ahrens, 1988).

10.	*the*	110.	*our*	210.	*land*
20.	*of*	120.	*think*	220.	*four*
30.	*and*	130.	*because*	230.	*need*
40.	*your*	140.	*things*	240.	*let*
50.	*up*	150.	*number*	250.	*times*
60.	*other*	160.	*name*	260.	*sentence*
70.	*could*	170.	*under*	270.	*knew*
80.	*my*	180.	*next*	280.	*hear*
90.	*water*	190.	*looked*	290.	*want*
100.	*know*	200.	*want*	300.	*turned*

Such words would reside in our Tier One category, which includes words that are likely learned from everyday experiences.

Nation's (2001) category of academic words are those common across domains of academic texts, which typically make up about 10% of running words in adult texts. Here Nation cites Coxhead's *New Academic Word List* (2000) as a good database. Coxhead's list of 570 word families was drawn from a corpus of 3.5 million running words from academic journals and university textbooks in four broad academic areas: arts, commerce, law, and natural science. Both frequency and dispersion—the extent that words appear in several domains—were considered in selecting the words, such that all word families on the list occurred in all four academic areas and were used at least 100 times across the texts being analyzed. Nation views academic words as essential to teach because of their range of coverage over various types of text and the meaning they bring to a text. These words would overlap our Tier Two category.

The two other categories in Nation's (2001) scheme, technical words and low-frequency words, cover the remaining 10% of running words, with each approximated at 5%. Technical words are those closely related to a specific topic or subject area, but not so common beyond it. Nation's technical words are similar to our Tier Three words, and he has asserted, as we have, that teaching such words makes sense only when learning the specialized subject matter.

The approaches espoused by Stahl and Nagy (2006), Nation (2001), and Beck and McKeown all inherently view judgment as a key component, in that these approaches describe criteria for choosing words rather than procedures for identifying specific words. Despite the objective procedures in the systems proposed by Biemeiller and Hiebert (2005), each finally comes to require subjective judgment to overcome problems within their systems. Biemiller and Boote (2005) acknowledged this aspect in two ways. First, Biemiller and Boote discuss the lack of clear criteria for distinguishing teachable and too-hard words, saying that they are "left with testing and some uses of intuition for identifying word meanings for instruction" (p. 4). Second, they mention their research group's need to evaluate "word importance" to distinguish words that are most useful to learn. Hiebert also acknowledges the judgment component in discussing implications for teachers, for example, pointing out the relative utility of [the] words *checkpoint* and *cautiously* that appear in the same text (pp. 260–261).

We summarize the instructional implications of issues discussed in this section by noting that Biemiller and Hiebert (2005) would select a set of words that are generally of higher frequency, tend to be more concrete, and are often acquired from everyday experiences. We—like Stahl and Nagy (2006) and Nation (2001)—would consider the utility of words for use in both comprehension and composition as the priority. Such words are more abstract and associated with written language; thus, they are more unlikely to be learned through everyday language.

Moving from using everyday language to being a literate language user can be difficult. A term used by Corson (1985, 1995)—the *lexical bar*— underscores that point and also suggests why learning the vocabulary of written language is so important. According to Corson (1985), a barrier (i.e., lexical bar) exists between everyday meaning systems—the words in conversations—and the meaning system created by academic, literate culture, or book language. Academic success is possible, according to Corson (1995), only if learners cross the lexical bar. So if students are to become successful in academic life, they need to be able to get meaning from text, which in turn means being able to build meaning using the more sophisticated vocabulary of written language.

In the rest of this chapter, we focus on that sophisticated vocabulary, which we refer to as Tier Two words.

IDENTIFYING TIER TWO WORDS IN TEXTS

To get an idea of the process of identifying Tier Two words, consider an example. Below is the opening paragraph of a retelling of an old tale (Kohnke, 2001, p. 12) about a donkey that is under a magical spell that forces him to do the chores for a group of lazy servants. The story would likely be of interest to third and fourth graders.

> Johnny Harrington was a kind master who treated his servants fairly. He was also a successful wool <u>merchant</u>, and his business <u>required</u> that he travel often. In his absence, his servants would <u>tend</u> to the fields and cattle and <u>maintain</u> the upkeep of his mansion. They <u>performed</u> their duties happily, for they felt <u>fortunate</u> to have such a <u>benevolent</u> and trusting master.

The underlined words are those we identified as consistent with the notion of Tier Two words. That is, most of the words are likely to appear frequently in a wide variety of texts and in the written and oral language of mature language users. (Note: We chose this paragraph because there were so many candidate Tier Two words; however, most grade-level material would not have so many words in only one paragraph.)

One "test" of whether a word meets the Tier Two criterion of being a useful addition to students' repertoires is to think about whether the students already have ways to express the concepts represented by the words. Would students be able to explain these words using words that are already well known to them? If that is the case, it suggests that the new words offer students more precise or mature ways of referring to ideas they already know about. One way to answer the question is to think about how average third and fourth graders would talk about the concepts represented by the Tier Two words. We think that students would be likely to offer the explanations shown in the accompanying list.

Tier Two words	Students' likely expressions
merchant	salesperson or clerk
required	have to
tend	take care of
maintain	keep going

performed	did
fortunate	lucky
benevolent	kind

Adding the seven target words to young students' vocabulary repertoires would seem to be quite productive, because learning the words would allow students to describe with greater specificity people and situations with which they already have some familiarity. Note that these words are not simple synonyms of the familiar ones, however, instead representing more precise or more complex forms of the familiar words. *Maintain* means not only "keep going," for example, but also "to continue something in its present condition or at its present level." *Benevolent* has the dimension of tolerance as well as kindness.

SELECTING FROM A POOL OF WORDS

Now consider which of the words will be most useful in helping students understand the above paragraph. For the seven words noted there, our thinking is that *fortunate* is particularly important because the fact that the servants thought they were lucky is an important condition of the story. Similarly, *benevolent* plays an important role in setting up the story, as the servants appreciate their master's kindness and do not want to upset their pleasant living situation. If one other word were to be selected, a good choice would be *merchant*. *Merchant* is a word that comes up in fourth- and fifth-grade social studies textbooks in discussions of colonization of the Americas (e.g., "European merchants were eager to locate new resources like tobacco and indigo, which could be found in the colonies"; or "Colonial merchants were dismayed by the taxes on English goods, which meant higher prices for their customers but no more profit for themselves"). The other candidate words—*tend, required, performed,* and *maintain*—are also words of strong general utility, and the choice of whether to include any more words is based solely on considering how many words one thinks students can usefully handle.

■ YOU TRY IT ■

Below is another excerpt from the tale about the donkey under the magical spell described above (Kohnke, 2001, p. 12). You might find it useful to try your hand at identifying Tier Two words. You will get to see our choices below the excerpt, so that you can compare your selections with ours.

> The servants would never comment on this strange occurrence [finding the kitchen clean even though none of them were seen doing the cleaning], each servant hoping the other had tended to the chores. Never would they mention the loud noises they'd hear emerging from the kitchen in the middle of the night. Nor would they admit to pulling the covers under their chins as they listened to the sound of haunting laughter that drifted down the halls to their bedrooms each night. In reality, they knew there was a more sinister reason behind their good fortune.

Which words did you select? Trying to be all-inclusive, selecting any words that might fit Tier Two, we chose *comment, occurrence, tended, mention, emerging, admit, haunting, reality, sinister,* and *fortune.* We considered them Tier Two words as we viewed them as fairly "general but sophisticated words." That is, they are not the most basic or common ways of expressing ideas but they are familiar to mature language users as ordinary as opposed to specialized language. The concepts embodied in each word are ones that students already have some understanding of, as shown in the accompanying list.

Tier Two words	Students' likely expressions
comment	something someone has to say
occurrence	something happening
tended	took care of
mention	tell
emerging	coming out
admit	to say you did something
haunting	scary
reality	being real
sinister	scary
fortune	luck

Now, the notion of tiers of words is not a precise one, and the lines between tiers are not clear-cut, so your selection may not match ours. Thinking in terms of tiers is just a starting point—a way of framing the task of choosing candidate words for instruction (see the accompanying box). Even within Tier Two, some words will be more easily familiar and some will be more useful than others. For example, our hunch is that *admit, reality,* and *fortune* are likely known to most fourth or fifth graders; that *tended* is not often used in a way that is key to understanding; and that fifth graders may already associate *haunting* with scary things—a Halloween context— which is fitting for this story. Thus we ended up with *comment, occurrence, mention, emerging,* and *sinister.* We judged the first four of these to be most useful across a range of contexts, and we chose *sinister* because it is a strong word with emotional impact that is used in literature to describe fictional characters as well as in nonfiction, such as when describing a group's sinister plans to invade another's territory.

SOME CRITERIA FOR IDENTIFYING TIER TWO WORDS

- Importance and utility: Words that are characteristic of written text and appear frequently across a variety of domains. For example, *categorize* ranges broadly, as most things can be categorized. Everything from words to kinds of governments can be categorized. Similarly, *technique* is widely useful, such as someone's technique for remembering telephone numbers or a city's technique for collecting parking tickets.

- Conceptual understanding: Words for which students understand the general concept but provide precision and specificity in describing the concept. For example, students understand that things can be in the way, but *hindrance* is a sophisticated way to express that idea. Similarly, that there is enough of something is recognized by young children, but that there is *sufficient* is a more mature way of expressing the idea.

- Instructional potential: Words that are more than one-dimensional, and offer a variety of contexts and uses to explore. For example, *aid* doesn't mean much more than "help"; in contrast, *establish* is similar to *start*, but it also means "to put on a firm basis," as in to establish a business or form of government or to establish a reputation. *Establish* also means "to put beyond doubt," as in to establish a person's innocence.

SELECTING WORDS FROM INSTRUCTIONAL TEXTS ACROSS DOMAINS

Here we want to raise an issue about the dilemma that teachers of upper elementary students face in selecting words to teach. The curricular resources for these students present vocabulary not only in reading but also in math, science, social studies, and spelling. For example, consider the table below. The lists of words come from materials sent home with one author's great-nephew who is in the sixth grade. Parents and caregivers are provided with the list of spelling words and lists of the science, social studies, math, and reading words with definitions. The expectation is that students will study the words so they can do well on chapter or unit tests.

Spelling	Science	Social studies	Math	Reading
musician	chloroplasts	monsoon	perimeter	mournfully
politician	cell wall	deity	circumference	emerge
historian	nucleus	reincarnation	composite	sodden
comedian	chromosomes	caste	number	sporadic
novelist	DNA	artisans	prime number	vanquished
scientist	genes	raja	prime	douse
tenant	dominant	export	factorization	leaped
student	recessive	import		flung
patient		epic		swerved
resident		meditating		dredge
				traitorous

Looking at the lists raises some important questions: Are these really vocabulary words? Are the meanings of the words worth learning because they are useful in a variety of contexts? Will teaching the meanings of the words contribute to students' verbal functioning? Let's consider the potential of each list.

The spelling list includes words that foreground spelling patterns and suffixes that indicate noun forms, specifically people. For a sixth grader, the meanings of the words are not difficult to understand, and teachers can gauge student understanding quickly as the words are pronounced and introduced and provide explanations as needed. Instruction does not need to be focused on word meanings (vocabulary) but on patterns in word structure (spelling). Nor does practice and review of meanings need to be incorporated.

The words in the science list are quite different. We would label these as Tier Three words, words that are limited to a very specific topic. The words on the science list comprise two clusters of words that describe particular concepts: genetic inheritance, including *chromosomes, DNA, genes, recessive,* and *dominant*; and cell structure, including *chloroplasts, cell wall,* and *nucleus.* The instruction for these kinds of words would rightly focus on building content knowledge rather than vocabulary knowledge. The danger here is reducing content knowledge to lists of isolated words. Nagy and Townsend (2012) emphasized this point, explaining that students need repeated opportunities to practice such words in authentic contexts "in which they both garner and support meaning of technical or theoretical ideas" (p. 96).

Like the science words, the social studies words are important for understanding a well-defined topic; in this case, aspects of the cultural, economic, and social life of ancient India. Although some of the words (such as *import* and *export*) can be used in a variety of contexts, the other words are quite specific to a social studies unit on the history of India. We would label these as Tier Three words. Instruction for these words would involve engaging students in developing an understanding of aspects of life in ancient India rather than focusing on the meanings of individual words.

The math words are also Tier Three words. They describe very specific mathematical features and actions. Learning the meanings of the words is not the point. Rather, students need to recognize the concepts and procedures that the words refer to when they encounter them in word problem contexts.

The words on the reading list come from three chapters of a novel that the sixth graders were reading. This list provides the richest source of Tier Two words, words that students can use in a variety of contexts. We would provide instructional attention and time for students to learn: *mournfully, emerge, sodden, sporadic, vanquished, chaos,* and *constriction.* These words are multidimensional and have high potential for students to develop rich representations. They can be used in a variety of contexts. They also provide the kind of precision and specificity that would allow students to provide rich descriptions and explanations. Four of the words—*emerge, sporadic, chaos,* and *constriction*—are clearly academic words in that they are likely to appear in expository texts as well as in narratives.

In an ideal world, teachers would be aware of the words on all the lists for a given time period and would design instructional activities to include words from across the lists when possible. For example, if *sodden* were one of the words selected for instruction, students could be asked to explain why *sodden* might be used in describing the effects of a monsoon. Or if *constriction* were selected for instruction, students could be asked to describe how the caste system *constricted* opportunities for many people in India.

The important point that we're getting at here is that teachers need to make decisions about how to deal with the words students are expected to "learn" in a given time period. Some word meanings can be introduced or reviewed quickly and not given sustained attention. Some words represent concepts that need to be developed as part of knowledge about topics within a specific content domain, rather than isolated, defined, and placed in novel contexts. For sustained vocabulary development, teachers should opt for those words that will provide students with the most leverage—Tier Two words. Those are the words that should be the focus of the kind of instructional attention we describe in the following chapters.

CONSIDERATIONS BEYOND TIER TWO

There is nothing scientific about the way words are identified for attention in school materials. Some words are obvious candidates, such as selecting the word *representation* for a social studies unit on the American Revolutionary War era. But beyond the words that play major roles, choices about what specific set of words to teach are quite arbitrary. Teachers should feel free to use their best judgment, based on an understanding of their students' needs, in selecting words to teach. They should also feel free to treat words in different ways. As Chapters 3, 4, and 5 will show, Tier Two words are not only words that are important for students to know, they are also words that can be worked with in a variety of ways so that students have opportunities to build rich representations of them and of their connections to other words and concepts.

In many texts, however, there may be several unfamiliar words that do not meet the criteria for Tier Two words but which nevertheless require some attention if students are to understand a selection. Consider the following excerpt from the short story "My Father, the Entomologist" (Edwards, 2001, p. 5):

"Oh, Bea, you look as lovely as a <u>longhorn beetle</u> lifting off for flight. And I must admit your <u>antennae</u> are adorable. Yes, you've <u>metamorphosed</u> into a <u>splendid</u> young lady."

Bea rolled her eyes and <u>muttered</u>, "My father, the <u>entomologist</u>."

"I heard that, Bea. It's not nice to <u>mumble</u>. Unless you want to be called a . . . Mumble Bea!" Bea's father slapped his knee and hooted. Bea rolled her eyes a second time.

The first day of fifth grade, and my father tells me I look like a longhorn beetle. Bea <u>shuddered</u> at the thought. She absolutely <u>detested</u> bugs. Why does Dad have to be <u>obsessed</u> with insects? She wondered. Why not football or golf like most fathers? The answer was simple. Bea's dad was weird. His weirdness made the whole family weird. And he had made Bea the weirdest of all when he named her Bea Ursula Gentry . . . B.U.G.

Suddenly, Bea felt angry. She flew into the kitchen where her father sat reading *Insectology*. She <u>hurled</u> her backpack onto the table.

"You know what, Dad?" she asked, tugging on one of her pigtails. "These are not antennae! Your bumper sticker, 'Have you hugged a bug today?' is not cool! And I <u>despise</u> eating in the dining room with all those dead bugs pinned to the walls!"

With fourth- and fifth-grade students in mind, we have divided the 12 underlined words from the story into the following three categories:

longhorn beetle	*obsessed*	*splendid*
antennae	*detest*	*shuddered*
metamorphosed	*despise*	*mumble*
entomologist	*muttered*	*hurl*

Most teachers would recognize that their students would not be familiar with the words in the first column; however, those words can be dealt with very quickly. *Longhorn beetle* does not call for attention—students will understand it as a type of insect, and more knowledge is not needed to understand the story. *Antennae* and *entomologist* are needed to understand the situation the author uses to set up the story, but the two words can be quickly described as "those things that stick out from an insect's head" and "a scientist who studies insects," respectively. More precise information is not required for this selection.

Metamorphosed can be explained as simply "changed or grown," but to get the humor intended here, the information needs to be given that it is the type of change that certain insects go through, such as when a caterpillar changes into a butterfly. But, again, no more precision is required, and this is not the place to go through the elaborate explanation about the process or how it occurs. That should occur in a science unit about insects.

The words in the next two columns have more general applications and are consistent with Tier Two words. The words in the second column—*obsessed, detest,* and *despise*—are most substantively related to the plot of the story, which is about a father who is obsessed with bugs and his daughter who detests and despises them. *Detest* and *despise* create a kind of "twofer" situation, in that they are very close synonyms that could be introduced together and used interchangeably.

The rest of the words do not play key roles in the story, nor is their unfamiliarity likely to interfere with comprehension. So, which other words are attended to, if any, is simply a matter of choice and convenience. That is, a decision as to the number of words taught might be made on the basis of how many a teacher wants to make room for at the moment. Factors in this decision may include, for example, how large the current vocabulary load is in the classroom, the time of year, and the number and difficulty of other concepts presently being dealt with in the curriculum.

Assume that there is room for several more words from this story. It might be convenient to teach *splendid* and *shuddered*, because they could take advantage of concepts already established for the story. *Shuddered* fits well, since something that is detested might well make one shudder. *Splendid* is also a good fit, as in "Bea's dad thinks bugs are splendid, but Bea detests them" or "If you're obsessed about something, you might think it's splendid." These two words would also be favored because they have a bit more dimension to them than *mumble, muttered,* or *hurl.* This is not to say that *mumble, muttered,* or *hurl* should not be taught but simply that, presented with the choice of words to work with, *splendid* and *shuddered* seem to lend themselves to a wider diversity of possible uses.

WHAT IF THERE ARE NOT ENOUGH WORDS?

Now let us consider a text that does not seem to offer much for vocabulary development because all of the words in the text are familiar to students. An approach in such a case could be selecting words whose concepts fit in with the story even though the words do not appear. For example, if the story features a character who is a loner, introduce the words *hermit, isolated,* or *solitary*; if a problem is dealt with, present it as a *dilemma* or *conflict*; if a character is hardworking, consider if he or she is *diligent* and *conscientious.* Think in terms of words that coordinate with, expand, or play off of words, situations, or characters in a text.

Bringing in words whose concepts fit with a story is especially salient when young children are just learning to read and there are only the simplest words in their text. Consider a story in which two children (Pam and Matt) try on a number of silly hats, some of which are very big and two of which are exactly alike. A number of words came to mind, and we chose *absurd, enormous,* and *identical.* Next we suggest how those words might be introduced to young children:

- In the story, Pam and Matt had very, very silly hats. Another way to say that something is very, very silly is to say that it is absurd. When something is absurd, it is so silly it's hard to believe.
- Some of the hats that Pam and Matt wore were so big that all you could see were their feet. Another way to say that something is very, very big is to say that it is enormous. *Enormous* means "very big— very, very big."

- Pam and Matt put on red hats that were almost exactly alike. A way to say that two things are exactly alike is to say that they are identical. *Identical* means "exactly alike."

Stories for older students have many concepts and ideas that are described and explained, but not necessarily labeled. This offers opportunities to connect an event or idea from the story to a potentially useful word. For example, a story about Devin, a boy who is getting ready for his first day at a new school, provides a context for introducing the words *foreboding* and *solace*.

- The boys in Devin's new neighborhood have teased him about the dangers at their school. Devin is terrified and thinks something bad will happen. Another way to describe the way Devin feels is to say that he has a foreboding. If you have a foreboding, you feel like something very bad is going to happen.
- Devin feels better when his big brother says he will walk with him to school. Another way to say that is that his brother is a solace to him. Someone who is a solace comforts you and makes you feel less frightened and sad.

AN EXAMPLE FOR OLDER STUDENTS

The examples provided thus far were drawn from texts for elementary students. Although the same principles apply to selecting words from texts for students in middle and high school, they may play out a bit differently. Thus, we present a discussion of the words that might be selected from Agatha Christie's "In a Glass Darkly" (1934), a story that is likely to be of interest to students in eighth or ninth grade. It is a rather brooding tale that moves from a murderous premonition to unrequited love, jealousy, and near tragedy before resolving happily. The story begins as the narrator, while staying with a friend, sees a vision of a man strangling a woman. The woman turns out to be his friend's sister, Sylvia, with whom he falls in love. But Sylvia is engaged—to the man he saw in his vision. He tells her of the vision, and she breaks her engagement. For years, the narrator is unable to tell her of his feelings for her. Finally, love is revealed and they marry. But he is deeply jealous, a feeling that results in his nearly strangling his wife—until he notices in the mirror that he is playing out the scene of his premonition.

The language of the story is sophisticated but not particularly difficult. Most words will likely be at least passingly familiar to many readers
in eighth or ninth grade. However, many of the words are probably not
of high frequency in the students' vocabularies, and thus an opportunity
presents itself for students to work with these words and gain fluency with
them. Here are the 30 words from the story that we identified as Tier Two
words:

essential	*appreciated*	*altered*
intervened	*decent*	*well-off*
attractive	*rambling*	*prospect*
valet	*throttling*	*complication*
gravely	*upshot*	*leisure*
disinterested	*scornfully*	*devoted*
absurdly	*endangering*	*inevitable*
entrenched	*gloomy*	*sullen*
savage	*unwarranted*	*abuse*
endurance	*revelation*	*sobering*

Of the 30 words, we decided to focus on 10 of them: *essential, altered,
well-off, devoted, entrenched, inevitable, sobering, revelation, upshot*, and *disinterested*. Ten words may be a lot to develop effectively for one story, but we
see it as a workable number because many of them will already be familiar.
Also, two of the words could be introduced rather briefly with little or no
follow-up work. These are *altered*, which could be defined simply as "permanently changed," and *well-off*, which could simply be given the synonym
wealthy. The reason for attention to these two words is that they could cause
confusion at the local level in the story if not understood.

Two other words were also chosen because they could cause confusion
in a part of the story. These are *upshot* and *disinterested*. The narrator talks
of the upshot of his decision to tell Sylvia that he saw a vision of her fiancé
choking her. Because of the context and feel of the story, we thought *upshot*
might be interpreted as some sort of physical violence, instead of simply "the
result of." The word *disinterested*, meaning "not being involved in a particular situation," is often confused with *uninterested*, meaning "not interested,"
and the story provides a good opportunity to introduce that distinction.

Five words seem to convey the mood and emotional impact of story
developments: *devoted, entrenched, inevitable, sobering*, and *revelation*. And the
word *essential* was chosen because "one essential detail" turns out to be a
key plot device—that is, in his premonition, the narrator notices a scar on
the left side of the choker's face. The essential detail he fails to account for

is that he is seeing this in a mirror, so the scar is actually on the right. The six words can be used to describe the plot as follows: The narrator is *devoted* to Sylvia, although *entrenched* in a jealousy that causes *inevitable* problems. Only a *sobering revelation* (that *essential* detail) saves him, his marriage, and his wife.

A couple of points should be emphasized here. The words were selected not so much because they are essential to comprehension of the story but because they seem most closely integral to the mood and plot. In this way, the vocabulary work provides both for learning new words and for enriching understanding of literature. This decision was made possible because there was a large pool of words from which to choose. Sometimes choices are more limited, and sometimes the best words are not so tied to the story. In such cases, a decision might be made to select words that seem most productive for vocabulary development despite their role in the story.

For the six words we consider to be most important to teach, some characteristics of the words themselves also drove our selections. *Sobering* was selected because its strongest sense for students might be as the opposite of drunk. So, the context of the story provides a good opportunity to overcome that and introduce its more general sense. The others, *essential, devoted, entrenched, inevitable,* and *revelation,* have wide potential for use and are not limited to specific situations or stereotypical contexts. Yet, they seem to be strongly expressive words that can bring emotional impact to contexts in which they are used.

AN EXAMPLE FOR YOUNG CHILDREN

We turn now to selecting words to enhance the vocabulary repertoires of young children—those who are just learning to read. We make two immediate distinctions between vocabulary work with students in upper elementary, middle, and high school, and work with students in the earliest grades, typically kindergarten though early second grade. The first is that we consider the best sources for new vocabulary to be trade books that teachers read aloud to children rather than the books children read on their own. In Chapter 4 we will make our case for that position.

The second distinction is that in contrast to introducing words before a story, in our work with young children we have found it most appropriate to engage in vocabulary activities after a story has been read. There are two reasons we decided that vocabulary activities for young children should occur after a story. First, if a word is needed for comprehension, since the teacher is reading the story he or she is available to briefly explain the word at the point in the story where it is needed (e.g., "A *ukulele* is a kind of guitar"; or "When ducks *molt*, they lose their feathers and can't fly until new ones grow"). Second, because the words that will be singled out for vocabulary attention are words that are very likely unfamiliar to young children, the context from the story provides a rich example of the word's use and thus strong support for the children's initial learning of the word.

The basis for selecting words from trade books for young children is that they are Tier Two words and words that are not too difficult to explain to young children. Here, we present our thinking for selecting three words for instructional attention from *The Popcorn Dragon* (Thayer, 1953), a story targeted to kindergartners.

In our review of *The Popcorn Dragon* (Thayer, 1953) for Tier Two candidate words, we first identified the following seven: *accidentally, drowsy, pranced, scorched, envious, delighted,* and *forlorn*. From the pool of seven, we decided to provide instruction for three: *envious, delighted,* and *forlorn*. We considered three issues in making our choices. First, we determined that the concept represented by each word was understandable to kindergartners; that is, 5-year-olds understand the concepts of wanting something someone else has (*envious*), being very happy (*delighted*), and being very sad (*forlorn*). Second, it is not too difficult to explain the meanings of those words in very simple language, as illustrated in the previous sentence! And, third, each word has extensive possibilities for use. In particular, the words are found in numerous fairy tales; that is, there is often some character who is *envious* of another, and there are characters who are *delighted* or *forlorn* about the turn of events. The words, however, are not restricted to make-believe; they can all be used in describing people in common situations.

We found the other candidate words—*pranced, accidentally, scorched,* and *drowsy*—interesting and potentially useful, but we saw *scorched* and *pranced* as narrower than the ones we chose, and *drowsy* and *accidentally* as not quite so interesting. We hasten to make the point that this is all a matter of judgment. The final decisions about which words to teach may not be as important as thoughtful consideration about why to teach certain words and not others.

WHAT ABOUT WORDS BEING ON GRADE LEVEL?

A concern that surfaces in deciding which words to teach is whether words are appropriate for students at certain grade levels. Key to this concern is to understand that no formula exists for selecting age-appropriate vocabulary words despite lists that identify "fifth-grade words" or "seventh-grade words." There is simply no basis for determining which words students should be learning at different grade levels. For example, that *coincidence* is an "eighth-grade word" according to a frequency index means only that most students do not know the word until eighth grade. It does not mean that students in seventh or even third grade cannot learn the word or should not be taught it.

There are only two things that make a word inappropriate for a certain level. One is not being able to explain the meaning of a word in known terms. If the words used to explain a target word are likely unknown to the students, then the word is too hard. The other consideration for word selection is that the words be useful and interesting—ones that students will be able to find uses for in their everyday lives. Of course, this is a matter of judgment, best decided by those who know the individual students. Work we have done with kindergarten and first-grade children shows that sophisticated words can be successfully taught to young children. For example, kindergartners readily applied *nuisance* to disruptive classmates, and understood what was happening when a *commotion* occurred in the hall; first graders could easily discern *argumentative* peers from those who were more collaborative and congenial!

SUMMARY

In evaluating words as possible candidates for instruction, here are three things to keep in mind:

1. How generally useful is the word? Is it a word that students are likely to meet often in other texts? Will it be of use to students in describing their own experiences?

For example, students are likely to find more situations in which to apply *typical* and *dread* than *portage* and *brackish*.

2. How does the word relate to other words, to ideas that students know or have been learning? Does it directly relate to some topic of study in the classroom? Or might it add a dimension to ideas that have been developed?

For example, what might knowing the word *hubris* contribute to a middle school student's understanding of the battles at Lexington and Concord, which set the Revolutionary War in motion?

3. What does the word contribute to a text or situation? What role does the word play in communicating the meaning of the context in which it is used?

A word's meaning might be necessary for understanding a text. Or understanding its meaning might allow an enriched insight about the situation being presented, such as in the case of *absurd, enormous,* or *identical* as words to describe a variety of hats. Keep in mind that there is no formula for selecting age-appropriate vocabulary words despite lists that identify "fifth-grade words" or "seventh-grade words." As long as the word can be explained in known words and can apply to what students might talk or write about, it is an appropriate word to teach. We provide compelling evidence for this claim in Chapter 4, which focuses on the success of young children in learning sophisticated words.

YOUR TURN

We invite you to use what you have learned in this chapter to make some decisions about which words you will teach.

1. Select a text that your students will be reading. It can be a story, or an excerpt from a chapter book or novel, or a social studies textbook.

2. List all the words that are likely to be unfamiliar to students.

3. Analyze the word list:

   - Which words can be categorized as Tier Two words?
   - Which of the Tier Two words are most necessary for comprehension?
   - Are there other words needed for comprehension? Which ones?

4. On the basis of your analysis, how will you deal with the words?

   - Which will need only brief attention?
   - Which will you give more elaborate attention to?

CHAPTER 3

Introducing Word Meanings

Consider these three possible scenes of introducing meanings of vocabulary words:

Scene 1

Ms. T: Our first vocabulary word is *covet*. Sam, do you know what *covet* means?

Sam: It's like not out there, like a secret something.

Amber: Oh! Yeah, like covet operations on *NCIS*!

Aaron: Like covet it up?

Scene 2

Ms. T: Our first vocabulary word is *covet*. Sam, please read the definition.

Sam: (*reading from the dictionary/glossary*) "To wish for greatly or with envy."

Ms. T: Okay. So, what's something you might covet?

Maria: I covet an iPhone—that's what I want for my birthday.

Scene 3

Ms. T: Our first vocabulary word is *covet*. Here's our friendly definition: "If you covet something that someone else has, you want it and wish it belonged to you." Have you ever coveted anything?

Eli: Ooh—my cousin got this cool new bike! When I saw it, I wanted it so bad!

We might call the three possible scenes above "Lost," "Nearing the ballpark," and "Got it." In the first one, students are going on vague memory traces that turn out to be wrong, and begin piling up. In the second one, a standard dictionary definition hasn't given enough particular information to differentiate *covet* from general wishing. In the third scene, a student is already right on target with his example.

In this chapter, our goal is to help students get off to the most effective possible start on learning new words. A strong start is important, because learning new words is a journey that goes well beyond being presented with information about their meaning. Even rich, meaningful explanations of word meaning will not result in deep or sustained knowledge of a word. Multiple encounters over time are called for if the goal is more than a temporary surface-level understanding and if new words are to become permanently and flexibly represented in students' vocabulary repertoires. In this chapter we focus on how to present words initially in ways that help them take root in students' vocabularies.

INTRODUCING WORDS: WHEN, HOW MANY, AND HOW?

Before we open the discussion of how to initiate building students' understanding of word meanings effectively, we consider for a moment a couple of initial decisions that need to be faced—*when* in the course of a lesson to introduce new words and *how many* to introduce at once. The most common answer to the first decision is before a text is read. Let's consider if that is always the right decision. The reasoning behind introducing words before reading is to make unfamiliar words available for students when they encounter them as they read. This makes sense as a way to alleviate comprehension difficulties, particularly if students are reading a text independently.

But if reading is done together with a group, the best time to introduce meaning of an unfamiliar word is right when it is encountered in the context. So, if the text says, for example, "The whole thing was turning into a calamity," just pause briefly and say "a *calamity*—that means it's a disaster." No need for any further information or additional examples at this point, because in the midst of a text, the focus should be on understanding text ideas, not learning vocabulary. Word meaning is introduced at this point only to further the main comprehension goal.

Keeping the comprehension goal in mind should also influence the number of words introduced either before or during reading. It should be few—only those words that might have the potential to disrupt comprehension of major ideas. If too many words are introduced before reading, students are unlikely to recall the meanings accurately as they meet the words in text. If too many words are introduced *during* reading, the flow of building comprehension is interrupted.

Note that this recommendation does not restrict the number of words to be taught overall. Words that you want to provide instruction for and that appear in a text being read—but that are not essential for comprehension—can also be introduced after the text is read. There may be words of interest or general usefulness that appear in a text but whose unfamiliarity may not be disruptive to overall comprehension. These words can be introduced following reading.

When working with words after reading, the focus changes from text comprehension to vocabulary development. Thus, here is where additional contexts and activities can be offered. In fact, we consider an important part of introducing a new word as getting students active with it, in a quick and spirited way. We provide some examples later in this chapter.

The heart of a robust vocabulary approach is to select a set of words to be introduced and sustained over several days. So, how many words should be in these sets? In our research, we have worked with sets of from 6 to 10 words over a period of 5 to 9 days. In our original study with fourth graders, we worked with sets of 10 words over a week, and we introduced all 10 words at once on the first day. We look back at that and scratch our heads a bit—10 new words at once seems like a lot. In more recent studies, we've introduced between three and five words in a lesson, and then introduced the rest either later in the day or in the next day's lesson.

The rest of this chapter expands on the "how" of introducing words—elaborating on how to get across a word's meaning initially and how to get students actively engaged with the word. But one final note here is a caution about how *not* to introduce new words: Avoid asking students, "Who can tell me what X means?" when your best hunch is that the word may be unfamiliar to many or most students. It's tempting, we know—you would like to know what students have in their minds about various words they may have encountered previously in their reading. But for the sake of students' learning, avoid that temptation! The reason to avoid the "Who can tell me what X means?" question is that most often students begin to guess the meaning, and incorrect guesses pile up as the teacher calls on more students, trying to ferret out knowledge (see Scene 1 above). Two consequences are likely, first, valuable time—which students could have spent learning the word's meaning—is wasted; second, and more problematic, is that students will remember those incorrect associations and have a harder time learning what the word actually means, as researchers such as Nichols's (2007) work demonstrated, and similar to the false memory effect explored by researchers such as Roediger (e.g., Roediger & McDermott, 2000).

PROVIDING INITIAL WORD MEANING INFORMATION THROUGH DEFINITIONS

If one asks teachers how they first introduce a word, there is a high probability that *definition* will be in their responses. Indeed, definitions are still synonymous with vocabulary instruction in many classrooms. However, the reality is that traditional definitions are not an effective vehicle for learning word meanings. Studies that provided dictionary definitions to students and asked students to create sentences with the words or answers to brief questions about the words revealed that:

- Sixty-three percent of the students' sentences were judged to be "odd" (Miller & Gildea, 1985).
- Sixty percent of students' responses were unacceptable (McKeown, 1991, 1993).
- Students frequently interpreted one or two words from a definition as the entire meaning (Scott & Nagy, 1989).

Problems with Dictionary Definitions

To understand why dictionary definitions are so often unhelpful, it can be useful to know a bit about how definitions end up in the form they do. Formalized definitional practice can be traced to the time of Samuel Johnson's mid-18th-century *Dictionary of the English Language* (Johnson & Walker, 1828). The traditional form of definitions is based on describing a word by first identifying the class to which something belongs and then indicating how it differs from other members of the class. A classic example is *bachelor* defined as "*a man* who is *unmarried*."

The most overriding consideration for definitional format, however, is that definitions in dictionaries must be concise because of space restrictions. Lexicographers, those who develop dictionaries, have called this constraint "horrendous." Indeed, one lexicographer made the point that "almost every defining characteristic common to dictionaries can be traced to the need to conserve space " (Landau, 1984, p. 140), and another has said that dictionary definitions have led to "some remarkable convolutions in dictionary prose style" (Hanks, 1987, p. 120).

So there is nothing "official" or "scientific" about the form in which definitions appear. For this reason, combined with the fact that definitions are not particularly helpful for student learning, we prefer to introduce new vocabulary by explaining a word's meaning rather than providing a definition for the word. When we examined definitions by putting ourselves in the place of a young learner trying to make sense of the information, we came up with four characteristic features of definitions that get in the way of understanding word meaning.

The first feature we called **weak differentiation**, which means that the definition does not differentiate how the target word is different from other similar words—how it is a specific case of a more general idea. For example, consider *conspicuous* defined in a junior dictionary as "easily seen." This definition weakly differentiates *conspicuous* from the general domain of *visible*. After all, unless it is dark or one has poor vision, nearly everything is easily seen. But something conspicuous is not just easy to see, rather it pops out at you because of its size or color or inappropriateness to a situation.

The second problem of dictionary definitions is that they are often stated in such **vague language** that they provide little information. As an example, consider *typical* defined as "being a type." At best, a learner might manage to ask, "A type of what?" It is unlikely that a young student would make enough sense of the definition to develop much, if any, idea of what *typical* means.

A third problem of definitions is that there may be a **more likely interpretation** of meaning than the one intended. This can happen when a definition uses familiar words in unfamiliar ways. For example, consider the definition for *devious*: "straying from the right course; not straightforward." The idea of straying from a course is likely to be interpreted by a young learner in a concrete, physical way. The learner may conclude that *devious* has to do with crooked walking or getting lost, such as "The boy was devious on his bike."

The fourth problematic characteristic is that some definitions give **multiple pieces of information** but offer no guidance in how they should be integrated. For example, consider the definition for *exotic*: "foreign; strange; not native." A learner might wonder what relationship to draw among these parts. Is something exotic if it is strange but not foreign, or only if it is both foreign and strange? The concept for *exotic* that needs to be captured is that when something is exotic it may be strange or unusual or special *because* it comes from a distant place.

The problematic features of dictionary definitions as exemplified by those provided above, the evidence that young students do not learn effectively from dictionary definitions, and the complaints of lexicographers themselves all point to a need for those of us who are engaged in teaching to do better than dictionaries may do when presenting word meaning information. Toward this goal, we present three constructs for developing *initial* word meaning information: student-friendly explanations of words, instructional contexts, and opportunities for students to interact with word meanings in ways that oblige them to think about what a word means.

▪ YOU TRY IT ▪

Select a few words that are unfamiliar to your students, and ask them to look up the words in a classroom dictionary and read the definitions. Then, ask students to talk about what they think the definition means. What was most helpful to them in understanding the definition? What was confusing?

Developing Student-Friendly Explanations

Giving a definition of a word—even for words we know well—is not an easy task. Toward developing student-friendly explanations, two basic principles should be followed: (1) Capture the essence of the word and how it is typically used and (2) explain the meaning in everyday language.

Capture the Word

When introducing words to students, it's important to try to capture what is particular about a word: What is its role in the language and what is communicated when we use that word? For example, consider the word *controversy*, which dictionaries define as "a discussion marked by opposing views" or simply "a disagreement." While these are true, neither definition captures the contentious nature of controversy. Students might differ in their opinions of which video games are best, but that wouldn't be called a controversy. Consider what kinds of things are described as controversies— not only is there the students' disagreement, but there is strong opposition on each side. An explanation of the word that comes closer to "capturing" the heart of its use might be: "A controversy is a strong disagreement about something that often involves a lot of discussion and angry feelings."

As an exercise in capturing a word's essence, consider the word *tamper*. What comes to mind when you think of that word? Possibly that if you tamper with something, it doesn't work anymore; also, that tampering is often done secretly to try to trick or harm someone. But consider a definition for *tamper* taken from a dictionary: "to interfere in a secret or incorrect way." This definition would seem to include simply meddling in someone else's affairs as a busybody. It lacks the sense of messing up something in a possibly sinister way. A more student-friendly explanation, crafted to highlight the notion that *tampering* with something damages it, might be "to change something secretly so that it does not work properly or becomes harmful."

Explain Meanings in Everyday Language

Developing effective meaning explanations for students calls for taking care to explain the concept in language that is readily accessible so students can understand the concept with ease. So, for example, avoid defining the word *ally* as "one associated with another." That seems more puzzling than helpful.

To move the definition of *ally* into accessible language, think of how to communicate the concept of "association" in student-friendly terms. Perhaps something like "somebody who does things with you" or "somebody you hang around with." Now, consider whether that captures the characteristic meaning of *ally*: It seems to miss the role of an ally as helping in some common cause. Picking up on that aspect, we might come up with an explanation such as "someone who helps you in what you are trying to do, especially when there are other people who are against you."

Another aspect of creating an explanation with an eye toward accessible language is developing it in such a way that students will attend to the whole explanation. This is to ensure that some words within an explanation do not take on unintended emphasis and lead students to choose just part of the explanation as the entire meaning. For instance, explaining *meticulous* as "extremely or excessively careful about small details" gives prominence to the word *careful*. Using the most obvious sense of *careful*, students could interpret the word as relating to being cautious about danger. Adding *neat* might help students understand the appropriate sense of *careful*. A student-friendly form of the definition might then be given as "being very neat and careful about small details."

Consider a few more words and how we might work our way from dictionary definitions to student-friendly explanations.

> *covert:* **kept from sight; secret; hidden**

What are students likely to make of this definition? The clearest part, for students, would seem to be the word *secret*. So, students might well interpret the word as a synonym for *secret* without even stopping to realize that the word is an adjective rather than a noun. Beyond this possible misinterpretation, the definition sounds as if it applies to something or someone that you want to hide. This is at odds with the way *covert* is most often used—to describe an action done in a secretive way. To define *covert* as "describes something that is done in a hidden or secret way" makes it much clearer to students how the word is to be applied.

disrupt: break up; split

This could easily be interpreted as physical breaking, as in "We disrupted the candy bar so we could all share it." What's the nature of *disrupt* that needs to be captured? It would seem to be that disrupting is like rudely stopping something that's going on, or causing a problem that makes some activity cease. Using these ideas might lead to the student-friendly explanation: "to cause difficulties that stop something from continuing easily or peacefully."

illusion: appearance or feeling that misleads because it is not real

This is a good example of a vague definition. An "appearance that misleads" is rather hard to make sense of. Might it be something that looks good but isn't—like a stale piece of cake? Or considering "feeling"—how does a feeling mislead? How is a feeling not real? The core of *illusion* is something that looks real but isn't, or appears to be something but isn't there at all. Those ideas could be put together in a definition such as "something that looks like one thing but is really something else or is not there at all."

improvise: to make, invent, or arrange with whatever is on hand

This definition seems to lack a key component of improvisation, the idea that you use whatever is on hand *because* you don't have exactly what's called for. Also, the "make, invent, or arrange" trio makes the whole concept a bit vague. A definition that better characterizes *improvise* and is more concrete and accessible might be "to make something you need by using whatever is available at the moment."

morbid: not healthy or normal

This definition really pushes the limits of failing to characterize a word! Something *morbid* is well beyond not healthy. Imagine a student telling his or her mother, "I think I need to stay home from school today—I'm feeling morbid!" The definition has to be explicit about the connection to death or gruesome thoughts. Perhaps a more student-friendly explanation is "showing a great interest in horrible, gruesome details, especially about death."

Note that all the above student-friendly explanations are quite a bit longer than their dictionary counterparts. The brevity of many dictionary definitions leaves too much assumed, and young learners often make incorrect assumptions or are unable to put the ideas together at all. Fuller, more explicit language is needed to promote students' development of word meaning. As teachers, we do not have the constraints imposed on lexicographers, so we can provide the kinds of explanations that will be most helpful to students.

If you review the student-friendly explanations above, you will also notice that they often include words such as *something, someone*, or *describes*. These terms anchor the meaning for students so they can begin to get an idea of how to use the word.

Resources for Developing Definitions

As we mentioned at the outset of our discussion of definitions, it is difficult to form a good definition off the top of your head, even for words that you know well. So in trying to come up with friendly definitions, it's good to start with some resources. A valuable resource for creating definitions is "learner's dictionaries." These were developed specifically for students learning English as a second language, but they are very useful to any student of the language. They present definitions in much more accessible language than traditional dictionaries, even dictionaries created for students. A notable learner's dictionary is the *Collins COBUILD English Language Dictionary* (Sinclair, 1987). This dictionary provides discursive explanations for words rather than traditional definitions. For example, the meaning for *defiant* is presented as follows: "If you are defiant, you show aggression or independence by refusing to obey someone or by refusing to behave in the expected way." Another useful learner's dictionary is published by Longman (Delacroix et al., 2007). Longman uses only the most frequent 2,000 words in English as the language of its definitions. In Longman, *defiant* is defined as "refusing to do what someone tells you to do, especially because you do not respect them."

Because COBUILD and Longman have somewhat limited word stock, you'll need to consult other dictionaries as well. And guess what—there is a website that will bring definitions from dozens of dictionaries to you! It's *onelook.com*. Work with definitions from these resources and tweak the best among them for the language level of your particular students.

■ **YOU TRY IT** ■

You might find it useful to try your hand at creating some student-friendly explanations.

1. Select some words that your students are currently learning.
2. Look up the definitions for the words provided in one or, preferably, more dictionaries or glossaries.
3. Think about the definitions from a young learner's point of view.
   - What difficulties might the definitions pose to such a learner? (Refer to pages 43–45 for a discussion of potential definition difficulties.)
   - How might you characterize the words so that their meanings are specific?
   - What everyday language might you use to craft explanations?
4. Create student-friendly explanations for the words you selected. Anchor your definition by including words such as *something, someone*, or *describes* in your explanations.
5. Share the explanations you created with your students. Ask them to compare your explanations with the definitions provided in a dictionary or glossary.

DEALING WITH MULTIPLE MEANINGS

The notion that many words in our language have more than one meaning is a common observation and presents a dilemma of how, how many, and which meanings to deal with in vocabulary instruction. The *Common Core State Standards* have foregrounded the importance of dealing with multiple-meaning words. The first anchor standard in vocabulary acquisition and use is to "determine or clarify the meaning of unknown and multiple meaning words and phrases based on [grade-level content]" (National Governors Association Center for Best Practices, Council of Chief State School Officers, 2010, p. 25).

So what exactly constitutes multiple meanings? The term *multiple meanings* often refers to *homographs*, which are words that are spelled the same, usually pronounced the same, but have different meanings. For example, consider *sound*, as in what we hear; *sound*, as in sturdy; *sound*, as in the name for a body of water. These are different words, whose origins are from various old English and European languages and they are no more related to each other than, say, *volume, sturdy*, and *island*. We wouldn't see an advantage for teaching the latter three words together, so there is little reason to teach the first three words together. The point is that the three words have no common semantic features—the meanings are not at all related, they just happen to be spelled the same. So if they were taught together, there is a good chance of confusing students.

Multiple meanings can also refer to words that have multiple *senses*, which are semantically related. This begins to get us into difficult territory, because the distinctions between different uses of a word, different senses of a word, and separate meanings of a word are not sharply drawn. Multiple senses of a word are related around a core meaning; that is, there is a common semantic origin. Various senses of a word emerge because language is flexible and ever changing as we use it. For instance, think of the word *mock*, which comes to us from the Middle English *moker*, via Old French *mocquer*. The original meaning is roughly "to mimic." Suppose the word *mock* appeared in a story the class was reading and was used in the sense of making fun of someone in a mean way. In that case, we would likely not also introduce the sense of an imitation of something, such as a mock battle. Although both uses come from a common core meaning, they are far enough apart that it would seem unhelpful to introduce them together.

We see a somewhat grayer area with the word *model*. The central sense here is a representation of something. Consider *model* used in the sense of a model student—which, in essence, means the best possible representation, or ideal representation, of "studentness." This sense is quite close to the use of *model* as a verb, as in "to model oneself after." The verb form usually connotes wanting to be like some excellent or ideal representation. Thus, we would likely introduce that sense of being a model and also use *model* as a verb in the same instructional set—probably not the first day the word was introduced, but in follow-up activities on a subsequent day.

Would it also make sense to talk about *model* in the sense of miniature versions of something, often used as toys or collectibles? This use seems to move farther away from the notion of ideal representation, yet the sense in which such a model represents something is rather readily understood. So this puts us right in the middle of a gray zone. Depending on the students and the time allotted to vocabulary, it could make sense to teach it or skip it. One teacher might decide that talking about that sense would enrich students' understanding, perhaps based on the knowledge that students have experience with these kinds of models. Another teacher might decide that the "miniature model" sense is not that important and that students are likely to learn it on their own, or that it may be distracting to include the extra information. Both decisions seem legitimate.

One case where it *is* a good idea to touch on multiple meanings occurs when introducing a word that has a meaning that students already know. For example, if you introduce the word *fast* as "not eating," it makes sense to say that the word also "has a meaning that we probably all know—if something moves very quickly, we call it *fast*." Thus, even though the two meanings do not have a common core, the fact that the word form—pronunciation and spelling—is already attached to a familiar meaning suggests confusion is best avoided if the likeness is explicitly pointed out.

Many Tier One words have multiple senses or even multiple meanings. Consider *like, run,* and *give* to name just a few. But this is not much of a problem for native language speakers. Children learn these words in their contexts early and encounter them with high frequency. For students who are English learners (ELs), and any student who seems to get confused by multiple meanings or senses, the best approach may be to talk about the idea that language grows and changes and we often use the same word in a number of different ways. Provide examples such as *see,* and *light,* and then refer to that idea when less familiar uses of words are encountered.

Perhaps even for ELs, however, multiple meanings may not be the most pressing problem. Since so many of the multiple-meaning words are in Tier One, the EL students will be exposed to many uses of them in regular conversation. These experiences mimic initial language acquisition when the frequent, contextualized use of words allows a learner to build knowledge of the words with relative ease, compared to words that are more likely to appear in text than in conversation. When instances of confusion occur, clear them up. But there is no need, even for EL students, to cover all senses of words or even introduce additional senses for every word that is taught.

When you do want to communicate multiple senses of a word, how to do so can be tricky. Try, as much as possible, to portray a core meaning rather than showing the distinction among senses of a word. For example, the meaning of *distinction* could be presented as two separate senses as follows:

1. A *distinction* <u>between</u> two things is a definite difference between them.
2. To do something <u>with</u> *distinction* means it is done really, really well.

Or the core meaning of *distinction* as a clear difference could be preserved, and the word explained as:

A *distinction* has to do with a definite difference between things. When things have a distinction between them, they are easy to tell apart. If a person does something <u>with</u> *distinction*, he or she does it really, really well. It is different from the way other people usually do it, because it is much better.

As demonstrated in the example of *distinction*, the notion of multiple meanings is another reason not to depend on definitions but to move toward thinking about providing word meaning more in terms of explaining word use and presenting examples. So, to practice the word *distinction*, rather than asking students to recall its definition, elicit examples in a context, such as "What is something that you would like to be able to do with distinction?" and "Is there a distinction between how sixth graders and seventh graders feel about homework? Why?"

The reason for emphasizing core meaning is that it benefits students to understand words as flexible items of language rather than numerous items with the same name and different meanings. Vocabulary knowledge is a network of connected concepts, and higher-quality connections are complex—picture an interconnected web. So it is more helpful to students to build many different connections to each word they learn rather than separate connections to multiple versions of a word.

As students encounter instances of the same word forms that have distinctly different, unrelated meanings, they may well exhibit confusion. That is part of learning language. But the more that students understand language as a living, growing phenomenon rather than a list of items with definite meaning boundaries, the less of a problem that will be. Learning vocabulary is really learning to use language. That learning has to include figuring out how far meanings go—how much to maneuver or stretch what you know about a word in applying it to a context. This process will surely have its ups and downs for students, and what they need in order to negotiate it successfully is abundant practice using words and abundant talk around word uses. The next section takes up how to initiate such practice.

SOLIDIFYING THE INTRODUCTION TO WORD MEANINGS— A.S.A.P.

Introducing word meanings with student-friendly explanations is only part of what it takes to help students establish an initial understanding of a word. The other part is to ensure that students actually deal with the meanings right away. There are numerous short and lively activities that can require students to process meanings. We next provide several that we have found to be engaging for students. The activities below come from the vocabulary research studies that we engaged in and which we noted in Chapter 1.

Word Associations

After having presented explanations for *accomplice, virtuoso, philanthropist,* and *novice*, we asked students to associate one of their new words with a presented word or phrase, such as the following:

- Which word goes with *crook*? (*accomplice*)
- Which word goes with "gift to build a new hospital"? (*philanthropist*)
- Which word goes with *piano*? (*virtuoso*)
- Which word goes with *kindergartner*? (*novice*)

In each case, students were then asked *why* they decided on the connection they had made. Building explicit associations between a known word and a newly learned word reinforces even further the meaning of the new word. Note that the associations are not synonyms; rather, the student must develop a relationship. For example, in the case of associations between *crook* and *accomplice*, one student might say that an accomplice helps a crook, another might say that an accomplice is learning to be a crook, and yet another might suggest that crooks want accomplices to help them in their wrongdoings. Having students explain their reasoning is an essential component of the kind of instruction that requires learners to process information—directly deal with information by considering and mentally manipulating it.

Have You Ever . . . ?

This activity helps students associate newly learned words with contexts and activities from their own experience. Thus, it helps students understand that they have a place for the word in their vocabularies. In the activity, students are asked to "Describe a time when you might *urge* someone, *commend* someone, *banter* with someone."

Applause, Applause!

For this activity, students are asked to clap in order to indicate how much they would like (not at all, a little bit, a lot) to be described by the target words: *frank, impish, vain, stern*. And, as always, *why* they would feel that way.

Which Would . . . ?

Form questions around target words by asking students which they would prefer between alternatives:

Which would you rather *anticipate*—your birthday or a dentist appointment? Why?
Which would you rather *interact* with—sharks or polar bears? Why?
Which would be easier to *confine*—butterflies or cats? Why?

There are many variations on activities that get students actively engaged with word meanings. They can be as simple as asking questions such as the following about newly introduced words:

When might you . . . ?
How might you . . . ?
Why might you . . . ?

The key to effective activities is that they require students to attend to a word's meaning in order to apply it meaningfully to an example situation.

SUMMARY

In introducing words, here are some things to keep in mind:

- Make word meanings explicit and clear. Develop student-friendly explanations for discussing word meanings.
- Get students actively involved with thinking about and using the meanings right away.

Full understanding and spontaneous, appropriate use of new words develops gradually, but a strong start is essential to allowing those processes to occur.

YOUR TURN

We invite you to use what you have learned in this chapter to develop some ways to introduce words you will teach.

1. Select words from a text that your students will be reading.

2. Create a student-friendly explanation for each word by:
   - Thinking about what specific elements make the word different from other words.
   - Using everyday language.

3. Create some brief activities that will initiate students' engagement with the words and their meanings.

CHAPTER 4

Bringing Vocabulary into the Earliest Grades

As part of their robust vocabulary activities in a primary grade classroom, the following exchange occurred when the teacher asked a question about the target word *strut*. Notice that a student not only responded to *strut*, but used two other target words in her response (in italics):

MR. W: Okay, are you ready? If a rooster *strutted* into this classroom right now, what would he do?

JANELLE: He might . . . he might like be happy and he might be *jubilant* walking in here because he doesn't know anybody and then he wants to try to *improve* his skills.

One of the biggest changes that has occurred since the publication of *Bringing Words to Life* is the focus on vocabulary for the youngest learners. This includes studies of vocabulary instruction that we and others have done with children from preschool to first grade (e.g., Beck & McKeown, 2007b; Collins, 2009; Coyne, McCoach, Loftus, Zipoli, & Kapp, 2009; Silverman, 2007). Research on younger learners has been sufficient for researchers to conduct a meta-analysis to examine results of vocabulary instruction for young children from many different studies. The analysis concluded that "children's oral language development benefited strongly from these interventions" (Marulis & Neuman, 2010, p. 322).

Many of the studies of vocabulary for young learners have taken a perspective similar to ours, that effective vocabulary instruction calls for

multiple encounters in varied contexts and active processing of word meaning (Marulis & Newman, 2010; Nagy & Townsend, 2012). Most of the
interventions begin with storybook reading and provide explanations of
word meaning and a variety of activities that allow children to explore
and apply word meaning. Many have also focused on Tier Two words,
or "sophisticated" words, in their instruction, for example, *peculiar, irri-
tated,* and *regretful* (Coyne et al., 2010), *solitary, murmur,* and *risky* (Silverman,
2007). In this chapter we provide examples of the books, words, and activities that we used in our studies. We begin with an overview of the research
studies that we have conducted with young children.

RESULTS FROM STUDYING ROBUST VOCABULARY
WITH YOUNG CHILDREN

We conducted two studies with kindergarten and first-grade children from
a low-achieving elementary school in which classroom teachers provided
vocabulary instruction of Tier Two words selected from story read-alouds
(Beck & McKeown, 2007b). The first study compared the number of words
learned for children who were directly taught the words and for children
in the same school who received no instruction. Instruction was developed
for several words from each of seven stories. The vocabulary instruction
occurred after a story had been read, thus taking advantage of the story's use
of the words to build initial understanding. The study found, as expected,
that children in the experimental group learned significantly more words.

In the second study reported in Beck and McKeown (2007b), we
compared kindergarten and first graders' word learning using two different amounts of instruction. Words were introduced and then follow-up
activities were provided for some of the words for 3 additional days. The
vocabulary gains for words that received more instruction were twice as
large. Twice the instruction for twice the gains may seem a rather obvious
result. But at the time we conducted the studies, some colleagues suggested
that the gains we obtained in the first study might indicate a ceiling for the
learning of sophisticated words for young children.

In both studies, vocabulary learning was assessed using a picture task
with a format similar to the Peabody Picture Vocabulary Test (PPVT;
Dunn & Dunn, 2007) in that children selected, from a set of four pictures,
the one that represented a target word. However, the processing required
by our picture task was more complex because the task did not ask for a
direct matching between a picture and an object, but rather asked students to decide which picture portrayed a situation described by a target
word. For example: "Which shows someone glancing? . . . someone who

is satisfied? . . . something being revealed?" Responding to such questions involved interpreting the semantic elements of the word in light of novel situations.

For the second study, a verbal test was added that involved asking children to respond (yes or no) to four questions about each word. Two questions (one true and one false) asked whether a presented meaning matched a given word (e.g., "Does *extraordinary* mean very special?" "Does *extraordinary* mean very hungry?"). Two questions asked whether a brief context exemplified a word's meaning (e.g., "Would it be *extraordinary* to see a monkey at the zoo?" "Would it be *extraordinary* to see a monkey teaching school?").

The measures we developed for the kindergarten/first-grade studies were designed to require students to do more than simply identify word meanings. However, the measures did not ask them to engage in the kind of higher-level processing required in text comprehension. Given that the eventual goal of vocabulary instruction is to affect language comprehension, we believed it essential to explore vocabulary instruction effects on measures of comprehension in young students. So for our most recent research with young students, we examined the effects of instruction with a series of tasks that addressed word knowledge, comprehension, and production (McKeown & Beck, 2012). Our purpose was to consider what the instruction enabled children to do with their language.

The study compared two approaches to vocabulary instruction. The instructional approaches represented prototypical vocabulary instruction found in instructional materials and research studies. One approach built on repeated readings of a storybook with explanations of word meanings during reading (repetition instruction) and the other began with story reading but moved to robust interactive instruction (interactive instruction). Instruction in the repetition condition focused on learning the meanings of the target words, and included activities such as concentration, in which students turned over cards to match words with their definitions, and yes/no games, in which students had to signal whether a word was paired with its correct definition. Thus the only content being practiced was the definition, but the formats of the activities were designed to be fun and engaging.

Activities in the interactive instruction condition were based on robust instruction, prompting students to think about and use the word meanings. For example, students were asked to make choices about the use of words and to explain why the choice was made (e.g., "Which would be more *astonishing*: seeing a robin in the spring or hearing your dog say hello to you . . . why?") and to create contexts for words (e.g., "What could you do that might *astonish* your friends?").

Following instruction, we gave students the same knowledge measure used in the 2007 studies, which required recognition of word meanings and simple uses of words in a yes/no format. We hypothesized that both the repetition and interactive instruction would be effective in helping students to learn the meanings of words, and so we did not expect a difference on this measure between the conditions, and no difference was found.

We then gave students two different measures to tap comprehension. One assessed context integration—the ability to integrate one's understanding of a word into a context in order to make sense of the context. Context integration has been shown to be a key process in comprehension (Jenkins, Pany, & Schreck, 1978; Kame'enui, Carnine, & Freschi, 1982; Perfetti, 2007). We had used a similar task in our work with fourth graders (McKeown et al., 1985), and found that it showed a difference between types of instruction. An example from the present study (McKeown & Beck, 2012) is "Megan's mom could tell that Megan was *reluctant* to ride her new bike. Why did she feel that way?" To respond to the item, students had to understand that Megan was unsure about riding her bike, and use that understanding to infer reasons for that. The results showed an advantage for the interactive instruction over the repetition instruction. Students in the interactive condition were more likely to give responses such as "Maybe she might fall off."

The second comprehension task tapped listening comprehension and was meant to represent text comprehension. The task asked students to listen to brief stories that contained taught words and then recall the stories. Results of the task showed no differences between the interactive and repetition groups. On one hand, this result surprised us, because we have found differences in past research on text recall tasks for interactive instruction (McKeown et al., 1985). On the other hand, we had not used a listening comprehension task with students as young as kindergarten before. The requirements of such a task include, in addition to vocabulary knowledge, ability to sequence ideas, knowledge of story structure, knowledge of syntax, and short-term memory capacity. Thus any advantages from knowledge of the vocabulary may be overwhelmed by these other requirements for young students, who may be less likely to have these other aspects under control relative to older students.

Finally we administered a production task designed to elicit use of the taught words. The production task was developed because learning words well enough to express them is an important learning goal, and having words in one's productive vocabulary is generally viewed as a good measure of word ownership. The task we developed explored students' ability to use newly learned vocabulary words in response to pictures that depicted features related to the words. For example, one picture showed a birthday party scene, including a girl digging through a gift box, to represent *rummage*; a boy who seemed to be lost in thought, to represent *ponder*; and a boy sitting with his arms folded, to represent *patient*. Students were not asked to label the pictures but to talk about what they saw happening in them, as an attempt to capture spontaneous use of the words. The results for this task were similar to the context integration measure in that the interaction instruction showed an advantage over the repetition instruction.

The studies we have cited and discussed provide the evidence that young students can benefit from robust vocabulary instruction. The rest of the chapter focuses on describing the activities that can provide those benefits. We begin with a discussion of sources for words to teach young children, primarily texts that are read aloud to children rather than read by children. We then examine activities that introduce words in a way that takes into account the support that young children need to make sense of those words. Finally we present examples of follow-up activities that are needed to provide substantial learning benefits.

SOURCES OF WORDS
FOR YOUNG CHILDREN'S VOCABULARY DEVELOPMENT

We start this discussion by noting where words for young children's vocabulary development do *not* come from—and that is from the text materials that children are asked to read early in the course of reading acquisition. This is because, given beginning readers' word identification limitations, the text materials used in the early phases of learning to read should comprise words children know from oral language, that is, Tier One words like *run* and *ball*. Indeed, learning to read is learning a new representation for the language young children know from speech. As such, the early text materials are not good sources for adding new words to children's vocabulary repertoires. Emphatically, however, this does not mean that adding to and enriching children's vocabulary repertoires should be put on hold; it only means that enriching young children's vocabulary cannot be best developed through the words in the materials that young children read themselves.

Young children's listening and speaking competence is in advance of their reading and writing competence. That is, they can understand much more sophisticated content presented in oral language than they can read independently. As children are developing their reading and writing competence, we need to take advantage of their listening and speaking competencies to enhance their vocabulary development rather than holding back adding vocabulary to children's repertoires until their word recognition becomes adequate. Although the words in stories that young children read themselves do not offer good candidates for vocabulary growth, the *ideas* in the stories can still be a useful resource because some of the ideas in the simplest stories can be characterized by sophisticated words. Thus, after a story has been read, the teacher can describe a character or incident with an interesting word. Consider, for example, a story from an early first-grade basal reader in which some children make cookies. The story is mostly built around pictures, with the vocabulary limited to some children's names and words such as *pass, pat, pan,* and *cookies*. The story ends with the children eating the cookies and saying, "Mmmm. Good!"

The teacher could remind the children that after the characters in the story ate the cookies they said, "Mmmm. Good!" and explain that another way to say that is that the characters thought the cookies were *scrumptious*. She could explain the word further by saying that when something is scrumptious it tastes great. *Scrumptious* lends itself to a variety of other possible interactions. Children could be asked to think of foods that they think are scrumptious, as well as suggesting foods that they do not think are scrumptious. The notion could go further with asking the children what would be scrumptious to a mouse? . . . to a cat?

The teacher could also mention that in the story the children ate up all the cookies really quickly, explaining that another way to say that is that they *devoured* the cookies. The children could be asked to suggest foods that they would devour. Even further the teacher might suggest that the reason the children devoured the food is that they were *famished*. So, even though the stories that young readers read do not offer words to teach, the stories are still a resource for the teacher to use in generating target words.

An excellent source for words that will expand young students' vocabularies are trade books that are designed to be read aloud to children. As we found in our work, these delightful books are chock-full of Tier Two words. When we examined children's trade books for Text Talk (Beck & McKeown, 2001), a research and development project aimed at capturing the benefits of read-alouds, we identified about 1,500 words as potential candidates to teach to children. A word was considered a good candidate if it seemed likely to be unfamiliar to young children and yet a word whose concept they could identify with and use in normal conversation—that is, Tier Two words. From that list we pared down our choices and selected words from each story for direct teaching following a reading of the story.

We taught different numbers of words in the different studies, ranging from three per story to 10 per story. Initially we provided three words per story, but increased that as we discovered that primary grades children were readily able to handle that number and likely more. Our second study increased to six words over a week's time and our most recent study provided instruction for 10 words over a 7-day cycle of instruction. In each case, learning was successful. Thus the decision on the number of words taught can be made based on time constraints and what else is going on in the classroom. The table below provides examples of the words we selected from several stories:

Story	Words selected	
A Pocket for Corduroy (Freeman, 1978)	*reluctant*	*patient*
	insist	*drowsy*
	affectionate	*inspired*
Doctor DeSoto (Steig, 1982)	*protect*	*delicate*
	quiver	*morsel*
	timid	*stumbled*
The Patchwork Quilt (Flournoy, 1985)	*dread*	*anxious*
	glanced	*plead*
	masterpiece	*ruin*

A larger list of books and selected words is presented in *Creating Robust Vocabulary* (Beck et al., 2008).

■ YOU TRY IT ■

Select several favorite read-aloud books and read through them to find words that you might want to consider for teaching. If you are a first- or second-grade teacher, read some of the stories that your students read early in the school year and think about ways of labeling events, characters' qualities, and the like with sophisticated words. Use the criterion we described earlier: the word is unfamiliar to young children, but the concept represented by the word is one they can understand and could use in conversation.

FORMAT FOR INTRODUCING WORDS TO YOUNG CHILDREN

In our vocabulary interventions for young children, direct instruction in vocabulary occurs after a story has been read, discussed, and wrapped up. Initiating vocabulary instruction after story reading provides a strong context with which to begin word meaning introduction. But note that in cases where we thought that a word was needed for story comprehension, we suggested that the teacher stop and briefly explain the word, and then go on with the story. So, for example, in reading *Six-Dinner Sid* (Moore,

1991), when Sid the cat was taken to the vet, the teacher said, "A vet is a special doctor for animals."

Our introductions of word meaning for young learners is similar to the word introductions described in Chapter 3 in that they are built around providing a student-friendly explanation of word meaning and getting students active with the word immediately. But in our work with younger learners, we created a more systematic introductory format, and we present that here, exemplified by the activities we developed to introduce vocabulary from *A Pocket for Corduroy* (Freeman, 1978), a story about a teddy bear (Corduroy) that spends the night at a laundromat. We begin with the activities for *reluctant*:

> In the story, Lisa was *reluctant* to leave the laundromat without Corduroy. *Reluctant* means you are not sure you want to do something. Say the word with me.
>
> Someone might be reluctant to eat a food that he or she never had before, or someone might be reluctant to ride a roller coaster because it looks scary.
>
> Tell about something you would be reluctant to do. Try to use *reluctant* when you tell about it. You could start by saying something like "I would be reluctant to _____."
>
> What's the word that means you don't want to do it?

Note how the instruction for *reluctant* was presented:

- First, the story context for the word was reviewed (In the story, Lisa was *reluctant* to leave the laundromat without Corduroy).
- Next, the meaning of the word was explained in a child-friendly way (*Reluctant* means you are not sure you want to do something).
- The children were asked to repeat the word because pronouncing a word helps build a memory for the sound and meaning of the word (Say the word with me).
- Examples in contexts other than the one used in the story were provided (You might be reluctant to eat a food that you never had before, or you might be reluctant to ride a roller coaster because it looks scary).
- Children interacted with examples or provided their own examples (Tell about something you would be reluctant to do. Try to use *reluctant* when you tell about it. You could start by saying something like "I would be reluctant to _____"). Finally, children said the word again to reinforce its phonological representation and meaning (What's the word that means you don't want to do it?).

Vocabulary instruction always began with the context from the story, because it provided a situation that was already familiar to children and provided a rich example of the word's use. However, it is important to move beyond this context in providing and eliciting examples of the word's use. This is not only because multiple contexts are needed for learners to construct a meaningful and memorable representation of the word. It is also important because young children have a very strong tendency to limit a word's use to the context in which it was initially presented.

Consider the following exchange, which took place when a class of kindergarten children was asked to talk about something they might be reluctant to do:

LUCY: I would be reluctant to leave my teddy bear in the laundro-mat.

MS. K: Well, that's just like what Lisa did in the story. Try to think about something you might be reluctant to do that is not like Lisa.

CHINA: I would be reluctant to leave my teddy bear in the super-market.

MS. K: Okay, that's a little different than what Lisa was reluctant to do, but try to think of something that you would be reluctant to do that is very different than what Lisa was reluctant to do.

GRADY: I would be reluctant to leave my drums at my friend's house.

MS. K   That's pretty different from what Lisa was reluctant to do, but can we think of something that you would be reluctant to do that isn't about leaving something somewhere?

ANJELA: I would be reluctant to change a baby's diaper!

Two of us were present when that exchange occurred, and we both agreed that because of the diaper example most of the children in that class would remember the meaning of *reluctant* with ease!

The tendency to limit a word's use to a single context does not occur only at the earliest levels, however; we have seen this at many grade levels. One example was a visit to a fifth-grade class in which the word *desperately* had been introduced through an example of a character desperately looking for car keys. We visited several days after the initial introduction, and when the students were asked to provide examples of *desperately*, every example provided was about desperately looking for something (lunch money, house key, bus pass).

In trying to reduce this tendency, it is very important that examples be provided that are beyond the original context. But notice that even though the instruction for *reluctant* did provide two additional example contexts—being reluctant to eat something and being reluctant to ride something—the children in the above example transcript all went back to the context for *reluctant* that was in the trade book. Thus, in addition to providing other contexts, and often multiple other contexts, teachers need to work with their students, as the one in the foregoing example did, to help them move the word beyond one context or one use.

More Examples of Word Introductions for *Corduroy*

Below we provide the instructional activities for *insisted* and *drowsy*, two other words from *A Pocket for Corduroy* (Freeman, 1978) singled out for instruction. Notice that the components discussed above are present.

> In the story, Lisa's mother *insisted* that she leave the laundromat when it was closing.
>
> *Insisted* means to say that something MUST be done—you won't take no for an answer. Let's say the word aloud.
>
> Your mother might insist that you wear mittens when it is cold outside. She doesn't just TELL you to wear them, she makes sure you have them on before you go out!
>
> If you were in charge of helping your class get ready to go on a trip, think of something you would insist that everybody do. Try to use the new word when you tell us. You could start out by saying "I would insist that _____."
>
> What's the word that means it must be done?
>
> In the story, Corduroy felt *drowsy* when he landed in the laundry basket after his adventures in the laundromat. *Drowsy* means feeling as though you are going to fall asleep. Let's all say our word together.
>
> Sometimes riding in the car makes people feel drowsy, as though they want to take a nap. What might make you feel drowsy, loud drum playing or soft music? Why?
>
> When might you feel drowsy? In the middle of your favorite TV program or after swimming on a hot day? Why?
>
> What's the word that means feeling sleepy?

Wrapping Up Word Introductions

Lessons provided for three to five words to be introduced in one sitting. After the target words for a lesson had been presented as described above, there was an activity in which all words from that lesson were brought together. In the case at hand, that activity is as follows:

> We talked about three words: *insisted, reluctant*, and *drowsy*. Let's think about them.
>> Show us how your mother might look if she insisted you go to bed.
>> Show us how you would look if you felt reluctant about taking your little sister to the park.
>> Show us how you would look if you sat down in a comfortable chair and started to feel drowsy.

A CLOSER LOOK AT COMPONENTS OF INTRODUCING WORDS TO YOUNG CHILDREN

The first component of the introductory sequence we developed for young vocabulary learners, contextualizing a word for its role in a story, is quite straightforward (e.g., In the story, Lisa was *reluctant* to leave the laundromat without Corduroy). The second component, developing an explanation, or what we have also called a student-friendly definition, was discussed in Chapter 3. The two features we identified for developing student-friendly definitions—capturing the word and explaining the meaning in everyday language—hold for young children. The latter is perhaps even more important.

Definitions for Young Children

Below we provide some examples of the kind of language we used to develop student-friendly definitions for young children:

- If something is *dazzling*, that means that it's so bright that you can hardly look at it. After lots of long, gloomy winter days, sunshine on a sunny day might seem dazzling.
- *Strange* describes something different from what you are used to seeing or hearing.
- *Exhausted* means feeling so tired that you can hardly move.
- When people are *amusing*, they are usually funny or they make you happy to watch them. A clown at a circus is amusing.
- When someone is a *nuisance*, he or she is bothering you.

Note that some of the definitions have an example embedded in them. For some words it is particularly hard to describe their meaning in general terms to young children given the limited vocabulary they have. That is, it can be hard to make new words clearly differentiated through words that are understandable to young children. Hence, folding an example into the definition can help to clarify and pinpoint the word's meaning.

Uses of the Word Beyond the Story Context

Beyond sometimes folding examples into an initial definition, it is very important to provide examples of the word's use in contexts beyond its use in the story. A good way to create examples is to start by thinking about places young children are familiar with (e.g., school, home, park, street, playground); things they do (e.g., eat, sleep, play, go to school, watch TV); things they like and are interested in (e.g., animals, food, clothing, toys, books, nature). Consider the examples we developed for the words defined above:

- For *dazzling*: a big diamond ring; teeth after getting them cleaned at the dentist.
- For *strange*: a dog that meows; a fish that barks.
- For *exhausted*: how someone probably feels after running a long, long race, or after cleaning the house all day.
- For *amusing*: watching animals play at the zoo; seeing someone perform magic tricks.
- For *nuisance*: a baby brother or sister making a mess; someone who keeps interrupting you when you are talking.

ACTIVITIES THAT ENCOURAGE CHILDREN TO INTERACT WITH WORDS

The final component in the introductory activity for each word provides opportunities for children to interact with the target word, often by responding to and explaining examples as well as creating their own examples. As you review the ones below, notice the extent to which children will have to deal with the word's meaning in order to complete the task.

Questions, Reasons, and Examples

- If you are walking around a dark room, you need to do it *cautiously*. Why? What are some other things that need to be done cautiously?
- What is something you could do to *impress* your teacher? Why? What is something you could do that might impress your mother?

- Which of these things might be *extraordinary*? Why or why not?
  - A shirt that was comfortable, or a shirt that washed itself?
  - A flower that kept blooming all year, or a flower that bloomed for 3 days?
  - A person who has a library card, or a person who has read all the books in the library?

Making Choices

- If any of the things I say might be examples of people *clutching* something, say "clutching." If not, don't say anything.
  - Holding on tightly to a purse
  - Holding a fistful of money
  - Softly petting a cat's fur
  - Holding on to branches when climbing a tree
  - Blowing bubbles and trying to catch them
- If any of the things I say would make someone look *radiant*, say "You'd be radiant." If not, don't say anything.
  - Winning a million dollars
  - Getting a hug from a favorite movie star
  - Walking to the post office
  - Cleaning your room
  - Having the picture you painted hung up in the school library
- I'll say some things; if they sound *leisurely*, say "leisurely." If you'd need to be in a hurry, say "hurry."
  - Taking a walk in the park
  - Firefighters getting to a fire
  - Runners in a race
  - Sitting and talking to friends
  - A dog lying in the sun

USING ALL THE WORDS

As shown earlier in the vocabulary activities for the three words from *A Pocket for Corduroy* (Freeman, 1978), the lesson concludes with a short activity in which all the words that had been considered during that lesson are brought together. Each of these is initiated with a statement something like "We've talked about three words (words are specified). Let's think about them some more."

Relating Words

To develop a concluding activity, a good way to start is to see whether there is anything about the words that is related. In the case of *reluctant, insisted,* and *drowsy,* we noticed that each word might be expressed through facial expressions, so we asked children to show how they would look if they felt reluctant to do something, if they were insisting that someone do something, and if they felt drowsy.

Sentences

Sometimes more than one of the instructed words can be used in a single sentence. For example, in the case of *prefer, ferocious,* and *budge,* we could develop the following question:

- Would you *prefer* to *budge* a sleeping lamb or a *ferocious* lion? Why?

Choices

In the case of *pounce, sensible,* and *raucous,* we could ask children to choose between two words:

- If you get your clothes ready to wear to school before you go to sleep, would that be *sensible* or *raucous*?
- If you and your friends were watching a funny TV show together and began to laugh a lot, would you sound *pounce* or *raucous*?

One Context for All the Words

Most of the time, however, it is difficult to find relationships among the target words. What can be done, though, is to use a single context. For example, notice how the words *immense, miserable,* and *leisurely* are used in the questions below:

- What would an *immense* plate of spaghetti look like?
- Why might you feel *miserable* after eating all that spaghetti?
- What would it look like to eat spaghetti in a *leisurely* way?

Same Format

Finally, one can bring some coherence to an activity by using the same format for all three words. Several examples follow:

- If a dog was acting *menacing*, would you want to pet it or move away? Why?
- If you wanted to see something *exquisite*, would you go to a museum or a grocery store? Why?
- Is *imagine* more like dreaming or sneezing? Why?
- Is *snarl* something a fish might do or a lion might do? Why?
- Is *grumpy* a way you might feel or a way you might move? Why?

Children Create Examples

In some of the examples above, the format asked the child to make a choice and to explain the choice. The explanation is the most important part, because it requires the child to explicitly think through how the word fits the choices in order to express the relationship between the example and the word. Another format we used to prompt children's thinking of how a word fits a context was to have them create examples such as these:

If there was an *emergency* at an amusement park, what might have happened?

If you had a friend who watched TV all the time, how might you *coax* him into getting some exercise?

The "Using All the Words" activities we created to conclude a lesson were both a way to get another encounter with each word and a way to bring all the words together to begin the process of having them become a natural part of the children's language rather than isolated, specialized items.

■ YOU TRY IT ■

Select three words from a children's trade book that you would like to share with your students. Develop activities for students to interact with the words through one or more of the following formats as described on pages 66–69:

- Questions, Reasons, and Examples
- Making Choices
- Using All the Words
  - o Relating Words
  - o Sentences
  - o Choices
  - o Children Create Examples

INTRODUCTORY FORMATS FOR SEVERAL MORE WORDS

Having taken apart the instruction to analyze the processes that the activities are intended to promote, we now put it back together again by providing some complete examples. Our thinking in providing them is that taking a leisurely stroll through several sets of activities may develop a rich mindset for developing such activities. Below are the vocabulary activities from Text Talk (Beck & McKeown, 2001) that were developed for one story each from kindergarten, first, and second grades.

Doctor DeSoto (Steig, 1982) was a favorite among the kindergarten classes in which we worked. Doctor DeSoto is a dentist who happens to be a mouse. Although he usually refuses to treat dangerous animals, he and his dental-assistant wife take pity on a fox suffering from a toothache. After being treated, the fox decides to eat them, but the DeSotos outwit him by creating a concoction that makes his jaws stick together. The words from the story that we chose to deal with after the story had been read and discussed are *timid, morsel,* and *protect.* Following is the instruction that was developed:

> In the story, it said that the DeSotos wouldn't even treat a *timid* cat. *Timid* means "shy, maybe a little scared." Let's say the word together.
> People can be timid, too. For example, if you walked into a big room full of people you didn't know, you might feel a little timid.
>
> - Show how you would look if you felt timid.
> - Show how a timid cat might act.
>
> Let's say the word together.
>
> In the story, the fox thought of Dr. DeSoto as a tasty *morsel.* A morsel is a very small piece of food. Let's say the word together.
> The fox thought of Dr. DeSoto as a morsel of food because in comparison to a fox a mouse is very tiny.
> If the food that I name is a very small piece of food, say "morsel." If it isn't a morsel, don't say anything.
>
> - One Cheerio
> - A whole pie
> - A raisin
> - A turkey dinner
> - A cake crumb
>
> What's the word that means a tiny piece of food?

In the story, Dr. and Mrs. DeSoto had to come up with a plan to *protect* themselves. *Protect* means "to keep something safe." Let's say the word together. You protect your feet from getting wet by wearing boots. A mother cat protects her kittens by keeping them close to her.

I'll say some things, and you tell me how they could protect you.

- A pot holder
- A smoke alarm
- Mittens
- Seat belts

What word means staying safe?

Let's think about all three words: *morsel, timid,* and *protect.*

- If a little boy walked out on a stage and saw a lot of people in the audience, would he feel *timid* or *morsel*?
- Would someone wrap a baby in a warm blanket to *protect* him or *timid* him?
- Is a *morsel* more like a slice of cake or a crumb of cake?

Beware of the Bears (MacDonald, 1999) was a very popular book in first grade. Goldilocks and the three bears from the well-known story are the main characters in this tale. The bears, angry about the fact that Goldilocks made herself at home at their place, decide to follow her and behave in the same bad-mannered way in her home. They have a grand time, sampling different types of cereals, trying out all of the bathroom products, and the like. They have a pillow fight that is interrupted by Goldilocks, who informs them that this is not her house but the wolf's house. The words selected from this story were *launch, gleeful,* and *astonished.*

In the story when the bears were playing and throwing the cereal around, Daddy Bear *launched* some spoonfuls of cereal in the air. *Launch* means to toss or move something upward fast. Say the word.

If what I say could be launched, say "That could be launched." If you think they are not things that could be launched, say "No way."

- A rocket
- An elephant
- A paper airplane
- A tree
- Some fireworks

What's the word that means it goes way up?

In the story, the bears watched for Goldilocks's reactions *gleefully*. *Gleeful* means "so happy that you feel a little silly or giggly." Say our word.

Which would make you feel gleeful—so happy you might want to giggle?

- A party in school or extra work to do for homework?
- A trip to an amusement park or a trip to the dentist?
- Having your best friends move away or having them stay over for the whole weekend?
- Staying home from school because you're sick or because of a big snowstorm?

What's the word that means funny and silly?

In the story, the bears were *astonished* when Goldilocks started laughing at the big mess they'd made. If something makes you *astonished*, that means it is so unusual that you are surprised and shocked by it. Say our word.

Would you be astonished if:

- You met someone from Cleveland or from the planet Venus?
- Your dog said hello or your baby cousin said hello?
- Your mother served spaghetti for dinner or if she served a big banana split?

What is something you might be astonished to see in the sky? Start your sentence with "I'd be astonished. . . ."

What's the word that means really surprised?

We talked about three words: *launched*, *gleeful*, and *astonished*. Let's think about them some more.

- Which would you more likely want to *launch*—a kite or a car?
- If your teacher was making you feel *gleeful*, what would he or she probably be doing or telling you?
- What would make you more *astonished*—to find a dinosaur bone or a bird's bone?

We used *Chestnut Cove* (Egan, 1995) in the second grade. It's about a town called Chestnut Cove where people take the time to really enjoy life and help one another when needed. Then the king offers his kingdom to the person who grows the best watermelon, and everyone gets greedy. The citizens begin to tend to their gardens and stop being nice to each other. The need to rescue a pig causes the citizens to realize that the contest was destroying their town, and they decide to have a picnic and eat all of the watermelons. The next day the king came and declared the watermelons "disappointing." But the citizens were very satisfied. The words selected were *entire, incredible,* and *emotion.*

> In the story the king said that the winner of the contest would get his *entire* kingdom. That means that person would get the whole thing, all of it. Let's say the word.
> Let's think about what *entire* means.
>
> - If I said the entire class is here—what does that mean?
> - If I said the rug covers the entire room—what does that mean?
> - If it rained for your entire vacation—what does that mean?
>
> Now see if you can say a sentence to answer my question about *entire.*
>
> - How would you feel if you ate an entire cake yourself? (Encourage children to begin "If I ate an entire cake. . . .")
> - How would you feel if you ran the entire way to school? (Encourage children to begin "If I ran the entire way. . . .")
>
> What's the word that means the whole thing?
>
> In the story, when the king came to Chestnut Cove, he made an *incredible* announcement, saying that the person who could grow the biggest watermelon could have all his riches. *Incredible* means "unbelievable." Let's say the word.
> Sometimes people might tell you things that sound incredible. That means it's hard to believe that it's true.
> Which would be incredible?
>
> - A cow that can fly or a cow that eats grass?
> - A talking teacher or a talking horse?
> - First graders driving their own bus to school or first graders riding in a school bus?
> - Finding a live dinosaur or finding dinosaur bones?
>
> Has something incredible ever happened to you? Maybe it was something so good or so lucky that it felt incredible. Tell us about it.

Try to use *incredible* when you're telling us about it. You might start by saying something like, "Here's something incredible that happened to me. . . ."

What's the word that means you can't believe it?

In the story, when everyone rescued Mrs. Lark's pig, Eloise, her eyes were filled with *emotion*. That means she was feeling things deeply and maybe she wanted to cry because she was so thankful for people's help. Let's say the word.

We all have a lot of emotions—we laugh and cry and get angry and scared. All our feelings are called emotions.

When different things happen, we feel different emotions, like some things make us feel happy and loving, others sad, or disappointed, or angry. I'll name some situations, and you tell me what emotion you might feel if it happened to you.

- Learning that your best friend can stay with you all weekend
- Losing a pet
- Getting a big hug from your grandmother
- Hearing that a big storm is coming when you're alone at home

What's the word that means the way we can feel?

We talked about *entire, incredible,* and *emotion.* Let's think about those words some more.

- Which is more *incredible*—a plane landing at the airport or a plane landing on the school yard?
- On Saturdays, what is your favorite way to spend the *entire* day?
- If you watch a football game and at first your team is winning and then they lose—what kinds of *emotions* do you feel??

■ YOU TRY IT ■

The sections above have presented principles and examples for teaching young children useful, interesting, and sophisticated words. The basic instructional format is as follows:

1. Read the story.
2. Contextualize the word within the story.
3. Have children say the word.
4. Provide a student-friendly explanation of the word.

5. Present examples of the word used in contexts different from the story context.
6. Engage children activities that get them to interact with the words.
7. Have children say the word.

Select a story that you would like to share with young children. Choose three words from the story. Design activities for one of the words using the instructional sequence described above.

THE TEACHER'S ROLE IN SUPPORTING CHILDREN'S LEARNING

An important element for developing children's understanding of word meanings is the teacher's reinforcement of those nascent understandings. Especially for young children it is important that the teacher give voice to the elements of developing word meaning that may be difficult for children to express on their own. And it is equally important that the teacher reveal aspects of word meaning that may not be readily apparent to young learners. No matter how well planned a lesson may be, a major part of all teaching is that combination of thoughtfulness and improvisational skill that allows a teacher to respond productively to children's comments. In this section, we provide some of the ways teachers responded to what children said to enhance children's understanding of words, as well as to encourage them to respond to comments offered by their peers.

Reinforcing Connections between Words and Meanings

When children contribute examples, it is important to acknowledge the appropriateness of the example, and a good way to do that is for the teacher to include elements of the word's meaning in his or her response to a child's comment. For example:

Ms. S: Who can tell about something that would be *absurd*?

NATE: A rock that can walk.

Ms. S: A rock that can walk would really be absurd, because that doesn't make any sense at all!

Ms. S: How might you *rescue* a cat that was stuck high up in a tree?

ALANA: Once my cat was up in a tree and I climbed up.

Ms. S: You climbed the tree—that would be a good way to rescue the cat.

Ms. S:	Tell us about something that would be a *feast*.
Brailee:	Taking a picnic to the park.
Ms. S:	Sure, a picnic at a park could be a feast, because you might bring lots of different kinds of food—chicken, potato salad, sandwiches, pie.
Ms. S:	What is something you might *gaze* at on a hot day?
Hunter:	I'd gaze at a swimming pool.
Ms. S:	Okay. If it's a hot day you might gaze at that swimming pool, because what would you really want to do?

Adding to Children's Network of Related Words

Asking children how a new word relates to words they already know helps them understand how words fit into their previous knowledge and gives them ideas of how they can use the new word. For example:

Ms. K:	When you're *exhausted* you're really tired. Tell us how it feels.
Samson:	Sweaty.
Glory:	Like I want to lay down.
Ladson:	Out of breath.
Ms. K:	If somebody is *grumpy,* how are they acting, what do they do?
Mara:	Mad.
Troy:	Got a mean face.
Dayvon:	Being ugly.

Suggesting Ways to Apply the Word

Prompting children to think about situations in their lives that relate to a new word increases the chances that children will recall and use the word when appropriate circumstances occur. Some examples follow:

Ms. L:	When you come in from recess, you could say "I'm *exhausted.*" When you climb the stairs, you could say, "I'm exhausted." When else could you say you were exhausted?
Anjela:	After riding my bike.
Richie:	When I stay up late.

DAYVON: When I run to see who wins.

Ms. L: I need to *remind* myself to stop at the store on the way home from school. Sometimes I remind you to bring in your homework. When are some times you might have to remind someone to do something?

LEANNA: Remind my mother to help me plant seeds tomorrow.

MICHAEL: Remind my brother it's my turn to say the [TV] program to watch.

Getting Children Involved in Responding to Peers' Comments

In many cases, connections between children's examples and word meaning can be provided by the children themselves. Prompting children to do this helps them develop the kind of thinking that promotes the building of such connections. Having other children play this role also spreads around the thinking by getting several children involved. And, furthermore, it makes it more likely that children will attend to their peers' examples if they know they might be asked to comment on them. After a child offers an example of how a word might be used, a teacher might follow up by posing questions such as those below, to elicit comments from other students:

- Does what Jack just told us sound *festive* to you?
- What do you think of that—could a new bike be *dazzling*?
- What does it mean that Shana is *reluctant* to eat spinach?"

FOLLOW-UP ACTIVITIES

We acknowledge that the introductory activities we've presented go beyond what is typically done in classrooms or typically prescribed in reading programs. However, they are not sufficient for children to fully develop understandings of new words. Practice and reinforcement in ways that engage children in thinking about and using the words, over time, are needed—as the findings of our research both with young children and middle grades children have shown. That is simply the nature of word learning. Words are learned incrementally through the creation and strengthening of many connections to the new words. In this section we offer the activities we provided that followed word introduction. These activities were presented over 2 or 3 days in lessons that took from 10 to 15 minutes per day.

    The follow-up activities presented are for three words from *Doctor DeSoto* (Steig, 1982): *delicate, morsel,* and *stumble.* The teacher begins each lesson by reminding children that they are working with words from *Doctor DeSoto*, and points to each word on a poster or word card while reading it aloud. Typically two or three of the activities would be engaged in each day, depending on the time available.

Review Meanings with Questions

- Does *delicate* mean something small and easily broken or something big and heavy?
- Which would probably be more delicate: a water pitcher made of glass or a pitcher made of plastic?
- Does *morsel* mean a big meal or a small piece of food?
- Which would probably be a good time to eat just a morsel: when you are tasting something for the first time or when you are starving?
- Does *stumbled* mean to trip and almost fall or to be gentle?
- Who would probably stumble more: a man who had difficulty seeing the road or a child walking slowly home?

Situations and Examples

- If a woman bought a fine lacy dress, you could say "It is delicate." When else might you talk about something being delicate? (As children provide examples respond by stating the connection between the word and its meaning. For example, "Yes, *X* is small and easily broken so we could say it is delicate"; "I'd say *X* is delicate because it broke so easily.") What are some things around your house that are delicate? (For example, china plates, glass vases, some plants or flowers.)
- If you did not like the smell of a certain food and only wanted to taste a small bit of it, you could say, "I'll have a morsel." When else might you talk about people or animals eating morsels? (For example, hamsters might only eat a few morsels of lettuce at a time.) If a bird were eating a morsel of bread, what would it be doing? (For example, eating just a small bite of bread.)
- Sometimes when you wear new boots, you tend to stumble because you are not used to walking in them. What are some other things that make people stumble? (For example, rocks on the ground, cracks in the road.) What are some reasons that an older person might stumble? (For example, not having a cane, not being able to see well.)

Find the Missing Word

Tell children that you will say a sentence that is missing a word and that they have to say one of the new words that fits into the sentence. Tell them that either: *delicate, morsel,* or *stumble* will fit in the blank. (Any time children have difficulty completing the sentence, repeat the three possible words.)

- If you were walking to the edge of a mountain, you would not want to <u>blank</u>.
- Pigeons often eat a <u>blank</u> of popcorn left on the ground.
- A baby's tiny fingers are <u>blank</u>.
- Horses in a race sometimes <u>blank</u> and hurt their legs.
- If you are very hungry, you eat most everything on your plate and leave only a <u>blank</u> of food.
- A beautiful butterfly would be <u>blank</u>.

Word Association

Tell children that you will say a word and they are to tell you which of the three new words it makes them think of. (As needed repeat the three possible words.)

- Which word does breakable make you think of? (*delicate*) Why did breakable make you think of delicate? (If necessary, provide explanation. For example, breakable goes with delicate because something delicate is easily broken or hurt.)
- Which word does bite make you think of? (*morsel*) Why did bite make you think of morsel? (If necessary, provide explanation.)
- Which word does trip make you think of? (*stumble*) Why did trip make you think of stumble? (If necessary, provide explanation.)

Finish the Sentence

I have some sentences that need endings. I'll start with a sentence and ask you to think of an ending. I'll show you one for practice. The sentence starts out: "The vase was so delicate that. . . ." Let's see, "The vase was so delicate that I was afraid to touch it for fear it would break!" Who can think of another way to end that sentence? "The vase was so delicate that. . . ."

- I wanted to eat just a morsel of green beans because . . .
- The puppy stumbled on the sidewalk because . . .

Yes/No

I have some sentences that make sense and some that don't make sense. You decide—if it makes sense, everybody say "yes"; if it doesn't make sense, say "no." Listen carefully! (For several of the sentences, ask a child to explain why it does or does not make sense. For example, "The sentence 'After eating a morsel of bread, you are full' does not make sense. Morsels are small bites so you would not get full.")

- Many flowers are small and delicate. (yes)
- People can stumble when they do not watch where they are going. (yes)
- The trunk of a tree is delicate. (no)
- Eating a morsel of chocolate might make you want more. (yes)
- Runners hope they will stumble. (no)
- After eating a morsel of bread, you are full. (no)

Final Review

- What's the word that means small and easily broken? (*delicate*)
- What's the word that means a small bite of food? (*morsel*)
- What's the word that means to trip and almost fall? (*stumble*)

The formats of the above activities are very flexible and can be used with nearly any set of words and across grade levels. In Chapter 5, we present follow-up activities as part of the examples of full instructional sequences for upper elementary, middle school, and high school. In the Appendix, we also include a Menu of Instructional Activities, which we have reprinted from *Creating Robust Vocabulary* (Beck et al., 2008). The Menu provides examples of a variety of formats.

SUMMARY

This chapter has focused on an instructional sequence, comprising systematic word introductions and follow-up activities for several days, to enrich the listening and speaking vocabularies of young children. The words come from the sophisticated language found in children's trade books, which teachers share with children by reading them aloud, or from labeling ideas in the simplest stories with sophisticated words. The vocabulary selected for teaching meet the criteria for Tier Two words of importance and utility, instructional potential, and conceptual understanding. That is, the words are ones that children will be able to use in many contexts, the words can be used in a variety of instructional activities, and the concepts to which the words refer are within the intellectual grasp of the children.

YOUR TURN

We invite you to use what you have learned in this chapter to create some lesson plans for a week of vocabulary instruction. Select a book that you would like to share with the children. Decide which words you would like the children to learn. After the story has been read—which may or may not be on the same day—provide explanations of the words in context and create activities in which children have to engage with the meanings of the words. You may find that the Menu of Instructional Activities in the Appendix is a useful resource here.

CHAPTER 5

Instructional Sequences for Later Grades

Mr. W challenges his sixth-grade students to use their vocabulary words whenever they can. Two of his students converse in the cafeteria at lunchtime:

> KYLIE: What's with these lunch packets—how is it that the ingredients don't spoil even after a couple of weeks?
>
> TREVOR: Well, aren't you inquisitive!
>
> KYLIE: I'm more apprehensive than inquisitive. They have a bunch of chemical additives. I don't trust what these chemicals do once they're inside me.
>
> TREVOR: Well if the chemicals preserve the food, maybe they help preserve you, too!

When effective instruction is part of classroom practice and students are encouraged to use the sophisticated words they are learning, they begin to take true ownership of the words that are presented. Their ownership can be seen in the playful way with which they insert the words into exchanges like the one above.

The purpose of this chapter is to describe the kind of instruction that inspires and supports word ownership by students. We provide examples of the sequences of activities that engage students from upper elementary, middle school, and high school through frequent and robust instruction.

FEATURES OF EFFECTIVE INSTRUCTION

One of the strongest findings about vocabulary instruction is that multiple encounters are required before a word is really known (e.g., Stahl & Fairbanks, 1986), that is, if the word is to affect a student's comprehension and become a useful and permanent part of the student's vocabulary repertoire. So, the vocabulary instruction discussed in this chapter is toward that end. The design of the instruction, and many of the examples used, come from vocabulary studies conducted by Beck and McKeown and their colleagues (Beck & McKeown, 2007b; Beck et al., 1982; McKeown et al., 1983, 1985). The key features of that instruction are frequent and varied encounters with target words and robust instructional activities that engage students in deep processing.

Frequency

The basic design used in our initial vocabulary work was to introduce about 10 words per week and present follow-up activities around the words daily. By the end of the week, each word had been the focus of attention some 10 times or more. An important aspect of the encounters is that they were varied in order to show different contexts of use and different nuances of a word's meaning.

Robustness

By "robust" instruction, we mean instruction that goes beyond definitional information to get students actively involved in using and thinking about word meanings and creating associations among words. Robust instruction was implemented through follow-up activities that varied widely, but that also conformed to a pattern that was similar each week. We began with the kind of word introduction described in Chapter 3 that involved discussion around a student-friendly explanation. Students had log sheets of the words and their meanings that they kept in a vocabulary notebook.

Throughout the rest of the week, we made sure to provide opportunities for students to:

- Use the words.
- Explore facets of word meaning.
- Consider relationships among words.

Students' Use of Words

Having students create uses for words was important to ensure that the word was an active part of their vocabularies. If students were unable to create a context around a word, then the word would remain just an isolated piece of information. Engaging students in talking about situations a word could describe or in considering instances when the word would be an appropriate choice were important ways to support the word becoming part of a network of ideas.

Facets of Word Meaning

Students were asked to respond to various characteristics of words to help them see a word not as a single block of meaning but as having different facets to its meaning. The purpose was to make students' word knowledge flexible so that they could both understand the word and apply the word to a variety of contexts. If a student's understanding of a word is limited to a narrow definition or stereotypical contexts (e.g., *delighted* is always used in association with receiving a gift), then many applications of the word will not be readily comprehended and the student will have only limited opportunities to use the word in speech and writing.

One way we commonly used to reveal facets of meaning was a follow-up activity in which students were asked to differentiate between two descriptions by labeling them as an example or a non-example of the target word. The descriptions were quite similar, differing only in features that were critical to the word's meaning. For example:

banter

A husband and wife argue about what to have for dinner.	A husband and wife kid each other about who ate more at dinner.

impatient

A boy tells his friends about his birthday party and hopes they can come.	A boy counts the days until his birthday and wishes the time would go faster.

retort

The player comes back with a quick answer after the referee calls a foul on him.	The player complains to the coach after the referee calls a foul on him.

glum

The class decides to have a party indoors when they learn that the picnic has been rained out.	The class learns that the picnic has been rained out and they have to do work instead.

berate

A police officer yells at a driver whose car is blocking traffic.	A police officer calls a tow truck to move a car that is blocking traffic.

Relationships among Words

As a way of moving words beyond narrow associations, we designed follow-up activities around relationships among words. In one activity, we presented questions that juxtaposed two target words, such as "Could a *virtuoso* be a *rival*?" In pairing words that were not obviously related, the purpose was to make students pause and truly consider whether a relationship existed. One student began to answer the *virtuoso/rival* question, saying: "No, because a virtuoso is somebody who is good at music and a rival—" He stopped in midsentence, and then continued with some excitement about his insight—"Oh! Yeah, it could be somebody who was good at music who was trying to be better than somebody else who was good at music!" So, suddenly this student saw the words not as straight, closed roads but as intersecting paths from which more complex ideas could be created.

Relationships are also important because of the way individuals' word knowledge is stored in networks of connected ideas. Thus, the more connections that can be built, the more opportunities there are for an individual to "get to" the knowledge of a word when it is encountered in a new context. Chances become greater and greater that words met will set off associations in the network and allow the learner to derive meaning from the contexts in which a word is used.

Additional Features: Alternative Definitions and Time Constraints

Other follow-up activities provided students with opportunities to interact with alternative definitions and to respond to words under time constraints.

Definitions for target words appeared several times during each week, and for each appearance we altered the definition somewhat. This was done so that students were not simply memorizing the definition but had to process the description of the word in a meaningful way. This helped ensure that students were learning the concepts represented by the words rather than the mere wording of a definition. Here are examples of the definitions used over the course of a week's sequence for two target words:

ambitious

1. Really wanting to succeed in becoming rich or important.
2. Wanting to get ahead by becoming powerful.
3. Wants great success in life.

stern

1. Being very strict about how you look and what you do.
2. Very demanding about how you and others behave.
3. Acts hard and serious.

Follow-up activities that were done under time constraints were included to help students develop rapid responses to the meanings of the words so that when the students met the words in a context—in a stream of speech or print—they would be accustomed to accessing the words' meanings quickly. In an activity called "Beat the Clock," students were given one and a half minutes to complete 14 true/false items. Their score was the number of items completed, minus any errors. Here are some sample items:

- *Shrill* sounds can hurt your ears.
- *Gregarious* people would rather be alone.
- It might be hard to have a conversation where there's a *commotion*.
- *Frank* people keep their thoughts to themselves.

RESULTS OF FREQUENT, ROBUST INSTRUCTION

What were students able to do after participating in frequent, robust instruction? Over the course of our vocabulary research, we compared groups of students who had received robust instruction to two kinds of student groups: one group who had not been instructed, and another group who had received traditional, definition-based instruction. We also compared the effects of less frequent with more frequent encounters. We examined students' learning on a variety of measures, and the pattern of results was that students who received robust, frequent instruction did better on a variety of measures. They were able to respond more quickly to word meanings in a timed task, and they showed better comprehension of stories containing the target words.

In a final rather complex task, context interpretation, students who received robust instruction performed especially well compared to those who did not. In the context interpretation task, students respond to questions about sentences in which a target word was used in a somewhat atypical context. As such, the sentences and questions were constructed to require some complex thinking, in addition to knowledge of the word being assessed. For example, students were shown this sentence: "After the prize winners were announced, Stacy ran up to console Meg." Then they were asked, "How do you think Meg had done in the contest?" Since the overall context about prize winners invites the notion of congratulations, students had to apply their knowledge of *console* to reason that if Stacy was consoling Meg, Meg must not have done very well.

Students who had participated in robust instruction were quite successful on this task. Students who had participated in the definition-based instruction, however, were less successful. They often responded to the questions by giving the definition of the word. So, in some sense they "knew" the word, but that knowledge did not help them where it counted. That is, they could not use it to bring meaning to a context. This seemed a particularly compelling result, because what literate people most often need to do with words is use them, not present definitions of them.

Beyond the results from the assessments, our observations in the classrooms demonstrated some other processes at work in these word-rich environments. Specifically, we noticed what we came to call "word ownership" in the students. They knew the words well, and used them easily and appropriately. They also reacted to uses of the words with relish and took obvious pleasure and pride in using them themselves. Another characteristic we noticed developing in the students was "word awareness." That is, not only were the students aware of target words that appeared in their environment but they also began to take notice of words in a more general way. Students even began drawing our attention to words that they thought we should have included in the program!

■ YOU TRY IT ■

Select one or more of the following activities to complete:

- Create three alternative definitions for words that your students are learning.
- Develop example and non-example scenarios for words that your students are learning.
- Pair words that your students are learning and pose a question about them to engage students in considering how the words might be related.

★   ★   ★

In the rest of this chapter, we present examples of instructional sequences. These sequences comprise how words were introduced and the subsequent follow-up activities presented for upper elementary, middle school, and high school students.

EXAMPLE OF INSTRUCTIONAL SEQUENCE FOR THE UPPER ELEMENTARY GRADES

As an example of an instructional sequence for upper elementary students, we chose words from *Dead End in Norvelt* by Jack Gantos (2011), the 2012 Newbery Award winner. The book is about a boy named Jack Gantos who lives in Norvelt, Pennsylvania, a town named after Eleanor Roosevelt. Norvelt was built in 1934 as one of the homestead projects that provided housing, work, and a community environment for unemployed workers and their families as part of the New Deal. The story takes place in 1962, when many of the original citizens of the town are dying. Jack is grounded for the summer and has to assist Miss Volker, the town historian, medical examiner, and obituary writer. Through Miss Volker's obituaries, Jack learns about the history of his town.

The book is rich in interesting and precise language. For this example, we selected seven words from the first half of the book. The instruction is arranged for a 5-day cycle. Students are introduced to the words on Day 1 and engage in follow-up activities on Days 2–4. On Day 5, students' knowledge of the words is assessed. We should note here that there is nothing magic about a 5-day cycle. Depending on how many words are being presented and the learning goal, less than a 5-day cycle and indeed more than a 5-day cycle can be appropriate. It is important, however, that attention be given to words on at least 3 days, so that there is some follow-up to simply introducing words.

Day 1

Introduce the words to students on the first day by providing student-friendly explanations and describing how the words are used in the story.

Target words	Story context	Student-friendly explanation
admiration (pages 13, 230, 261); *admire* (pages 229–247)	Jack's mother spoke of Miss Volker with admiration because Miss Volker was wise. Throughout the book, Miss Volker expressed her admiration for the women of Norvelt.	If you have admiration for people, you respect them and think about them with approval and sometimes wonder or surprise.

exasperation (page 36); *exasperated* (pages 12, 103)	Miss Volker was exasperated when she found out that Jack didn't know how to type.	When you're exasperated, you are annoyed and irritated by something.
abscond (page 30)	When Miss Volker wrote an obituary for Emma Slater, she told how Emma absconded with her life after being captured by Indians.	When you abscond, you leave suddenly and secretly, usually to avoid being seen.
implored (page 109)	When Jack visited Mrs. Dubicki, she implored him to stay longer.	To implore is to ask for something with great urgency or need.
conceded (page 117)	Mom wanted Dad to get help in fixing the airplane runway in their yard, but conceded when Dad said that he wanted to keep the project in the family.	To concede is to give in or agree that someone is right or has a good reason for doing something.
forlornly (page 131)	When Jack's dad told him that he still had to finish digging the bomb shelter, Jack shrugged his shoulders forlornly because he had to help Miss Volker.	Forlorn means miserable or unhappy.
incredulously (page 167); *incredulous* (page 175)	When Miss Volker told Jack that she wanted to bury the mice that she had poisoned, he was incredulous.	Incredulous means not willing to believe that something is true or real.

It is important for teachers to display the words that students are learning on a word wall or poster so students can refer to them throughout the week. Students should also keep their own records of the words and their meanings, such as in a vocabulary notebook.

Days 2–4

We design follow-up activities so that students interact with the words in scaffolded ways. For example, initially, we ask students to select words that relate to a scenario. Later, we ask students to develop their own scenarios for words. Here are some follow-up activities for the words above:

Example/Non-Example

If I say something that might make you feel forlorn, say "Oh no" in a forlorn voice. If not, don't say anything.

- Finding out that your best friend is moving to another state.
- Reading that your favorite pop star has a new record.
- Discovering that you left your backpack out in the rain.

If I say something that might exasperate you, say "No way" in an exasperated voice. If not, don't say anything.

- Learning that the schedule for your volleyball practice has been changed for the tenth time.
- Finding out that your little sister has been using your closet for a playhouse.
- Discovering that your dog has hidden one of your shoes again.

If I say something that would evoke your admiration, say "That's admirable." If not, don't say anything.

- A high school student walks his young neighbor to the bus stop each school day.
- A nurse volunteers with the Red Cross on weekends to help in areas struck by disaster.
- A young man sits in the handicapped section of the bus because he wants a seat but he has no disability.

Word Associations

Which comment goes with a target word? (*concede, implore, incredulous, abscond*)

- I told my mom how much I really wanted to go to the concert even though it was on a school night.
- We knew the game was over when the other team scored a touchdown with 10 seconds left.
- The news story told how the thief had concealed the shoes he had stolen.
- No one could believe what the mayor said because it was so unlike her.

Generating Situations, Contexts, and Examples

The following questions hold the situation constant and challenge students to find ways to apply different target words to it:

- What would make someone say:
    "I am totally exasperated!"
    "I am filled with admiration!"
    "I am incredulous!"
    "I am ready to concede."
    "I am really forlorn today."

Word Relationships

Ask students to describe how two vocabulary words might be connected
or related.

- *incredulous/admire* (A person might do something so heroic and admirable that people would be incredulous when they read about it.)
- *implore/concede* (After much imploring, a person might concede or give in.)
- *exasperated/forlorn* (A person might be exasperated and then become forlorn because a situation is not improving.)

Writing

Provide students with sentence stems such as the following. The value of
this format is that it prevents students from producing minimally informative sentences ("I felt admiration.").

- The citizens were incredulous when . . .
- The dog absconded with . . .
- The candidate refused to concede that she had lost the election because . . .
- You could see how forlorn people were when they found out that . . .
- The chef was exasperated with the waiter because . . .
- The principal spoke of the retiring teacher with admiration, explaining that . . .
- The little girl implored her friend to . . .

More extended writing can be generated by formats such as:

- Think of a time when someone might need to concede. Write a little bit about that.
- Think of someone you admire. Write about why you admire the person.
- Think of a situation that involves someone absconding. Write a headline about the situation using the word *abscond*.

Returning to the Story Context

Having students return to the context in which they met the words is a powerful way to reinforce the connection between understanding vocabulary and understanding story ideas.

- Find three examples of times when characters in the story were exasperated.
- Select two situations in the story when you were incredulous.
- After reading the obituaries in the story, which of the women did you most admire? Why?

Ready, Set, Go

An activity that works well as the last instructional activity—the one before the next day's assessment—is a timed activity called "Ready, Set, Go." It consists of four activity sheets, or "laps," that students complete as a partner times them. Each sheet lists the words on one side and the definitions on the other, and the students have to match them by drawing lines to connect each word and definition. The order of the words for each lap should be changed, and the wording of the definitions altered a little to ensure that students are not just associating specific words with a target word. The goal is to see if one could get faster across the laps.

Day 5

The culmination of an instructional sequence is an assessment. We take up the notion of assessing students' vocabulary learning in Chapter 6. Here we present examples of three formats that might be used for the set of words under discussion.

Select the word that best completes each sentence.

admire	*concede*	*implore*	*exasperate*
abscond	*incredulous*		*forlorn*

1. Because of her great knowledge of the town's history, people in Norvelt came to _____ Miss Volker.
2. After listening to the presentations for and against school uniforms, the principal had to _____ that the students had some valid objections that needed to be taken into consideration.

3. My dog looked _____ as she watched me leave for school each morning.
4. The firefighters watched as people tried to _____ with items from the burning mansion.

Respond to each question below.

1. Would you admire someone who absconded with your new baseball cap? Why or why not?
2. How might you express your exasperation with someone who kept imploring you to go to a movie that you didn't want to see?
3. When might your teacher or coach be incredulous about something that you did?

Choose the word that best completes each item.

1. People condemn villains, but they _____ heroes.
2. Soothing or pleasing people is the opposite of _____ them.
3. If you are convinced that something is true, then you are not _____.
4. If you are guarding a treasure, you are not trying to _____ with it.

EXAMPLES OF INSTRUCTIONAL SEQUENCES FOR MIDDLE SCHOOL AND HIGH SCHOOL

Vocabulary work in middle school and high school should allow deeper explorations of language—how language gives meaning and how words mean what they mean. This kind of approach makes an especially stark contrast to vocabulary as synonyms. Teaching new words as synonyms for known words is a common way to present vocabulary to students, perhaps particularly so for students at middle schools and high schools where often the goal is to prepare students for various standardized tests. But the synonym approach, although handy for providing a quick anchor point for a word, is a bankrupt way to teach word meaning. Building understanding of language comes through developing knowledge of both the similarities and the differences among words and the precise roles they can play. A focus here is on exploration of complex dimensions of a word's meaning and the relationships that exist to other words along some of those dimensions—how the word may be related to others through some components but not others.

The vocabulary work at upper grade levels can also be more rooted to a text and dealt with in a way that both teaches the words and brings enriched understanding to the text. It can bring attention to how authors use words, the deliberateness with which an author chooses a specific word, and thus what role it plays in what the author is communicating. These kinds of things can indeed be done with younger students, but there can be a more rigorous focus with older students.

Middle School Example

The example we provide is based on an excerpt from Mark Twain's *The Prince and the Pauper* (1881/1992), the story of Tom, a young pauper who switches identity with a prince and is subsequently crowned king. The text is rich in language, offering abundant possibilities for vocabulary work. In the segment of the story we use for this example, it is Tom's second day as king, and he is faced with determining the fate of a man who has been accused of poisoning someone.

We have selected 10 target words. None is really crucial to understanding the story, but several embody the theme of the selection. *Compassion* most captures the theme of the segment. *Homage* and *imperious* tie in with Tom's present royal situation, and *indecorum* is a source of concern for Tom in his present role. The other words could be of help in local comprehension, potentially playing a role in understanding a specific sentence or so. To provide a flavor of the story and its language, we present the context in which each word appears in the story as well as the friendly definition we would use.

Target words	Story context	Student-friendly explanation
tolerable	Tom said the words which Lord Hertford, who had become his friend, put into his mouth from time to time, but he was too new to such things, and too ill at ease to accomplish more than tolerable success.	Just barely good enough, but not of high quality
sufficient	He looked sufficiently like a king, but he was ill able to feel like one.	Enough of something for a certain purpose
homage	But there was a lifting of his cloud in one way—he felt less uncomfortable than at first; he was getting a little used to his circumstances and surroundings . . . he found that the presence and homage of the great and afflicted embarrassed him	Great respect and honor toward someone, usually someone in authority

less and less sharply with every hour that drifted over his head.

compensation	In truth, being a king is not all dreariness—it hath its compensations and conveniences.	Something done to balance or make up for something else (it can be a payment for work done, or something good that happens to make up for something bad)
compassion	Death—and a violent death—for this poor unfortunate! The thought wrung Tom's heartstrings. The spirit of compassion took control of him, to the exclusion of all other considerations.	A feeling of sympathy for people who are suffering and a desire to help them
blurt	His concern made him even forget, for the moment, that he was but the false shadow of a king, not the substance. Before he knew it he had blurted out the command.	To say something suddenly that you might have held in if you had thought about it
suppress	Then he blushed scarlet, and a sort of apology sprung to his lips; but observing that his order had wrought no sort of surprise in the earl or the waiting page, he suppressed the words he was about to utter.	To hold back from doing or saying something because you think it shouldn't be said or done
profound	The earl's face showed profound gratification, for he was a man of merciful and generous impulses—a thing not very common with his class in that fierce age.	Describes a feeling that is deeply felt or believed
indecorum	Another blush followed this unregal outburst, and he covered his indecorum as well as he could by adding, "It enraged me that a man should be hanged upon such idle, hare-brained evidence!"	Describes behavior that is not acceptable for the situation
imperious	How sanely he put his questions. How like his former natural self was this abrupt, imperious disposal of the matter!	Describes behavior in which someone commands others to follow

At this point, we will assume that the words and definitions have been introduced and the story read. We now pick up on follow-up activities we would use to further develop students' knowledge and understanding of them. These activities can occur over the next 3 to 5 days, with at least one activity per day.

Record the Words

As we mentioned in the upper elementary example, it is useful for students to keep a written record (e.g., a vocabulary notebook or journal) of words that are introduced. Students should add the words and definitions to whatever ongoing records are being used for vocabulary in the classroom. An example of the use of each word should also be added to the record, and developing examples for the vocabulary record is suggested as the focus of one follow-up activity. This activity might be best on the second or third day in the instructional sequence to give students a chance to get to know the words first. In that way, students will be able to create more meaningful examples.

Facets of Word Meanings

Begin with the context of the story as a basis for discussing the words. Talking about their applications in the story can prompt students to explore and elaborate on the meanings. This deepens students' understanding of the words and helps to build connections to other words and concepts they know.

The discussion could begin by asking which of the words best captures what the story is all about. *Compassion* is the most likely answer, although any candidates that can be defended are possible. When a candidate word is offered, reasons for why that word captures the story line should follow.

Here are discussion starters for the rest of the words:

- What might Tom have considered to be *compensations* for his present state?
- *Imperious* is often appropriate for describing a king. How appropriate is it to Tom?
- How do Tom's *blurting* out and *suppressing* his words relate to a judgment of him as imperious?
- What made Tom think he looked *sufficiently* like a king? Do you agree?
- Tom was afraid that he showed *indecorum* by sparing the prisoner's life. Why was that indecorum? Do you think Tom showed indecorum in his dealing with the prisoner?
- Who was paying *homage* to whom in the story? In what ways can it be said that: Tom paid homage to the prisoner; the earl paid homage to Tom; those around Tom paid homage to him as king?

- When Tom decided that the prisoner should not be boiled in oil, the earl's face showed *profound* gratification. What other profound feelings are shown in the story?
- Do you think that Tom showed *tolerable* success as king in this episode? Is *tolerable* an appropriate way to describe it?

Relationships among Words

The activity below pairs words so that students need to consider how meanings interact in order to respond to the questions. This activity can be done in a number of formats. It can be done completely orally as a discussion, students could respond to each question in writing in class or for homework, or pairs or groups of students could work on the questions. The key, however, is that if students write responses, sharing and discussion of the responses should follow.

- Would you pay homage to something tolerable?
- Would you have compassion for someone imperious?
- Would you suppress a profound thought?
- Would blurting out your thoughts be an example of indecorum?
- When would compensation not be sufficient?

Most of the questions are set up for yes or no answers, and although one response is more likely, either is acceptable if it can be justified. The point of the activity is for students to decide how they would respond and then support their response. For example, "Would you pay homage to something tolerable?" could be answered:

- No, if something was tolerable—like just okay, but not really very good—I wouldn't give it homage, or respect it.
- Yes, I might, if something was tolerable and all the other choices were not even tolerable. Then something tolerable could deserve homage.

Students' Use of Words

This activity gives students practice in using the words, and it doubles as a way to create examples for the vocabulary record. Divide students into groups and have each group develop sentences for several of the words. Students should strive to make the meaning of the word clear within the sentence. After sentences are developed, have them shared with the class and edited as desired or necessary. This will ensure that the examples are strong and appropriate, and optimally helpful for demonstrating word meanings.

■ YOU TRY IT ■

Select a story or excerpt that your students will be reading. Choose 5–10 Tier Two words that you would like them to learn. Develop definitions for the words. Then, pair the words in a question format so that students have to consider how meanings interact in order to respond. You may want to refer to the model on page 97.

High School Example

The example for high school is based on the opening chapter of *Wuthering Heights* by Emily Bronte (1847/1961), and it uses the text in a somewhat different way as the centerpiece for vocabulary work, and as such, blends vocabulary instruction with a character study. Instruction begins with several words from the opening paragraphs of the book, because what happens so early in the novel is that the persona of Heathcliff begins to be developed. The words we would introduce are *misanthrope, solitary, reserve,* and *inhospitable.* Additional words could be introduced later that have some connection to the concepts that the author is communicating about Heathcliff.

Target words	Story context	Student-friendly explanation
solitary	I have just returned from a visit to my landlord—the solitary neighbour that I shall be troubled with.	Existing alone; remote from civilization
misanthrope	In all England, I do not believe that I could have fixed on a situation so completely removed from the stir of society. A perfect misanthrope's heaven.	Someone who dislikes and distrusts humankind
reserved	I felt interested in a man who seemed more exaggeratedly reserved than myself.	Holding back in speech or manner; keeping one's feelings hidden
inhospitable	"What the devil is the matter?" he asked, eyeing me in a manner that I could ill endure, after this inhospitable treatment.	Not welcoming to guests

Follow-up activities to be presented over the next 3 to 5 days are provided below.

Facets of Word Meaning

In this activity, the words introduced are discussed in order to consider their similar core of meaning and how it relates to Heathcliff. The central concept here seems to be one of "distance"—in particular, Heathcliff's personal distance from human society. After discussion of the four initially introduced words, we add some additional words, not found in the text, that seem to fit the portrait of Heathcliff that the author is painting. The following outlines the basis for discussion:

- A *misanthrope* is defined as "someone who dislikes and distrusts humankind," yet a misanthrope is part of humankind. Can this word be used for animals?
- Would a misanthropic ape, for example, be one that hates other apes or that hates humans? (The point here is that the essence of the word is contempt or loathing for your fellows, making yourself distant from others of your kind. That notion of distance is an important one in describing Heathcliff and his environs.)
- What other words and phrases in the text support this picture of Heathcliff keeping himself apart? ("removed from the stir of society," "I beheld his black eyes withdraw so suspiciously under their brows," and "his reserve springs from an aversion to showy displays of feeling—to manifestations of mutual kindliness.")
- What kind of feeling does *solitary* give you? Does the word imply loneliness? Dislike of others' company? How is it used?
- What is the quality of Heathcliff's reserve? Here it would be important to bring up that *reserve(d)* is often associated with positive qualities, such as dignity or maturity. Or someone's seeming reserve might spring from shyness. But the essence is distance: "held or kept back" (also "cautious in one's words and actions").
- Consider introducing the words *alienate* and *estrange* into the discussion.
    alienate: to cause someone to become unfriendly to you or to your point of view
    estrange: to put at a [psychological] distance; most often used rather formally to describe what has happened to a relationship with a spouse or other family members

Is Heathcliff's reserve meant to alienate or estrange? Help students realize that these two words relate to the concept of keeping personal distance that is emerging about Heathcliff. Prompt students to note that an important distinction is that with these words the distance is more active—holding or pushing others back emotionally, not merely keeping back oneself.

- Is *inhospitable* active or passive? (Either could probably be defended.)
- Some further words might be added here that describe the manner of someone who is inhospitable: *terse, brusque,* and *curt.* They are very similar, although with shadings: *terse* is brief and emotionless; *brusque* carries the idea of roughness; *curt* is brief or terse, usually implying anger or at least impatience.
- Consider that a place can also be called inhospitable. What would such a place be like?
- Introduce the word *recluse,* someone who has removed himself from society. What does a recluse share with a misanthrope? What is the emotional component here?

The point of the activity is to get students to think about the words beyond their definitions, to explore how they fit together, and how they apply to the portrait that the author is depicting.

Record the Words

Have students record in their word journals the word meanings and some examples of how the words can be used. The examples can merely be notes from the discussion to help students recall the ideas that have been developed about the words.

Students' Use of Words

Have students write sentences for each word, but provide some hooks around which they can form their thoughts. Begin with a class discussion of questions such as the following, and then assign individually written sentences:

- Can you think of anyone you'd call a *misanthrope*? What does he or she do that would cause you to label him or her so?
- Do you ever feel *solitary*? What does it feel like?
- How do you respond to someone who acts *inhospitable* toward you?
- What are different ways people show *reserve,* and what different messages do they give?

As an alternative, students could be asked to write sentences for the initially introduced words (*misanthrope, solitary, reserve,* and *inhospitable*) and to include as many of the additional words as they can within those sentences.

Relationships among Words

The development of semantic relationships for older students can be done by adding more words to those under study. A good expansion to the collection of words in the example we have been considering is a set of words that is in opposition to the antisocial, distant concepts embodied in the target words. For example:

- *Philanthropist* is definitionally the opposite of *misanthrope*, but it is used very differently. Although *philanthropist* is defined as "a lover of humankind," it is used almost exclusively to designate people who give large sums of money to charity. It is unlikely to hear someone who enjoys the company of other people described as a philanthropist. From such discussion, prompt a search for a functional opposite to *misanthrope*.
- *Gregarious*, defined as "seeking and enjoying the company of others," seems in opposition to *solitary*—not alone or reserved. Discussion should note that the concept of *gregarious* includes not holding back but going out to others.
- In opposition to *inhospitable*, the word *solicitous* could be introduced. One could draw a sort of continuum from *inhospitable* to *welcoming* to *solicitous*, which represents eagerness to provide caring attention.

Another aspect that could be developed is that there seems to be two dimensions of loving or hating humankind: one is a caring for humans in general—a charitable nature. The other speaks to personal relationships. *Misanthrope* seems to apply to both dimensions, but the more positive words seem to lean toward one or the other: *Philanthropist* applies to the general. *Gregarious* and *solicitous* seem more on the personal side. On the general side, we might explore the following:

- *Altruistic:* showing concern for the welfare of other people in general, rather than putting oneself first.
- *Benevolent:* being kind, helpful, and tolerant.

After this variety of words has been introduced, students could be assigned to develop a character sketch of some character they have read about or seen on television or in the movies. The character should fit the description of a misanthrope, a recluse, or a philanthropist. Students could consider the character's actions in terms of at least three of the words that are being worked on, then write a description of how they fit or do not fit the character.

Another activity might be to write a letter to a newspaper editor on some issue from the point of view of a misanthrope or of a philanthropist; or a letter that alienates, or shows altruism, or is solicitous. Again, the assignment is more valuable if students are asked to include several of the words being worked with.

SUMMARY

Throughout this chapter, and indeed throughout this book, we have emphasized the importance of keeping vocabulary work going beyond the initial introduction of word meaning. The reason that this is so essential to learning new words is that words can only truly be learned through use. The nuances, subtleties, and characteristics of a word's role in the language can only be understood through repeated exposures to the word in a variety of contexts. A definition, no matter how well crafted, can never communicate all of this. Each context that students encounter can add dimension to what is known about a word. The need for multiple uses becomes even more critical at the upper grades because the words are more sophisticated and thus more multidimensional, and distinctions among them more subtle.

YOUR TURN

We invite you to use what you have learned in this chapter to develop some ideas for supporting students in thinking about a set of words that you have selected from a text that they are reading. Describe your rationale for selecting the words. Then, develop an instructional sequence with several days' worth of activities to help students use and respond to the words in meaningful ways. Refer to the Menu of Instructional Activities in the Appendix as a resource.

CHAPTER 6

Assessing and Maintaining New Vocabulary

In this chapter we attend to two topics beyond the sets of instructional activities that students encounter across several days to initiate their learning of new words. The first is assessment, which, as we mentioned in Chapter 5, is traditionally and appropriately the culmination of an instructional sequence. But the assessment should not be thought of as closing the door on learning a word. Students need to continue their interactions with words across a semester or school year. The more opportunities students have to think about and use the words that they are learning, the more elaborate their mental representations of the words will be. So, the second topic of this chapter is how to maintain attention to words that have been taught. This includes attention both within and beyond the classroom.

ASSESSING STUDENTS' LEARNING

Assessing what is learned about words relates to an issue we discussed at the outset of this book, that is, what does it mean to know a word? For example, a learner may be able to supply a synonym for a word but not know how to use it, or understand the context in which it appears but be unable to express its meaning. Such different configurations of knowledge would allow a learner to succeed on some kinds of assessments but not on others. So, when considering what kinds of assessment are appropriate, it is important to first consider the kind of learning that is the goal. The type of assessment selected will differ if, for example, you want to know whether students have developed an initial association to a word versus a deep understanding that will serve students' comprehension and composition.

A demonstration that different pictures of word knowledge emerge from different criteria was shown in Curtis's (1987) study in which she tested fifth graders on a set of words using several different measures. She found that on a checklist where students were asked to place check marks next to all the real words (also containing nonwords), the students identified an average of 80% of the real words. When asked to explain the meanings of the words, 70% could pass a very easy criterion such as describing *invent* as "to invent a machine." When the criterion involved giving an example or partial explanation, 50% of the responses were correct. Only 20% were correct for a criterion that required generating synonyms or complete explanations.

In an earlier study with college students, Curtis (1981) found that the completeness or precision of knowledge in an individual's vocabulary repertoire differentiates high- and low-ability college students. The undergraduates took a traditional multiple-choice test and then were interviewed about the tested words. From the interviews, Curtis discovered that low-ability students not only knew fewer of the tested words but also had less knowledge of the words they knew. Specifically, they were only able to provide correct explanations for about half the words they had gotten correct on the multiple-choice test. This finding highlights how different measures might lead to different conclusions about whether students know words.

The fact that different assessments can lead to different conclusions might suggest that a multipronged approach to assessment may be most informative of what students have learned. For example, a simple matching of word and definition could be offered along with an item that asks students for an example of how the word can be used. Then, rather than having an all-or-nothing picture of what was learned, the teacher can gauge the extent of the learning for each word and by different students.

In the rest of this section we offer a variety of formats for assessing learning of vocabulary taught in the classroom. As we do, we will make note of the level of knowledge that may be tapped in the various formats.

Traditional Formats with Both Traditional and Novel Applications

The most widely used measure of word knowledge is the multiple-choice format. The results of a multiple-choice test may be greatly influenced by the nature of the foils—the incorrect choices. Foils can introduce ideas that may confuse a learner by interfering with what the learner knows about a word. On the other hand, if the foils are very different from the meaning of the target word, a learner can get the item correct even with very limited knowledge of the word.

The changeable nature of multiple-choice items, however, can be used to advantage, to create tests that are purposely easier or more difficult and thus tap different levels of word knowledge. Consider, for example, a test item for *diligent* whose choices are (a) fast, (b) hardworking, (c) lost, and (d) punished. Compare that to the thinking required to select the correct choice for *diligent* from among (a) making a lot of money, (b) working at an interesting job, (c) always trying one's best, and (d) remembering everything. The changeable nature of multiple-choice questions has been exploited in an assessment development project by Judith Scott and colleagues (Scott, Vevea, & Flinspach, 2010). For the project, the researchers created a series of items to tap a progression of knowledge about each word. For example, one question required students to identify the word's semantic field (such as whether *pyramid* "has to do with" farming, noise, movement, or math), and the next question in the series asked students to choose the correct definition of the word.

Although some researchers have taken a pessimistic view of the usefulness of multiple-choice tests (Kame'euni et al., 1987), researchers including Curtis and Scott (Scott et al., 2010) are more positive about their usefulness. Curtis (1987) argues, for example, that despite their drawbacks, they do provide some useful information. They give reliable indications of the relative range of an individual's vocabulary and correlate rather strongly with measures of reading comprehension. As a school assessment measure, they give useful information about where a student stands in vocabulary development in relation to his or her peers.

Another old "work horse" format in assessment is the true/false item. These items, as with multiple choice, can be developed to be relatively easy as well as rather hard, thus tapping either shallower or deeper knowledge. For example, consider the word *seniority* and the two items below:

- People who have *seniority* have been someplace longer than other people.
- *Seniority* is related to time.

The second item is more abstract, likely requiring a deeper understanding of the word. But a true/false assessment can be taken to yet another level by requiring students to explain their answers for items like "*Seniority* is related to time."

Many of the formats that we used in the instructional activities developed for our vocabulary program can also be used as assessment formats. One of them is essentially yet another version of a true/false test. This is the example/non-example format that we have discussed earlier and is exemplified below.

- Present items that ask students to distinguish between an example of a word and a non-example of a word. Both the example and the non-example should be designed to present situations that have similar features and thus require student thinking that zeros in on the meaning of the target word.

    proclaim

    A woman refuses to talk to reporters about the election.   A woman tells reporters which candidate won the election.

    commend

    Your teacher tells you to have your parents come in for a conference.   Your teacher tells your parents how well you are doing in school.

    mention

    Our neighbors once told us that they had lived in Florida.   Our neighbors are always talking about when they lived in Florida.

Assessment Formats to Tap Deeper Knowledge

A variety of formats for robust instructional activities can be used to assess deeper levels of word knowledge. Such activities call on students to use what they know about the words to evaluate contexts and uses of the words, for example, or compare the learned words to other words. Consider the following:

- Have students create examples such as:
    Describe how someone acts that shows being *diligent*.
    Tell about a time that you were *perplexed*.
    Describe some things that could make a person feel *miserable*.
- Ask students to describe what is alike and/or different for pairs of words that are semantically similar. The following word pairs would be useful in such an assessment:

    berate/retort   **acquaintance/ally**
    exotic/unique   **extraordinary/peculiar**

In Chapter 5, we described a "context interpretation" task in which students responded to questions about sentences containing target words. The important point about this task is that it requires students to apply the word's meaning to understand the context of its use. In responding to the contexts in the task, students need to use knowledge of the words to draw an inference in order to make sense of the context. The task is inherently challenging, and can be made more or less so depending on whether the contexts show typical or not so typical uses for the target word. Note that in the examples below, the first item is particularly challenging, as someone is commended in an unexpected situation—for destroying something in anger; the other examples show more typical uses:

- When Father heard that Lisa had ripped up the letter from Steve, Father *commended* her for it. What do you think Father thought of Steve?
- When Sam and I arrived at Alvin's front door, I had to *urge* Sam to knock on the door. How do you think Sam felt about going to Alvin's house?
- Rhonda sent out wedding invitations to all the family, including Uncle Charles, who was a *hermit*. What do you think Uncle Charles's answer was to the invitation?
- Mr. Robinson, the high school principal, was in a very good mood after his meeting with the *philanthropist*. Why do you think Mr. Robinson was happy?
- Mary thought that Jim was *ridiculing* her when he said that the cake she made looked beautiful. How do you think Mary thought her cake looked?
- Jerome told us he was a *novice*, but when we heard him play the piano we knew he had been kidding us. What do you think Jerome's piano playing sounded like?
- Everyone whom Paul met at his new school was very much alike, except for Dan, who was an *extrovert*. How do you think Dan acted toward Paul?
- At the baseball game Tony thought his chances of hitting a home run were *thwarted* when Rusty came on to pitch. What do you think Tony thought of Rusty's pitching?

Assessments for Younger Learners

The examples of assessment formats presented so far are suited to students in upper elementary and above. Assessing vocabulary learning for the youngest learners presents some special issues, chiefly that it is challenging to create items to assess learning of Tier Two words that are accessible to young children in print. A solution we have found is for the teacher to present statements orally and have children answer them on a response sheet by marking YES/NO, or ☺/☹. For example:

- If something is *usual*, does it happen a lot?
- Does *drenched* mean very hungry?

Another issue to be aware of is that with yes/no items there is a 50% chance that a student can get an item correct through guessing, versus 25% in multiple-choice items. But a typical multiple-choice item offers four choices, which would be very difficult for children to hold in memory, with the item being presented orally. What we have done to address this issue is to essentially create four-choice items by developing clusters of four yes/no items, and asking each one separately. Below is an example, using *clever*. Notice that in the example below the first two items focus on a context in which the word might be used, while the third and fourth items focus on the meaning of the word. In presenting such an assessment to children, items for one word should be mixed together with items for other words in an instructional set so that all items for a particular word do not appear next to one another.

clever
- If you are a whiz at working puzzles, might someone say that you are clever?
- If you couldn't remember your phone number, might someone say that you are clever?
- Does *clever* mean trying hard?
- Does *clever* mean good at figuring out things?

Our major message about vocabulary assessment is that the assessments should match the goals. Assess for what you want to know about your students' learning. If fairly straightforward knowledge is the goal, then multiple-choice items can be appropriate. If deeper knowledge is the goal, then the more complex formats noted above are more likely to provide the kind of information that will allow teachers to determine whether students have gained complete, precise, or deep understanding.

▪ YOU TRY IT ▪

Select one or more of these assessments to develop:

- Write some sentence stems for words that your students are learning.
- Create some questions that have students choosing one of two vocabulary words as the answer.
- Design multiple assessment items in different formats for words that you have selected for your students to learn.

MAINTAINING ATTENTION TO NEW WORDS

Vocabulary research strongly points to the need for frequent encounters with new words if they are to become a permanent part of an individual's vocabulary repertoire. Those encounters should not be limited to the week in which words are the focus of instruction. Rather, students should have opportunities to maintain their vocabulary learning and elaborate their understanding of words by meeting words they have learned in contexts beyond the instructional ones. Keeping students' attention on words they have learned can be supported in a nearly infinite variety of ways. We will offer some of our favorites here.

Creating Classroom Reference Resources for Words

An ongoing vocabulary program should include some kind of record of the words being learned that includes the word meanings and sample uses for the words. This might be realized as a classroom dictionary or a set of index cards with one card per word. The advantage of using index cards is that the resource can then be used flexibly in a myriad of ways. Students can use it as a ready reference to check words they may have forgotten. The teacher can use it as a word bank to stimulate ideas for writing assignments. The teacher can ask students to sort words or select words that represent patterns, such as words to talk about characters' feelings, words that describe how a person or pet moves or acts, or words students would use to describe themselves. Or at transition times—like lining up for lunch or changing classes—the teacher can ask a volunteer to pick a word and talk about it, such as when it might be used, what it means, or creating a sentence.

Students at upper elementary levels and above should keep their own individual records of words that they are learning, in addition to there being a classroom shared reference. Students' personal records should include each word that is taught, its meaning, and example sentences. Students can add to it as the year progresses noting similarities between words, interesting uses they come upon, and so on.

Incorporating Words into New Situations

In our vocabulary studies, both teachers and students often noticed when words they had learned appeared in subsequent texts that were read in class. We also noticed occasions when, although a learned word did not necessarily appear in a text, it could be applied to the text situation. In these cases, teachers frequently challenged students to think about the vocabulary word that would fit. An example of this situation occurred in a first-grade classroom during a reading of *Curious George Goes to a Chocolate Factory* (Rey, 1998). In that story, George, the curious monkey, loves chocolate and nearly causes disruption in a chocolate factory by trying to find his favorite candy. But he ends up helping in an unintended way, and he is rewarded with a free box of chocolates for his efforts. The teacher asked the following questions that relate words learned from previous stories to the *Curious George* story:

- We learned some words in other stories that could fit here, too. How about the word *craving*? How does that describe something that happened in this story?
- Remember the word *deserve*? George got a box of chocolates as a present at the end. Do you think that he deserved to get that? Why?
- Does anybody remember a word that George might use to talk about the candy? It's a word we used to talk about the things the wolf baked for the chickens in *The Wolf's Chicken Stew* (Kasza, 1987). He thought the candy was _____ [*scrumptious*].

Even though this example is from a primary grades classroom, the same technique can be used all the way through high school. For example, recall the words taught in conjunction with *Wuthering Heights* (Bronte, 1847/1961) in Chapter 5. One could imagine that readers might encounter many future instances of inhospitable conditions, solitary characters, and examples of alienation as they continue delving into literature.

Another way to work words into the daily routine is to use them in getting the day started. In elementary, particularly primary, classrooms the day often begins with a "Morning Message." Vocabulary words can easily become a regular part of that—for example, "Today is Tuesday. It is a *lovely* day outside. The sun is *radiant*. I *insist* that we work hard this morning so we can all go outside at recess." At upper grades, a similar strategy might be used by beginning each day with a question formed around a vocabulary word, such as: "Did everyone have a *sufficient* breakfast this morning?" "What might you feel *adamant* about today?"

There are lots of fun ways to incorporate attention to words within a school day. One that has amused us is selecting humorous pictures—from Internet photos that have gone viral, for example—posting them in the classroom and challenging students to write a sentence that describes the picture and uses a vocabulary word. Silly pet pictures are always good for this purpose. A favorite picture shows a large dog being trailed by a line of tiny ducklings. Appropriate comments might include: "The dog seems to be *functioning* as the ducks' mother," "There is something *inherently* odd about this scene," or "That is not a *traditional* animal family." This activity could even be turned into a competition, where sentences are voted on and the favorite gets a star.

Maintaining attention to words can take very simple forms, such as keeping a list of words posted and making tally marks if someone in the class uses a word or finds it used in classroom materials. In classrooms where Text Talk was implemented, we have seen teachers place target words on a bulletin board next to the cover of the story from which they came, and then place the tally marks next to words when they were mentioned by the teacher or children.

The above illustrate just a few ways to tuck words into the corners of the day in classrooms. We offer them here to inspire further creative ways to keep attention on vocabulary and to demonstrate to students that knowing words is fun.

Extension Beyond the Classroom

Our final recommendation for maintaining attention to words that have been taught is to direct students to look for their words outside of school. There are important reasons to have students be attentive to sources outside school that use or embody their words. First, this helps students see the words they are learning are "real" and not just a classroom exercise. Second, if students find places for words in their own surroundings, the words are more likely to have a permanent place in their vocabulary repertoire—for example, if they think of their living room couch as *cozy*, or their Aunt Elsa as *loquacious*.

Word Wizard

We included a beyond-school component in our original vocabulary program and found that it was phenomenally successful! It was not an uncommon day to have every student in the classroom come armed with a word he or she had found the night before. In a later study, we found that there was measurably more learning when students had this "outside-of-class" component in their vocabulary program (McKeown et al., 1985).

The component we set up was a system called Word Wizard, in which students gained points by bringing in evidence of hearing, seeing, or using target words outside the classroom. The Word Wizard chart consisted of a list of students' names with space to add tally marks as they brought in sightings or uses of words that had been introduced to their class. Students could earn extra-credit points for reporting sightings of target words or for using them. The tally marks helped students keep track of their points and the extra credit that those points represented.

Before introducing the Word Wizard notion to our fourth-grade vocabulary research classrooms, we engaged in an "advertising campaign" about the opportunity to become a Word Wizard. Specifically, we distributed leaflets entitled "You Can Be a Word Wizard!" The leaflet described, with engaging graphics, the different categories that students could achieve, with the highest being, of course, Word Wizard. Other categories included Word Wildcat, Word Whirlwind, Word Winner, Word Worker, and Word Watcher. On another fold of the leaflet were descriptions of how points could be earned.

For example:

If you hear a word—on TV, on the radio, on the street, or at home—you can earn 1 point. Just tell your teacher where you heard or saw the word and how it was used.

On the back fold of the leaflet students were told to:

- Look for your name on the Word Wizard chart.
- Watch for special events for Word Wizard points.

Points were tallied every few weeks, and students received certificates based on their totals. The certificates were designed around the different categories.

To earn their points, students had to describe the contexts in which the words were used. An interesting feature of this activity that we discovered is that students' fabrications still accomplished the purposes of the activity. That is, sometimes students made up a story about using or hearing the word even though it did not occur. A long-remembered example was the boy who reported to the teacher, "I told my mother I was so *famished*, I was going to *devour* everything in the refrigerator, and that I didn't care whether it was *nutritious*." Three points! One could well question the veracity of the reported incident; what cannot be questioned, however, is that the student had used the words—appropriately and creatively—in a context beyond the classroom.

We can guarantee from our experience that this activity is successful! The fourth graders in the participating classes went absolutely wild with bringing in words. So much so that a constant topic of conversation at our meetings with the teachers was how to manage the enormity of tallying the students' points!

The discovery of examples of target words in various environments can be left up to the students' motivation, as in the case of doing so for extra credit and, indeed, for Word Wizard points. However, looking for examples of words in various environments can be primed somewhat. For example, the teacher can assign a word or several words for students to find or to invent an example or application for. The teacher might ask students to find the words *reasonable, inexpensive,* or *competitive* in newspaper or TV advertisements.

Another variation of assigning students to engage with words outside of school is to ask them to identify or create a situation that could be described by a target word. For instance, ask students to find something in the news that could be described as *whimsical,* or challenge them to find as many possible applications of a short list of target words (e.g., *ultimate, diverse, unique*) as they can in one evening—using sources such as the newspaper, books they read, TV programs, or their family's conversation. This could be an individual or team competition.

Since using the Word Wizard in our studies and describing it to teachers, we have seen teachers develop a host of variations that are useful for similar purposes and across various grade levels. In Ms. H's classroom, the Word Wizard device she created allowed first-grade children to "show off" their new vocabulary expertise. At any time that a child could explain the meaning of three of the words being studied, she or he received each of those words on cards, as well as a Word Wizard hat. Then, with the Word Wizard hat and the three cards, the child could go through the school and any adult could read the word on one of the cards and ask the child to explain its meaning. The other teachers, and in particular the principal, got into it, and there were many "oohs" and "aahs" heard when a Word Wizard was in the hall!

In the Media

In our latest vocabulary endeavor, Robust Academic Vocabulary Encounter (RAVE), which teaches academic words to middle school students, we have included an outside-of-school component that we call In the Media. It is a slightly revised version of Word Wizard created to appeal to older students and to be in tune with contemporary sources that students interact with. For In the Media, students are asked to find words in any media—such as video games, websites, television shows—or even books and magazines! Again we created a chart to track students' progress with students' names across the bottom and points tallied up the vertical. We collaborated with the classroom teachers to develop a reward system. So, students were able to earn free homework passes and quiz bonus points when they had reached the 10-point mark on the chart. Students reacted very enthusiastically to the challenge of finding words beyond the classroom.

To record their finds, students were given In the Media deposit slips where they had to record their name, the word, and the context in which they found it. A fun aspect of this activity for teachers and researchers was that it gave us some insight into how students were spending their time outside of school, when, for instance, examples from *Twilight* novels predominated, or a series of submissions mentioned the television show *Survivor*. The following is a sampling of students' contributions that show the uses of the words and the sources in which they found them.

Word context	Source of context
It is hard to *process* this. You are not making it clear.	*Desperate Housewives* (TV show)
Express your own *unique* style.	Window of a bridal store
It said this is a *dramatization*.	Clinique commercial
Calvin and Miranda are moving upstairs, stirring up household tensions in the *process*.	*Tyler Perry's House of Payne* (TV show)
Beauty expert Julie G. on makeup and nail *trends*	*The Wendy Williams Show* (TV show)
There will be *consequences*.	*How to Train Your Dragon* (movie)
This misery . . . pales in *significance*.	*Anne Frank: The Diary of a Young Girl* (Frank, 1993)
Malkin *dominated* the game.	Commentary during a Pittsburgh Penguins hockey game
These gloves are *compatible* with iPads, phones, etc.	JCPenney store ad
Using the Genius *feature*, you will be capable of. . . .	iTunes terms and conditions
This time around, debates are having *consequences*.	CNN.com
As soon as a body is *exposed* to the air. . . .	Book about mummies
They are *potentially* the strongest team.	*The Biggest Loser* (TV show)
On Facebook you have *mutual* friends.	Facebook

They climbed into *adjacent* holes.	*Holes* (Sachar, 2000)
Playtex has *unique* hold.	Tampon container
The eagle was *symbolic* to Native Americans.	YouTube
You have the *potential* to be a star.	*American Idol* (TV show)
We can *isolate* the storm.	TV news
Land *features*; land left *exposed*; *process* by which rock is broken down; layer of the atmosphere that *sustains* life	From students' science and social studies books

Beyond-school challenges can work in two directions. Either students can be asked to find examples of uses of their words, or find places where the words would fit. In the second case, students are recognizing the concept underlying the word—such as noting that a girl on a television show who was sent to her room might feel *isolated*. Whether it is recognition of the word itself or of its fit to a situation, both indicate attentiveness to vocabulary that has been learned and added to a student's repertoire. And the enjoyment of words is reinforced.

SUMMARY

In this chapter we discussed two topics that go beyond the introductory and follow-up instructional activities we have been describing. The first topic was assessment of students' learning about vocabulary. A key concept here is that many different kinds of activities can serve as assessments. What undergirds a decision on the kind of assessment to be presented is the goal of the learning. If you want to know whether students have learned words deeply, that will signal a different kind of assessment than if you want to know whether students can recall a brief association to a word. The second topic discussed was maintaining words in students' repertoires after the initial set of instructional activities—indeed, throughout the school year. We offered a number of informal, quick ways to keep students' attention on the words they have learned. We also stressed the value of prompting students to take their word learning outside the classroom and look for examples of the words they have learned elsewhere in their lives, such as in the media they interact with after school.

YOUR TURN

1. Select a set of four to six words that your class has been working with and create two assessment items for each word, based on some of the examples provided. Create one set of items to assess more shallow knowledge and one set to assess deeper understanding and use of the words.

2. Select several words, perhaps some that students learned earlier in the year, and develop a couple of ways to highlight those in the classroom to help students recall and reinforce their meanings.

3. Using that same set of words, develop a way to challenge students to find or apply them outside of school. Part of this should include a way of keeping track of students' contributions and coming up with a reward appropriate to the task.

CHAPTER 7

Working with Instructional and Natural Contexts

Nine-year-old Mark was reading a Hardy Boys book in his room when his mother walked by.

MARK: What does *rend-es-vus* mean?

MOTHER: How's it used?

MARK: It says, "The boys would *rend es vus* at the cave."

MOTHER: What do you think it means?

MARK: Eat. They are always eating.

MOTHER: [Goes over, looks at the page, and sees the word *rendezvous*.] Oh, it's *rahn-day-voo*. It's a French word that means "meet."

MARK: How was I supposed to know that?

Mark's attempt to use context to figure out the meaning of *rendezvous* didn't work. In Chapter 1 we made the point that the word context is frequently found in both research and instruction, but that there were several different meanings to *context*. We noted that there were **instructional contexts**, which are contexts that were intentionally written to support figuring out an unfamiliar word's likely meaning. Another use of *context* is connected to learning new words while reading **naturally occurring text.** In both cases the means to revealing word meaning is to use **context clues**, a well-worn suggestion, which has presently been given extra weight in the *Common Core State Standards* (National Governors Association for

Best Practices Council of Chief State School Officers, 2010). In this chapter, we deal with each of the three issues: instructional contexts, naturally occurring text, and context clues.

PROVIDING WORD-MEANING INFORMATION THROUGH INSTRUCTIONAL CONTEXTS

A common way, although far second to definitions, to convey word-meaning information is through instructional contexts. Instructional contexts are contexts that have been deliberately developed with the intention of providing strong clues to a word's meaning. To understand how instructional contexts differ from natural context, consider in which context the word *dire* appeared in Chapter 1.

> Gregory had done all he could to complete the task. When Horace approached his cousin he could see that Gregory was exhausted. Smiling broadly, Horace said, "You know there are *dire* results for your attempt."

The use of *dire* makes sense—it communicates well—*if* you know the meaning of the word. However, the natural context is misleading for readers who do not know the meaning because the situation described might lead such readers to think that *dire results* are good results. In contrast to the misleading natural context in which *dire* was found, one could develop an instructional context in which the meaning of *dire* is fairly easy to derive. For example:

> Gregory had not completed the task. When Horace approached he could see that Gregory had failed to do what he had promised. With an angry expression on his face, Horace said, "You know there are *dire* results for your attempt."

Even though instructional contexts are designed to make word meanings transparent, it is not enough to simply make an instructional context available to students. In one way or another, a definition or explanation of a target word needs to be developed. And the reasoning behind deriving a meaning for the target word needs to be made public for students. Mere exposure to an instructional context leaves introduction of word meaning incomplete. There is no guarantee that students will come to a clear or correct conclusion about a word's meaning. Making word-meaning information public ensures that all students will begin with a clear, explicit concept of the word. And making public *how* word meaning was derived from the context allows students to build a stronger connection between the word and its meaning. For example, if a student derives the meaning of *dire* as perhaps "bad things," the teacher needs to probe that student's thinking in ways that require the student to explain the parts of the context that helped him or her figure out that *dire* was not a positive description. So, let's go to Ms. T's class and see what such an exchange might be like:

Ms. T: Tell us how you figured out that Horace was saying Gregory's failure would result in bad consequences.

Tonia: Well, Horace had a mean—an angry face.

Lee: And Gregory didn't do what he promised.

Ms. T: How does not doing what he promised have to do with getting bad consequences?

Zoe: People don't like it when other people don't do their promises.

Ms. T: Yes, so Tonia was right; *dire* has to do with something bad. You figured that out because Horace's expression was angry and Gregory had failed in keeping his promise, so *dire* was unlikely to mean anything that was good.

Explaining their reasoning may be quite difficult for students. Therefore, it is a good idea to start out by having the teacher provide some models for deriving meaning from instructional contexts. As an example, consider the following:

The rider couldn't control the *obstinate* horse. She was getting angry that this horse acted this way often.

Modeling how one might derive the meaning for *obstinate* could go something like this (McKeown, 1985):

Obstinate must mean something that a horse could be, and it has to be something that would make a horse hard to control. Maybe scared, a horse could be scared, and because it was scared, it might act up and be hard to control. But it says the horse acted this way often and that the rider was angry about it. I don't think a rider would be angry at a scared horse. *Obstinate* must be a way a horse acts that riders don't like. It could mean stubborn, because horses can get stubborn and some horses can get stubborn often. When they do, it's hard for riders to get them to do what they want.

Such modeling can be useful, but teachers should use it sparingly because it puts students in the passive role of overhearing the teacher thinking aloud. However, such modeling is appropriate when students are being introduced to the idea of deriving meaning from context and when a complicated and subtle context is being explored. It is important, however, to emphasize that students should be made part of the deriving-meaning process as soon as possible, queried along the way as meaning elements are derived from a context.

The following examples show how one might scaffold students' attempts to derive word meanings from instructional contexts:

The deer would be able to eat all they wanted in the meadow, for there was an *abundance* of grass.

- Why would the deer be able to eat all they wanted?
- How much grass must be in the meadow?
- So, what do you think *abundance* means?

The train ride had been long, and I was tired of looking out the window. So I decided to eavesdrop on what two of the passengers sitting behind me were saying. I knew what they were saying was none of my business, but it might be interesting, so I tried to listen.

- What is this person up to? What told you that?
- What's this about if it was none of his business?
- So, *eavesdrop* means what kind of listening?

"Please don't eat the flowers, sir," said the waiter. "I don't think they are *edible*! They might make you sick!"

- What is the waiter telling the man about the flowers?
- If eating them might make you sick, what does that tell you?
- So, if you shouldn't eat things that are not edible, what does *edible* mean?

NATURALLY OCCURRING CONTEXTS

Our readers may be surprised that we have written about teaching students to derive word meanings from natural context, given our strong assertions about the difficulty of doing so. Emphatically, we do not retract the concerns we have discussed. Rather, we keep the concerns alive in our discussion of what might be done to help students gain word meaning information from natural contexts.

To set the scene for the kind of instructional recommendations we make in this chapter, let us provide a brief sketch of the road we traveled that led us to our current perspective. In our earliest forays into vocabulary instruction, we noticed that there was a kind of mantra about how to provide vocabulary instruction: "Have students use context clues." For decades, the theme of context clues seemed to dominate vocabulary instruction. The strongest variant of the theme involved working with categories of context clues that investigators seemed to believe were highly predictive of word meaning. The focus of work on vocabulary through the 1940s, 1950s, and 1960s seemed to be on identifying and refining these categories of context clues and promoting the teaching of them to students (e.g., Ames, 1966–1967; Artley, 1943; McCullough, 1943, 1958; Rankin & Overholser, 1969). Some examples of types of clues from the various classification schemes are presented below:

contrast

Unlike Sarah who was graceful and elegant, Milly was quite *clumsy*.

linked synonyms or appositives

The strongest of the group—all people of height, athletic ability, and *stamina*—were dispatched to protect the camp.

The results of studies directed at the use of the categories were usually somewhat successful in teaching students about the clue types. However, it doesn't take long to recognize that teaching such clues through contrived contexts—which is the only way one could do it—is unlikely to transfer to natural texts.

Our next major foray into the universe of context was an examination of the recommendations that several basal reading programs made for helping students derive meaning from context. We found two pervasive recommendations: teach specific types of context clues, such as the kinds noted above; and have students derive meaning in the course of reading. Having already rejected the first, we explored the second direction by engaging in the study discussed in Chapter 1, in which we categorized the types of information available in natural contexts (i.e., misdirective, nondirective, generally directive, directive) and demonstrated that even adults could only reliably gain information from the most directive contexts.

Our next turn on the vocabulary context road was to explore how students of high and low verbal ability actually use context (McKeown, 1985). The exploration focused on the process of deriving word meaning from context, in which a learner first recognizes a word as unknown, selects information in the context that constrains the word meaning, combines relevant clues into a hypothesis for the word's meaning, and refines that hypothesis upon encountering further information. A study was designed to examine that process by looking at the reasoning learners engaged in as they worked through series of contexts with increasing information for identifying target words, which you see below were nonwords (McKeown, 1985). The results of the study pointed to differences in the reasoning processes used by high- and low-ability students as they tried to figure out word meanings. The differences emerged as three characteristics that less-skilled students demonstrated more frequently than high-ability students did while attempting to derive word meaning through context.

One was a **limited use of context**, in that students focused too narrowly on the context and failed to consider key aspects that were needed to derive the meaning of a target word. As an illustration, consider the case of the pseudoword *laked* as a stand-in for *dragged*:

> The carpenter laked several heavy pieces of lumber to the middle of his workroom and carefully placed them against an old table.

Deciding that *laked* meant "burned" because "You can burn wood" is an example of one student's limited use of the context. The only consideration from the given context is that wood can burn. But it doesn't make sense that the carpenter would burn wood that he had "carefully placed."

The second characteristic that less-skilled readers engage in is **attributing the meaning of the entire context to the target word**. Classic examples of this date back to Werner and Kaplan's (1952) landmark study. As an illustration, the sentence "People talk about the bordicks of others, but don't talk about their own" was described by a young student as "People talk about other people and don't like to talk about themselves" (p. 15).

The third problematic characteristic is going beyond the limits of the meaning of the context and developing a **scenario** into which a meaning might fit. What happens in such cases is that the student selects a possible meaning for a word and then creates a rationale to accommodate that meaning. The result is a bogus relationship between the student's suggested word meaning and the context. For example, in the case of the context sentence, "Because I like corn I would like to <u>steen</u> some," a student responded, "It could be 'sell' because if you make some money, you could grow some corn and sell it."

The recommendation from McKeown's (1985) study was that instructional strategies needed to focus on the *process* of deriving word meanings, in contrast to the *product* of coming up with the right meaning of an unknown word.

USING CONTEXT CLUES

Earlier we made the point that even with instructional contexts it was important to support students in deriving word meaning—at least early on—and we offered examples of the kinds of questions that a teacher could ask to buttress students' inspection of a context. But supporting students to gain meaning from natural contexts is far more difficult. That is, attempting to support students in deriving word meaning from naturally occurring texts is a "horse of a different color."

Goerss, Beck, and McKeown (1999) attempted to address the problem. We started with lots of teacher modeling of how one might consider what an unfamiliar word in context might mean and gave lots of opportunities for students to interact with the context. To explore whether the instruction was effective, Goerss and colleagues took low-skilled readers through seven instructional sessions in which they were given a variety of natural contexts and supported in deriving word meaning information through the specific instructional procedures—which are specified in detail later—that had been developed for the study. Over the course of the study, students showed strong improvements in being able to identify relevant information from contexts and using that information to develop reasonable hypotheses about a word's meaning.

To provide a sense of the kinds of improvements that students made over the course of the study, we present a portion of a transcript of one student's interactions with context during the first training session, and a transcript from a later session. The student is Lisa, a 13-year-old sixth grader who had been in reading intervention programs since second grade. Prior to engagement in the study, she exhibited all of the problems described earlier in using context to derive meanings. One problem was her inability to separate a specific meaning for an unfamiliar word from the rest of the context. Below, is the example context. Lisa's response to the context with *huddling* provides an example of this problem.

> Even knowing help would come shortly didn't make it pleasant. Cobie sat down, huddling her arms and face against her knees for warmth.

The teacher led Lisa through the first several steps of the instructional procedure and Lisa recognized that in the sentence, Cobie was trying to get warm. However, when asked what *huddling* might mean, her responses still attributed the meaning of the entire sentence to huddling.

Ms. G: She could be trying to get warm.

The teacher attempted to describe *huddling* in order to help Lisa find a specific meaning, but Lisa was unresponsive. Finally, the teacher demonstrated *huddling* with her arms and face against her knees.

Ms. G: If someone was doing this, what would you call it?
LISA: She was cold.

This example is in sharp contrast to Lisa's approach to using context in the final (seventh) session. Here, she was able to distinguish the meaning of the word from the context and think of possible meanings for it. Consider the following context and how Lisa approaches uncovering what *conscientious* might mean:

> She wouldn't have forgotten. Sister Frances isn't like that. She's very *conscientious*; in fact, she says so herself and expects all of us to be too.

In the transcript below, Lisa begins to think through the context, describing several aspects she has identified as holding clues to the meaning of *conscientious*:

> What is happening is Sister Frances is talking or telling. Some clues might be *forgotten, Sister Frances*, and *expects all of us to be*.

Lisa then goes on to explore what these clues might yield as a meaning for *conscientious*. Notice that she is able to discern the most meaningful aspect of the context—that *conscientious* is a quality that Sister Frances has and expects others to have—and Lisa keeps on it as she generates possible meanings.

> *Conscientious* could be "nice," because she said so herself and expects everyone to be like that. Or "caring," because it is how she wants everyone else to be. "Friendly," because she is telling everybody that she is like that and she wants everybody to be like, that's how she is, the way she told people to act.

Lisa does not come up with the meaning of *conscientious*, but in the context provided there are not sufficient clues to allow her to do so. What she was able to do is provide some reasonable possibilities, and all the possibilities were in the right domain: *conscientious* is a positive quality. So, had she been independently reading the text, she would at least not have misunderstand the general notion. Moreover, having put *conscientious* into a positive domain, the next time Lisa comes across a context with the word, she may be able to build on what she had figured out and get closer to an understanding of the word.

THE INSTRUCTIONAL SEQUENCE IN GOERSS, BECK, AND MCKEOWN

The instruction we designed for our context research was to take students through the process of deriving word meaning and to allow them to see that different contexts offered different levels of information about word meaning. The instructional model started with an investigator modeling the process and then scaffolding it as responsibility was gradually released to the student. The instructional sequence included five components that started with the text being read and paraphrased, then moved to requiring the student to explain what the text was about and to provide an initial notion of the word's meaning. The sequence also required the student to consider whether the context would allow other potential meanings, and finally the information that had been established through the dialogue was summarized. The enactment of the instructional sequence is represented in examples from several transcripts in which Goerss interacts with students.

The purpose of the initial step, **read/paraphrase**, was to introduce the context and paraphrase it in a way that puts emphasis on the unfamiliar word. Either the investigator or the student could do the reading and paraphrasing. In the example below, the investigator does both.

As for Rusty, he scowled at Mary before stamping out of the room. "And I'm not coming back either, see!" Now, let's kind of reread these sentences to figure out what's happening. Rusty does this scowled thing at Mary and then stamps out of the room. As he does this he says, "And I'm not coming back either, see!"

As noted in the above example, the teacher does the paraphrasing, but as students get acquainted with the approach they are given the responsibility to figure out what is being said.

The second step in the instructional sequence was to **establish meaning of the context**. This is done in order to get students to fully consider the meaning of the context and prevent them from an isolated focus on the word. Toward requiring them to do so, after the initial reading of an item, a teacher can encourage students to consider the information by asking, "What's being said?" "What's going on?" and "Tell us what those sentences are all about." This in itself can go a long way toward helping students become sensitive to the relationship between a context and an unfamiliar word. Below, notice that the student is successful in establishing the meaning of the context:.

Ms. G:	What's happening in these sentences?
LISA:	Rusty is mad at Mary about something and he stamped out of the room.
Ms. G:	Good, is there anything else?
LISA:	Well, he yelled at her as he went out the door that he wasn't coming back.

Note that when the teacher asked, "Is there anything else?" she was looking for the student to examine the context further so that the student might generate some more information—beyond Rusty being mad—that might be helpful in generating possible meanings for the unfamiliar word.

In the third step, **initial identification/rationale**, the student was asked to provide some sense of what the word might be and a rationale for how the context supported that choice. You will notice that, in the example of this step below, the student is able to generate a plausible meaning of *yelled*, with a rationale that includes helpful context:

Ms. G:	What do you think *scowled* might mean?
LISA:	"Yelled."

Ms. G: Why do you think it is "yelled"?

LISA: Well, he is mad at her and then he yelled that he wasn't coming back.

If a student did not have a response at this point or failed to use context information, the teacher guided the student by reviewing the second step, the establish context meaning step, perhaps drawing attention to relevant context clues. Then, the student was encouraged to provide an idea of the meaning of a target word, not necessarily an exact word. In the dialogue below, which was quite typical, notice that the investigator returns to the context and specifically asks the student to generate possible meanings:

Ms. G: What do you think *scowled* means?

LISA: [no response]

Ms. G: Let's look at the sentence with *scowled* again: "As for Rusty, he scowled at Mary before stamping out of the room." When someone stamps out of a room, what do you think they are feeling?

LISA: Mad or upset.

Ms. G: Right, so if Rusty is mad or upset, what are some things he might do at Mary?

LISA: Yell or throw something.

The fourth step, **consider further possibilities,** was to help students examine more possibilities and refrain from the expectation that it is necessary or even possible to find one right meaning for every unfamiliar word. This step might proceed something like the dialogue presented here:

Ms. G: Can you think of some other possible meanings?

LISA: Make faces at her.

Ms. G: Why do you say "make faces at her"?

LISA: If you are mad at someone, you might make a face at them before you stamp out of the room.

Ms. G: Can you think of anything else *scowled* might mean?

LISA: Shake your fist.

Ms. G: What made you say that?

LISA: I shake my fist when I'm mad at my sister.

Notice that the student was able to generate two other possible meanings using the context and experience.

In the fifth and last step, **summarize**, the information that had been generated in the dialogue about the unfamiliar word was pulled together. The intent here was to bring together information so that it would be available to the student to reconsider and then draw conclusions about what was known about the word's meaning. As an example, consider the following:

Ms. G:	What do we know about *scowled*?
Lisa:	It is something Rusty did at Mary.
Ms. G:	And . . . ?
Lisa:	He was mad because he stamped out of the room telling her he wasn't coming back. It could be "yelled" or "shook his fist" or "made an angry face at her."
Ms. G:	Any one of those might be possible meanings for *scowled* based on these sentences. *Scowled* does mean one that you suggested—"made an angry face."

The whole point of the five steps is to get students to really think through what is being talked about and notice what information in the text might relate to a target word. From there, it becomes a trial-and-error process to see if a word that comes to mind fits the whole context and, if not, to generate alternatives. An important point, however, is the learner needs to be fully cognizant of the varying amounts of information that are available from contexts, and needs to know when to stop the process as it might not be possible to come up with a likely meaning of a word.

WORKING WITH A GROUP OF STUDENTS

The instructional sequence explained above can be used in a range of informal to formal situations, with one student to a whole class. And, depending on the situation, all the steps or just one or two steps can be used. The examples from the Goerss and colleagues (1999) study showed the use of all the steps and involved working with an individual student. But it has been our experience that trying to figure out the meaning of a word from context is enriched when a group of students, including a whole class, is involved. We provide some examples of the procedures used in whole-class situations.

In a section from *Charlotte's Web* (White, 1952) in which Wilbur, the pig, asks Templeton, the rat, "Will you play with me?" Templeton responds that he doesn't "know the meaning of the word." So, Wilbur describes some of the things one does when playing, to which Templeton says, "I never do those things if I can avoid them." At this point the teacher decides to pursue the meaning of *avoid* and the following dialogue occurs:

MS. J: What's Templeton saying here?

ALVIN: He doesn't like to do those things.

MS. J: What do you think *avoid* means?

ALVIN: Never do those things.

MS. J: So, *avoid* means "not to do something"?

STUDENTS: [Several students seem to agree.]

MS. J: *Avoid* does mean "to stay away from something."

In this case, identifying the meaning of *avoid* worked well. It worked well because the text information was adequate for inferring the meaning, but we also submit that it worked well because the teacher started with establishing the message of the text segment before going directly to questioning about what *avoid* might mean.

Below, we provide examples of situations when deriving a meaning is more difficult. The example below comes from the scene in which Templeton leaves Wilbur and goes into a tunnel that he has dug. Then, the text says:

Templeton was a crafty rat and he had things pretty much his own way. The tunnel was an example of his skill and cunning. The tunnel enabled him to get from the barn to his hiding place under the pig trough without coming out into the open.

The following exchange captures how the teacher pursues the meaning of *cunning*:

MS. J: What's happening here?

GELESA: Templeton goes in his tunnel.

MS. J: What do we know about the tunnel?

MARTIN: He made it.

PERRY: Nobody sees him.

Ms. J:	What's it mean, "The tunnel was an example of his skill and cunning"?
MELIA:	He was good at making the tunnel.
Ms. J:	Okay, he was good at it, so that's an example of his skill, but what do you think *cunning* means?
MARTIN:	His digging skill . . .
Ms. J:	Well, he did dig the tunnel, but *cunning* is telling us something more about Templeton. Remember when Perry [the third student who spoke] told us that he goes into the tunnel so nobody sees him. So, what's that say about Templeton?
SHANNEL:	He dug a deep tunnel so nobody could see him.
MARTIN:	He's smart.
SHANNEL:	He's sneaky.
Ms. J:	Great! Templeton is smart and sneaky! And that's what *cunning* means. *Cunning* means "to be clever and sneaky."

The *cunning* example is an instance of going through the process using a context that has several clues to the word's meaning, as well as information that could distract and lead to other possible meanings.

The next situation involves a text that has little and perhaps not enough information to provide a direction for a target word's meaning. It occurs in the text after Templeton declines to play with Wilbur and explains that:

[I want] to spend . . . [my] time eating, gnawing, spying and hiding. I am a glutton but not a merry-maker. Right now I'm on my way to your trough to eat your breakfast, since you haven't got sense enough to eat it yourself.

Ms. J:	What does this tell us about Templeton?
BEVERLY:	He doesn't want to play.
ALVIN:	He's going to eat Wilbur's breakfast?
MARTIN:	He thinks Wilbur is dumb because he didn't eat his breakfast.
Ms. J:	Okay, it also says that Templeton likes "eating, gnawing, spying and hiding. I am a glutton but not a merry-maker." What do you think a *glutton* is?
SHIKIA:	Somebody who doesn't like to have fun.

MARTIN: Like somebody who spies and steals things.

Ms. J: Those ideas show good thinking because those are ideas that are coming through about Templeton. But *glutton* means "somebody who likes to eat a lot and is very greedy about food." You know, there really was no way for you to figure that out for sure because there was lots of other information about Templeton, and it was hard to tell what information would have been useful for figuring out the meaning of *glutton*.

Given that the teacher had to tell the students the meaning of *glutton*, one can point out that time could have been saved had the teacher just told the students the meaning of *glutton* from the start and as such there was no advantage to students in asking them to try to use the context. We suggest that there is advantage. One is to underscore that it is exceedingly important that students learn that they may not be able to get potentially useful information from context, be it the actual meaning of a word or a sense of the word meaning or a sense of how it's used. In such cases students need to go to an outside source—a person or a dictionary. From our own practical experiences and that of colleagues, many students find looking words up in the course of reading annoying, and others just don't do it.

For a moment let us digress and offer several suggestions for alleviating the annoyance of looking up words' meaning in the course of reading. One is that students are permitted to ask the teacher what a word means. (How many of us ask a person in the room in which we encounter an unknown word whether they know the meaning of a given word?) The teacher's time in providing word meanings can be kept in control by setting up a ground rule such as for every word for which a student asks the teacher for an explanation, the student needs to look up another word in the dictionary. Another way to reduce the annoyance of looking up words in the course of reading is to ask students to lightly underline words (of course depending on the nature of the material that is marked) whose meaning they don't know, and offering points, yes points, for the number of words that were so marked. It is important that students understand that it is a good thing, at least certainly not a bad thing, that students acknowledge their unfamiliarity with certain words. Subsequently, the teacher can collect such words and deal with those worth class time. Of course, there are electronic and digital devices—handheld electric dictionaries, apps for smartphones, tablet computers as well as online dictionaries—that might be incorporated in useful ways. Teachers are creative, and with limited equipment many may have already developed ways to enable students to use them—perhaps taking turns with a mobile device, and collecting some words and then consulting a desktop computer.

Returning to our discussion of advantages for asking students to make their thinking public was demonstrated in the Goerss and colleagues (1999) study, where it was shown that students learned to actually think about what a word might be by querying the text around the word, and making hypotheses about word meanings—witness Lisa's efforts when trying to figure out the meaning of *conscientious* as it related to Sister Frances.

Practicing the procedure of inferring meaning from context helps readers develop a sensitivity to the relationship between a novel word and the context in which it appears. It is important for students to understand the relationship between words and the broader context; the word has to make sense within the context and that words bring meaning to context. Toward those ends, we have been involved in a research and development project that we discuss below.

ROBUST ACADEMIC VOCABULARY ENCOUNTERS

In our latest vocabulary instruction endeavor, Robust Academic Vocabulary Encounters (RAVE), the relationship between word and context is highlighted in the way we introduce words. We present the words in authentic contexts, provide friendly explanations of word meaning, and promote discussion about how the word meaning fits the context. The aim is to show students the types of contexts in which they may encounter the words and the role the words can play in communicating meaning. RAVE addresses two issues that are central to vocabulary instruction: learning words in naturally occurring contexts and learning academic words. Below we first consider the role of academic words in RAVE.

Academic Words

The contexts we used in the Goerss (1999) work were selected from fiction material. Presently there is concern that words that are more likely to appear in informational text (content-area and other nonfiction material) have not been given the attention that is needed. These words, which have been labeled academic words, are not the words that are tightly tied to specific content material (e.g., *meteorology, fjord, subsidy*). Rather, they are words that are common across various content-area texts.

As we described at the beginning of Chapter 2, Nation (2001) cites Coxhead's (1998) *Academic Word List* (AWL) as a good database. Coxhead's list of 570 word families is drawn from a corpus of 3.5 million running words from academic journals and university textbooks in four broad academic areas: arts, commerce, law, and natural science. To select words for inclusion in her database, a word family had to have occurred in all four academic areas at least 100 times to be included in the corpus. Nation views academic words as essential to teach because of their range of coverage over various types of text and the meaning they bring to a text. These words would overlap our Tier Two category.

In our current work we selected words—99 for each of two middle school grade levels—from the AWL and identified authentic contexts that included each word. We describe that work below.

Overview of RAVE

In RAVE, our focus is on informational texts, which for the most part, we drew from Internet-based resources such as journals, national newspapers, and professional blogs (e.g., Museum of Science), as well as some print sources to select contexts for target words. These authentic contexts serve as a starting point for discussing what a word means and how it is used within different contexts, such as a context for *confine* used to describe something that is physically limited in movement (the toddler was confined to her playpen) and another context for *confine* to describe how ideas can be mentally limited (suggestions made to students not to confine their ideas narrowly).

In RAVE, encounters with target words were systematically designed to reveal various nuances of meaning and to represent the kinds of contexts in which students would encounter the words. Friendly definitions, developed to present a core meaning for each word, are also presented to introduce each word.

Active processing is embodied in RAVE through follow-up activities that students participate in for several days after initial word introduction. The approaches used in such activities are similar to the kinds of robust vocabulary activities suggested in the first edition of *Bringing Words to Life* (Beck et al., 2002) and in the subsequent *Creating Robust Vocabulary* (Beck et al., 2008). For example, students are asked to make decisions about word use and to develop contexts around kernel ideas that are presented: "Would you *conform* if sixth graders started wearing right and left shoes of different colors? Why?" and "How could you *establish* yourself as the DJ for every school dance?" RAVE instruction features authentic contexts with teachers directing the sequence and discussion of those contexts.

To provide a sense of a RAVE lesson, we present the instructional materials for the first portion of a lesson, the introduction of the word *expose*. These materials include:

- An initial supportive context for a word (Context 1)
- Questions to direct student attention to the context
- Ideas to develop, which indicate specific aspects of the context to highlight
- A student-friendly definition for the word
- Questions to support students in integrating the context and definition
- A second context for the word (Context 2)
- Questions and ideas to develop as noted above
- Questions to support students in integrating Contexts 1 and 2
- Activate vocabulary, which prompts students to use the word in different contexts

Teacher Materials for the Introduction of *expose**

Context 1: Some miners work deep underground to dig out coal. Other miners blast off the top of mountains to *expose* layers of coal underneath. They often have to blast away 800 to 1,000 feet of rock before the coal is *exposed* (Goodell, 2006).

- To understand Context 1:
  - What does this context say about how coal is mined?
  - Ideas to develop: Some coal is mined by digging deep underground, and some coal is mined by blasting off mountaintops.
- Friendly definition:
  - If you *expose* something, you let it show or make it known.
- To integrate meaning and Context 1:
  - How does the meaning of *expose* fit Context 1?
  - Ideas to develop:
    - When mountaintops are blasted off, the coal underneath can be seen.
    - Follow up as needed: What do you mean by that? What does that have to do with *expose*?

---

*In Chapter 9 we provide examples of how this material is scaffolded for response to intervention (RTI) instruction and English learner (EL) instruction.

Context 2: Students can be *exposed* to the world of jazz music by attending jazz concerts and by listening to jazz CDs. A new CD, called *Second Set*, exposes students to jazz solos, backgrounds, bass lines, and parts for piano and percussion (samash.com, 2010).

- To integrate meaning and Context 2:
  - This context says students can be *exposed* to jazz. What's that all about?
- Ideas to develop:
  - Students can begin to know about jazz music by going to concerts and listening to CDs.
- To integrate meaning across both contexts:
  - From the two contexts, what do we know about how we can use the word *expose*?
  - If needed, summarize by pointing out: We use *expose* to mean showing something. It can be something hidden, like coal underground, or making something known, such as new ideas or new ways of doing things or new kinds of music.
- Activate vocabulary:
  - How could middle school students be exposed to what it will be like in high school?
  - How could you expose someone who was mistreating his or her dog?

In all lessons either the teacher or a student reads the contexts and friendly definitions aloud. Notice that the purpose of the upcoming question about the context is given ("to understand Context 1"). Next, the question "What does this context say about how coal is mined?" is the means toward understanding the context. If students have difficulty explaining the context "ideas to develop," prompt teachers with the goal of the question so that they might rephrase the question, have the context reread, or provide an appropriate response themselves if they thought it was needed to achieve the goal.

Second, the friendly definition is read. Then "to integrate meaning and Context 1" the question "This context says students can be *exposed* to jazz. What's that all about?" follows. The goal of the third step "to integrate meaning across both contexts" asks students, given knowledge of the two contexts, how the word *expose* can be used. Then a summary is provided.

The final entry in the lesson, "activate vocabulary," is the last step in the introductory portion of a RAVE lesson. Among its purposes is that students actually engage with target word meanings right after the word is introduced and to do so in contexts other than the two examples already provided. In a way it is kind of starting the "hardening" of word meanings in students' lexicon. Below we provide a transcript of students engaging in activate vocabulary for *expose*.

MS. R: Um, let me ask you a question. How could middle school students be *exposed* to what it will be like in high school?

TYLER: Because it's a big change . . .

MS. R: No, not because . . . let me ask . . . let me ask the question again. How could middle school students be exposed to what it will be like in high school?

SAVANNAH: You can, uh, take the students down to the high school and show them the classrooms and what they do and stuff.

ISABELLA: Yeah, take them to the high school and show them the classes. That would be exposing them?

TYLER: Um, get a high school student and bring them in here.

MS. R: There you go! All right, next question. How could you *expose* someone who was mistreating his or her dog?

DOMINIC: Call the Humane Society.

MS. R: And, how would that expose them?

DOMINIC: You could tell their name and what they're doing to the dog.

MS. R: Mmm, hmm. You would call the Humane Society and give their name and tell them what you, um, saw them doing to the dog. That would expose them. That would make it known. What else could you do to expose someone mistreating the dog?

DOMINIC: Put a camera in their bushes and record them overnight and then go to the people in the morning.

MS. R: Right, a camera! That would expose them. A camera would actually record what that person was doing to mistreat his or her dog. Okay, when you expose something you're making it known.

Notice that dealing with the different senses represented by "exposing students to high school" and "exposing a wrong-doer" was not a problem for students.

Some Results

So far, about 125 sixth graders have received RAVE instruction—20 in a short pilot study and 105 in an implementation over the school year. All students made impressive gains on a test of word knowledge given before and after the instruction. The results contrasted with those for some academic words not taught (for the pilot study) and for comparison classrooms (for the larger study), as we found no gains for words not taught and very small gains for comparison students who had not had RAVE instruction.

What this means is that, although these academic words do occur in the students' environment (indeed, students showed us many examples from their textbooks), students are not likely to learn them without direct instruction. For the pilot study (because analyses are not complete for the larger study), we also have results from a text comprehension task that consisted of oral recall of two expository passages, one with 27 instructed words and the other with 27 academic words not taught. Students produced more comprehensive recalls of the passage with instructed words compared to the passage with nontaught words. This suggests that comprehension effects can be an immediate result of robust instruction when students meet the taught words in new texts.

SUMMARY

If teachers want to hone their skills to support students' abilities to derive the meanings of words from natural contexts, the following advice may help:

- Anticipate that, at first, some students will tend to engage in inappropriate meaning-deriving characteristics: limited use of context, attributing the meaning of a word to the meaning of the entire context, and creating a scenario for a word's possible meaning.
- Keep in mind that natural contexts do not provide information in logical and systematic ways and vary widely in the amount of information they provide about a given word.
- Because of the unreliability of natural contexts, instruction needs to be presented as a *process* of figuring out meaning within an individual context, rather than focusing on the *product*—a word's meaning.
- When implementing instruction, always start with asking students to explain what is going on in the portion of text being read, and then what the word might mean.

YOUR TURN

1. Select some passages from expository text, and identify some words that students are unlikely to know. Use the *expose* lesson in this chapter as a guide to develop several lessons. Or you may want to start with some words and find some text in which words appear. Texts that are publicly available on the Web allow searches for contexts containing specified words. These sources are *Corpus of Contemporary American English* (Davies), *Dictionary Squared* (Kapelner), and *Wordnik* (McKean). The *Corpus of Contemporary American English* (COCA), created by Mark Davies, is the largest electronic corpus of English. It comprises 385 million running words of text, equally divided among spoken, fiction, popular magazines, newspapers, and academic texts. Sometimes the texts need to be adapted as they come from longer pieces and a context should not be much more than about 60 words.

2. Below are instructional contexts for three Tier Two words. For each, think of questions you could ask that draw students' attention to aspects of the context that provide clues to meaning and then lead students to deduce a meaning for the word.

   • The students prepared dozens and dozens of cookies for the bake sale because they <u>anticipate</u> lots of customers. They are sure that a bake sale is a good way to raise money.

   • Serena didn't know whether to vote for Nadia or Tony for class treasurer. She thought either one would do a good job, so she was <u>neutral</u> about who should win the election.

   • When the Nelson boys were small, they ran around on the field and kicked a soccer ball every day after school. Even though they are on a soccer team now, they would rather play video games. Their interest in soccer has <u>diminished</u>.

CHAPTER 8

Vocabulary and Writing

The notion that vocabulary knowledge is related to writing proficiency is intuitively compelling. Composition teachers certainly believe it. How many of us upon just glancing through a teacher's comments on a piece of our writing have noticed the same word, let's say, *important*, circled every time it appeared in close proximity? That's code for "You're repeating the same word." In fact, word choice is often one of the features included on rubrics used to evaluate student writing (e.g., Culham, 2003). Precision of word knowledge is another feature related to good writing as it enables the writer to say exactly what he or she wants to say. One demonstration of this is the many of us who when writing have paused and struggled to find just the right word. Corson (1995) suggests that it is the content of language, especially the use and diversity of vocabulary, that teachers look for when their students are communicating meaning.

READING AND WRITING AS RELATED PROCESSES

Historically, reading and writing have been thought of as contrasting processes with reading being identified as a receptive process and writing an expressive process. In the 1950s, the paradigm shift in psychological research from *behaviorism*, with its focus on observable behaviors, changed to *cognition*, with its focus on the mental processes in which individuals engaged in the course of carrying out various tasks (Miller, 2003). The cognitive orientation influenced educational thought, and new insights and understanding about reading and writing grew. For example, in the case of reading, the behavioral interest was focused on the product of reading—such as a reader's answers to questions or a reader's summary of what was read. In contrast, the cognitive interest was in what mental processes were engaged in generating the product. The paradigm shift to cognition affected research to such a large extent that it came to be called the "cognitive revolution" (Gardner, 1985).

In about the 1970s, the cognitive revolution stimulated thinking and research about reading and writing. Reading emerged from a passive, bottom-up activity to a constructive process in which readers actively engage with text to create meaning. Writing emerged from a focus on the product to a process of interactions between the writer and knowledge of language, topic, and audience (e.g., Applebee, 1982; Flower & Hayes, 1981). With cognitive and constructivist theories surfacing in both reading and writing, the metaphor of readers composing a text in their minds (Tierney & Pearson, 1983) encouraged greater focus and attention to the linguistic and cognitive similarities of reading and writing. With researchers examining the relationship between the two (Fitzgerald & Shanahan, 2000) a useful literature emerged.

The overall theoretical orientation of the similarities between reading and writing is that they are both constructive processes. So what is similar between these two constructive processes? Among the similarities, Fitzgerald and Shanahan (2000) discussed four types of knowledge that both readers and writers share and need to engage in the course of reading and writing to be successful. One is *metaknowledge about written language*, which includes knowing about the functions and purposes of reading and writing, awareness that as a reader, one needs to interact with text to understand ideas and as a writer to interact with ideas to create text. Metaknowledge also involves monitoring one's own meaning making. A second kind of shared knowledge is obvious—the *linguistic features of written language*, which include sounds within words (phonemes), spelling (orthography), morphology, semantics, syntax, and text features. It is hard to think of what among the features of written language are not shared by reading and writing. The use of certain features (e.g., phonemes and orthography) is most relevant to early readers and writers and may be more important to writing than to reading. But orthography is not irrelevant to reading—think about homophones: *straight/strait, told/tolled, sink/sync.*

A third category of shared knowledge is *procedural knowledge*, which includes knowing how to access and use knowledge during reading and writing. For instance in both reading and writing, it is not uncommon for an individual to become aware that knowledge beyond what is being read or what is being written is needed. At such times a person may attempt to interrogate his or her memory for such knowledge or know that the needed knowledge is not in memory. When that happens the individual needs to decide to go on without the knowledge or go to an outside source. Procedural knowledge also includes such intentional strategies as questioning and summarizing.

Fitzgerald and Shanahan (2000) also identified *domain knowledge and semantics* as a particularly important shared area between reading and writing. Domain knowledge, sometimes referred to as background knowledge or content knowledge, is what the reader or writer already knows about the content he or she is reading or writing about. The study of the role of background knowledge in reading has been of interest to reading researchers and the object of study for decades (Anderson & Pearson, 1984; Bransford & McCarrell, 1974; Spivey, 1997). Evidence that background knowledge affects reading comprehension is well established (McKeown, Beck, Sinatra, & Loxterman, 1992; Sinatra, Beck, & McKeown, 1993). Yet despite the obvious role of background knowledge in writing—after all, writing has got to be about something—little research has been undertaken (Fitzgerald & Shanahan, 2000; Flower & Hayes, 1981; Hillocks, 1986a, 1986b) and what there is has been hard to find.

Semantics, which Fitzgerald and Shanahan (2000) included in parallel with domain knowledge, in its broader sense refers to the meaning of language, but it is often used in association with word meaning, and word meaning in educational literature is referred to as *vocabulary*. We will stick with *vocabulary*, the words and word choices, which are the building blocks of reading and writing.

VOCABULARY INSTRUCTION AND WRITING

Among the few studies that consider the relationship between vocabulary instruction and writing, several directly incorporated the notion of improving writing by enhancing vocabulary. One set of studies discusses a unique approach to enhancing vocabulary toward affecting writing, and two quasi-experimental studies compare robust vocabulary instruction and traditional instruction on writing. We start with the work that focuses on a unique way to enhance vocabulary.

A Unique Approach to Vocabulary Instruction

A recent book by Scott, Skobel, and Wells (2008) described an approach to vocabulary that emphasizes enhancing writing through developing students' word consciousness. Teachers immersed students in rich literature and encouraged them to examine authors' use of words. The notion was that such a process would help students to value the power of words in writing, leading to wider vocabulary use and improved writing by the students. Students were encouraged to "gather Gifts of Words" from literature. For instance, Scott and colleagues provide examples of students' choices from the first chapter of *Half-a-Moon Inn* (Fleischman, 1980).

> A chill darted up his spine.
>
> He felt as restless as a chipmunk.
>
> He burst out of bed as though the sheets were a fire.

Such phrases are then deposited in a word bank and students are encouraged to draw on this bank of phrases in their own writing.

The work of Scott and her colleagues on developing word consciousness in classrooms has been going on for a number of years, first with a project titled Gift of Words (Henry et al., 1999; Scott & Nagy, 2004), and more recently with an intervention titled Vocabulary Innovations in Education (VINE) that was targeted to developing teachers' awareness and knowledge of words. Initial word consciousness work and more recently VINE work has resulted in several books, a number of book chapters, and a few journal articles that tend to show more positive outcomes for word consciousness classrooms compared to control classrooms.

In VINE, teachers met and shared ideas, but each teacher determined how word consciousness would be enacted in his or her classroom. Thus, although the goal among classes was the same, development of word consciousness through various activities and different enactments was going on across classrooms, including for instance Writers' Workshop, that may not have been implemented in every experimental classroom. So, there is no way to figure out whether one or several components were instrumental in results.

Comparison of Instructional Approaches

In another vein, one study directly explored the effect of two kinds of vocabulary instruction on writing. The researchers based their experimental instructional writing materials on the research about the kind of vocabulary instruction that supported reading comprehension. So before we describe the details of those studies, let us review the research that has been acknowledged throughout this book as the basis for the kinds of instruction that affect reading comprehension. We can do that easily by mentioning two meta-analyses (Mezynski, 1983; Stahl & Fairbanks, 1986) that pointed to promising effects on comprehension from vocabulary instruction.

Mezynski's (1983) meta-analysis reviewed eight vocabulary training studies designed to influence reading performance. All eight of the studies showed gains in overall word knowledge and three showed transfer to reading comprehension. Similarly, from their meta-analysis, Stahl and Fairbanks (1986) concluded that vocabulary instruction does seem to have an effect on comprehension. Their analyses reviewed comprehension effects on passages containing taught words and on standardized test passages that did not contain the taught words. Significant effects were found for both the passages containing taught words and for the standardized passages.

Of the studies that showed favorable gains in reading comprehension, instructional implications were drawn about the kind of word knowledge necessary to impact comprehension. Mezynski (1983) identified three features: (1) amount of practice of the targeted words, (2) breadth of word knowledge about the words, and (3) the use of active processing. Stahl and Fairbanks drew similar implications. In particular, Stahl and Fairbanks (1986) determined that methods that had the strongest effect on comprehension were those that included (1) both definitional and contextual information about the words, (2) multiple exposures to each word, and (3) deeper processing of the words. As you know from earlier chapters, these features are hallmarks of robust vocabulary.

Duin and Graves (1987) can be recognized for putting forth the notion that if vocabulary instruction can improve reading comprehension, then it may be possible to improve the quality of student writing by teaching vocabulary in the same manner in which it has been shown to impact reading comprehension. Thus, in their 1987 investigation, Duin and Graves developed writing instruction based on the research noted above that positively influenced reading comprehension. They targeted 12 sophisticated words for three groups of students. The first group received robust vocabulary instruction. Students in this group were also provided with specific writing activities designed to assist them in using the new words in their writing. The second group also received robust vocabulary instruction, but did not engage in any of the writing activities. The third group was taught using traditional vocabulary instruction and, like the second group, did not engage in writing activities.

Results indicated that students' knowledge of the target words in each of the robust vocabulary groups increased significantly from pretest to posttest, compared to students in the traditional group. The first group that received robust vocabulary instruction and writing instruction also did the best on a writing assessment. Although the trend in Duin and Graves's (1987) work was toward the impact of robust instruction, since only one of the two robust vocabulary groups received writing instruction, we are left not knowing the influence of vocabulary instruction on writing.

A COMPARISON OF TWO VOCABULARY APPROACHES
WITH WRITING INSTRUCTION

In her dissertation research, Lisa Yonek* (2008), Isabel's student, investigated the role of writing and two kinds vocabulary instruction on students' expository writing. That is, students in each of two groups received the same writing instruction but they differed in the kind of vocabulary instruction—traditional or robust—in which they were involved.

The study was implemented with two intact classes of fourth-grade students in an urban school district in a middle-sized city. Fifty-two percent of the students in the school were eligible for free or reduced lunch, and 70% of fourth graders were considered proficient as measured by results on the state's reading test. Analysis of those scores showed that each class's reading abilities were not different from the other. In fact, the means for each group were exactly the same: 2.75 out of a possible 4. There were 18 students enrolled in each class; 16 from each group were granted permission to participate in the study.

Yonek (2008) compared students' persuasive essays written in the early part of the year, October/November, and compared them to essays written toward the end of the year, May/June, after the interventions had been implemented in each of the two classrooms. The essays written in the fall were administered as part of a district policy in which all fourth graders were required to write persuasive essays as part of the district's grading system. The fall writing assessment was administered under the district's auspices after students had engaged in a 5-week unit on persuasive writing that was part of the district's core language arts program. The district made essays from two classrooms available to Yonek, which she rescored for use as a pretest for the study. The same writing assignment was administered as the posttest, 7 months later, after the two fourth-grade study classrooms had completed either robust or traditional vocabulary intervention. Thus, both groups had the same writing instruction at the same time, completed the postwriting assignment after that instruction, participated in either robust or traditional instruction for 5 days, and wrote the post-essays at the same time.

The writing prompt that the students received was taken from the core language arts program. It is provided below:

---

*We are grateful to Lisa Yonek, who graciously gave us permission to use material from her dissertation. Specifically, the material that appears on pages 144–151 was developed from Yonek's (2008) dissertation. The analyses of students' essays and the actual students' essays are presented verbatim from her dissertation.

Write an editorial for your local paper in which you tell readers why you think it is important to keep your city parks clean. Be sure your essay is at least three paragraphs long.

Yonek (2008) used an interesting approach to identify target words for use in the study. She reviewed the pretest essays for common ideas students had expressed that could be linked to Tier Two words that had not appeared in any of the essays. For example, a number of students wrote about how dangerous littering in parks could be to animals and people. *Hazardous*, a Tier Two word, was designated as an appropriate match for that particular concept. In another instance, a few student essays voiced concern that littering would cause their parks to be dirty and run-down. The Tier Two word *deteriorate* was linked to that particular idea. In this manner, Yonek identified the following nine Tier Two words: *hazardous, unfortunate, deprived, deteriorate, appealing, environment, recreation, accountable*, and *maintain*. In addition, three general words that could well be used in a persuasive essay were added: *imperative, sway*, and *numerous*, which could take the place of *important, convince*, and *many*, respectively.

Materials for robust instruction, which have been described in detail in previous chapters, were developed for the 12 target words for one of the two fourth-grade classes. Materials for the other fourth-grade class, the traditional group, were also developed. Those materials were modeled after basal readers' activities and workbooks as well as Yonek's (2008) observations of how vocabulary was taught in the district. Traditional instruction involved presenting students with a dictionary definition, possibly a context sentence, and an activity such as matching words to definitions or identifying words that were synonyms or antonyms for the target words.

Since a high number of encounters with target words is not characteristic of traditional instruction, yet is a hallmark of robust instruction, the number of encounters in the traditional group was increased to be the same as those in the robust group. This was essential because just the sheer number of encounters could have a significant effect on outcomes. So, the comparison is more correctly viewed as between robust instruction and extensive traditional instruction. Thus, both groups were taught the same 12 words, in the same order—over 5 days, with the same number of encounters of target words, and the length of lessons were similar.

Word-Level Assessments and Results

To determine whether there were differences in word knowledge achieved by students under the two conditions, two word-level assessments were administered. These were a multiple-choice test intended to measure basic word knowledge and a degree of word knowledge assessment designed to measure precision and depth of word knowledge. The multiple-choice test had the traditional format of a stem and five choices for each of the 12 words.

The degree of word knowledge items were sentences that included a target word and two blanks for students to complete. For example: Something *imperative* for a teacher is _____ because _____. Each of the 12 items was scored on a 4-point rubric according to the following scale: 3 (full word knowledge), 2 (partial word knowledge), 1 (vague word knowledge), and 0 (no word knowledge).

Findings showed that on the multiple-choice tests the two classes scored the same on both the pretest and posttest scores. Large gains were made by students in both conditions with posttest scores for each word across both groups ranging between 88 and 100% correct. One take-home message here is that a high number of encounters with either traditional or robust instructional approaches will produce gains on traditional word knowledge measures.

However, the depth of knowledge assessment told a different story. Both groups' pretest scores were virtually the same. But on the posttest with 36 as the highest possible score, the mean for the traditional group was 21 and the mean for the robust group was 33. So, the average student in the robust group missed 3 points and in the traditional group missed 17 points.

The implication of comparing the results of both groups' posttests on the two word-level assessments is quite revealing of the notion that we have been asserting for some years. That is, increasing students' word knowledge to the level of being able to respond correctly to multiple-choice items is limited. The kind of knowledge represented on a multiple-choice test may have a low probability of being activated for complex language tasks, such as comprehension and composition. It is our position that the most important goal of vocabulary instruction is to enhance students' ability to engage in complex language situations. The degree of knowledge assessment was a more complex task than the multiple-choice test.

Students' Essays

Writing is clearly a complex task and one primary goal of the study was to explore whether there were differences in the number of target words used and the quality of the essays that might be attributed to the different vocabulary instructional conditions.

An analysis of the number of words used in the pre-essays (written in fall before instruction) showed that students in each group barely used any of the words. However, for both groups, there were significant increases in the use of target words when the pre-essays were compared to the post-essays (written in the spring after instruction). The increase was almost four words for the traditional group, and almost twice as much, eight words, for the robust group.

It is important to mention that there was an attempt to keep the post-essay conditions as close to those for the pre-essay conditions as possible. The one difference was that after the researcher read aloud the probe that asked students to write the essay about keeping the parks clean, she told students in both groups to try to use some of the words they had been studying and pointed to a wall chart on which the words were displayed. That chart had been placed on the wall at the beginning of the interventions and stayed there during the composing of the post-essays. As such, the increases in use of the words in the essays probably should be considered a best-case scenario.

So why did students in the robust class use twice as many words in their essays as the traditional group? We assert that definition-based knowledge alone has a limited effect on complex tasks, such as writing to persuade. What does matter is the use of vocabulary to support the communication of ideas.

On both pre- and post-essays, quality of students' writing was rated on a 4-point scale ranging from 0 (below basic), 1 (basic), 2 (proficient), to 3 (advanced). From pre- to post-essay, both groups showed improvement; however, the amount of improvement was significantly greater for the robust group. Specifically, on the pre-essay the majority of students in both groups performed below proficiency, either basic or below basic, with only 6% of students in the robust group and 13% in the traditional group receiving a proficient score. Proficient post-essay scores increased to 44% of students in the robust group compared to 25% of students in the traditional group. Additionally, the percentage of students in the robust group who scored below basic on the pre-essay (25%) was reduced to 0. In the traditional group the mean percentage of students below basic (38%) remained in that category on the postwriting. Two individuals scored the essays independently and interrater reliability was computed at .89.

In order to provide a sense of the students' writing and changes from pre- to post-essays, Yonek (2008) made available to us for use in this book the pre- and post-essays for two students from the robust group whose posttest essay writing was rated one level higher than on the pretest. The two students' essays (the names are pseudonyms) are presented below with

Yonek's analyses of each essay provided first with the student's essay following.

Although the students' phrasing often appears immature, among several reasons this is the case, perhaps the words are still fragile. They are, however, using the words meaningfully to express their ideas. Students seem to be using the words to explore new arguments and ways to express their points. Certainly, the arguments are not well developed, but the post-essays show an increased number of ideas put forth in the essays.

Rolanda's Essays

ANALYSIS OF PRE-ESSAY

Rolanda's pre-essay was scored as basic mainly because of a lack of content and focus, which makes for a weak argument. Rolanda gives consequences for not keeping the park clean but fails to give reasons why keeping parks clean would be beneficial.

Pre-Essay (Basic)

Do you enjoy going to a park full of dirtballs? If not, help today! Do you want your kids to play in a dump? Well if you don't, help pick up trash from 2–4 pm. The park will be sparkling clean.

Do you like graphetti on your equipment? Then what are you waiting for, do something about it. Your children will repeat everything they've seen. Many people complain about dog business on the ground. All you have to do is buy a pooper-scooper. The park will be as good as new. Help now! and get involved.

ANALYSIS OF POST-ESSAY

In contrast to her pre-essay, Rolanda's post-essay is more developed and provides a more coherent argument about the importance of keeping community parks clean. Notice in the post-essay Rolanda still mentions the consequences of not keeping parks clean, as she did in the pre-essay, but adds other ideas such as how keeping the park clean and appealing will attract more people, and the idea about the clean-up team being accountable for maintaining the park. The language in the post-essay is clearly more mature than the pre-essay due to the addition of the target words, which gives the writing an overall better style and tone and clearly adds to the content. Because of these reasons, the post-essay was scored as advanced and the student moved up two levels from basic to advanced.

Post-Essay (Advanced)

It would be *unfortunate* if the *environment* in which your park is is nasty, so help clean it up! That is a place where you can do almost any recreation.

You should have numerous garbage and recycling cans. It would be *hazardous* if a baby was playing and got cut by a piece of glass.

Also, try to *sway* the parks owner to have a clean up team so they can maintain the parks cleanleness. They would be held *accountable* if there was any trash on the ground.

If the park is clean then it might be *appealing* to other people that never been there before. Kids will be *deprived* of playtime if it is dirty. So that's why you should help keep the parks clean.

Michael's Essays

ANALYSIS OF PRE-ESSAY

In looking at Michael's pre-essay, it is clear that the essay contains minimal content. Michael seems to almost lack understanding of the purpose of the writing task as evidenced by the opening statement in which the writer asked the readers to clean the park. Although Michael's essay presents a voice, the lack of content and focus contribute to this writing being scored below basic.

Pre-Essay (Below Basic)

Hey all you people, don't you want to clean up the park. I mean come on. There are litter, dog business, and a lot of other messy things. Would you want to step in or slip and fall on litter? It would be so much better if we all worked together and clean up our park. You wouldn't step or slip and fall on litter or go down dirty slides. It would be so much better if we all worked together and cleaned up the park. So if you do not want a dirty park and you want a nice clean park, lets all clean up the park!

ANALYSIS OF POST-ESSAY

The post-essay below contains more content than the pre-essay, although the content remains a bit vague. The Tier Two words used by Michael seem to give him some ideas to write about, but at times he seems to get in trouble by attempting to use too many of the words, which makes the writing seem contrived and unnatural. It is apparent that Michael has some understanding of the words, but needs to elaborate on the ideas in order to further develop the content. The post-essay is an improvement from the pre-essay and Michael moved up one level from below basic to the basic category.

Post-Essay (Basic)

It's very *imperative* to keep our park clean because litter is *hazardous* to the animals. Also, who would want to come to a park with *numerous* pieces of trash. It would look so *deteriorated* and it would feel so *unfortunate* to the people who like the park but can't go in it because it looks *deteriorated*. They would feel so *deprived*. So that's why it's *imperative* to keep the park clean. Now you're *accountable* for keeping the park clean!! We need to *maintain* it. Just go down to the park and pick up that nasty numerous pieces of garbage. If you don't that will hurt the environment.

What Can We Say about These Essays?

The feature that comes up the most in the analyses above is content. In fact, all four of Yonek's (2008) analyses of the essays included remarks about content—what the students wrote about. In the pre-essay analyses, the inadequacy of the content was a theme; in the post-essays that there was more content is acknowledged. In the two post-essays, Yonek commented about the relationship of the target words and what the students wrote about: "It almost seems as if the Tier Two words gave the writer focus and content that she didn't have when writing the pretest essay," "Target words . . . clearly add to the content," and "seem to give him some ideas to write about."

On another note, Yonek pointed out that "at times he seems to get in trouble by attempting to use too many of the words, which makes the writing seem contrived and unnatural." We have seen students do this in other environments and it appears that they find trying to fit as many target words as they can into a composition as kind of a challenge. Although Michael's attempt to jam so many target words into his post-essay makes for awkwardness, notice that Michael has not misused the meanings of the words. We suggest that using the words in ways that reflect a correct understanding of their meanings points to the writer having more than superficial knowledge of the words. What about the inappropriate syntax? Short answer: it is poor. It is our experience, however, that when new words are used with incorrect word form that behavior seems to get straightened out for a first-language speaker without direct instruction.

Another observation that Yonek made was that the students described some negative consequences of an unclean park, but barely mentioned positive consequences. We wondered whether a contributor to the less frequent statements of positive consequences of a clean park might be related to the relative "strength" of some of the words that potentially could be used to describe consequences, with our assessment that the negative words (*hazardous, deteriorate*) were stronger than the positive ones (*appealing, recreation*).

We close this chapter by returning to the issue of the content of students' essays. Words are just labels for concepts, and thus it is not surprising that the analyses of students' essays suggested that the target words stimulated their use of some of the content. Adams (2009) makes an important statement about what words are: "Words are not just words. . . . What makes vocabulary valuable and important is not the words themselves so much as the understandings they afford (p. 180).

SUMMARY

Although intuition suggests that there has to be a relationship between vocabulary and writing, there is a paucity of research about that relationship. This situation is in contrast to a useful amount of research on vocabulary and reading. What little research there is about vocabulary and writing tends toward affirming our intuition about the relationship. But what research there is supports the notion that it is not just any kind of vocabulary instruction that affects writing. Rather, to affect writing the instruction has to be robust.

YOUR TURN

1. You might find it interesting to try to replicate Yonek's (2008) study, but you will probably want to cut it down. One way you can cut it down is by reducing the number of words. For example, you could try another topic, for instance tornadoes. We thought of *humanitarian, catastrophe, devastate, demolish, facilitate*, and *compassionate*. Teach the words using robust instructional strategies. Then give students a writing probe, such as the following:

   • Write a descriptive essay about what an area that has been hit by a tornado looks like. Include discussion of the impact a tornado can have on people's lives, the kind of help they need, and what you would do to help if you could.

2. Identify a topic that would be of interest to your class. Choose about 10 words that might be used in an essay. Teach half of the words through robust instruction and the other half through a traditional approach. Then, provide a writing probe in which the words could be potentially useful. See whether you get a difference in the number of words from the two approaches that are used and the quality of students' use of the words in their writing.

CHAPTER 9

Differentiating Vocabulary Instruction

In this chapter, we describe approaches for differentiating vocabulary instruction. Specifically, we consider how robust vocabulary instruction can be used to address the needs of students who struggle with reading and students who are English learners (ELs).

STUDENTS WHO STRUGGLE WITH READING

In 2004, the Individuals with Disabilities Education Improvement Act (IDEA) was reauthorized, allowing for more timely and multileveled support for students who were having difficulty in school, most often difficulty in reading. One model for such support is response to intervention (RTI), which provides differentiated instructional approaches designated as tiers. Be careful not to confuse the instructional tiers of RTI with the tiers that we have identified for vocabulary words. There is no correspondence between them. To clarify this distinction, we spell out the numbers in our own tiers (e.g., Tier One) and use numerals for the RTI tiers (e.g., Tier 1).

In general terms, Tier 1 RTI instruction makes use of a core program with a curriculum that meets state guidelines, such as a basal reading program. Tier 2 instruction is in addition to the instruction provided by Tier 1 approaches. Based on assessment results, students who are assigned to Tier 2 receive targeted instruction in small groups to address areas such as phonics or fluency. Tier 3 instruction is designed to address the needs of students who are at high risk for academic failure and often involves one-on-one instruction. The instructional support offered at each tier increases in intensity, frequency, and duration.

Most of the RTI approaches for early intervention have focused on phonics and fluency. However, as Coyne, McCoach, and colleagues (2010) pointed out, focusing on beginning reading skills is not going to help students who are at risk for experiencing reading problems due to language and vocabulary. And there is sufficient evidence to indicate that the vast differences in children's vocabulary need to be addressed from the beginning of schooling if those differences are ever going to be mediated (Biemiller & Slonim, 2001; Coyne, Simmons, Kame'enui, & Stoolmiller, 2004).

There are some studies that have examined the impact of multilevel support for vocabulary development. One such study is dissertation research by Isabel's student Michelle Sobolak (2008, 2011) who investigated the impact of variations in the amount of vocabulary instruction on students' learning. Sobolak worked with first graders in a large public suburban school district. The school is in an economically disadvantaged area, with more than 30% of students on free or reduced-price lunch. She used resources from *Steck–Vaughn Elements of Reading: Vocabulary* (Beck & McKeown, 2004) to teach four six-word sets, one set for each of 4 weeks. She implemented three rounds of instruction, which correspond to the three tiers in RTI. In round 1, students participated in the four instructional lessons provided in the *Elements of Reading* program. In round 2, students who did not demonstrate an understanding of word meanings on an end-of-unit assessment were engaged in additional instructional activities with the words. These students were taught the words in 15-minute sessions for 3 more days. In round 3, students who had not demonstrated mastery of the word meanings after round 2 participated in 3 more days of alternative instructional activities. The activities in rounds 2 and 3 were based on the approaches described in the first edition of *Bringing Words to Life* (Beck et al., 2002) and provided opportunities for students to talk about word meanings in different contexts and to draw on their developing understanding of the word meanings to select appropriate uses of the words. The average number of word meanings that students learned increased across the two rounds of additional instruction. In addition, across the 4 weeks of the study, fewer students were identified as requiring round 2 and round 3 instruction because they were learning more words by participating in the initial instructional sequence. The success of the intervention designed by Sobolak demonstrates the power of instruction that provides students with more time and opportunities to develop rich representations of word meanings. Duration and intensity make a difference.

A study by Puhalla (2011) demonstrated the same kind of result with first graders also using instructional approaches described in the first edition of *Bringing Words to Life* (Beck et al., 2002). In the study, students were engaged in a read-aloud intervention focusing on topically related expository and narrative texts such as books focusing on specific animal species such as mammals. The read-aloud curriculum included instruction for Tier Two words (e.g., *survive, peculiar*) and Tier Three vocabulary words (e.g., *herbivore, hibernate*). In addition to that instruction, Puhalla designed what she called "booster sessions" for students identified as being at risk for academic failure. With these students, teachers implemented five 20-minute booster sessions with scripted lesson plans. An important feature of the lesson plans was daily review of word meanings and an entire session on the fifth day devoted to review. Because the booster sessions were conducted with small groups and involved more intense and frequent vocabulary instruction, they can be described as a Tier 2 approach in RTI. Results of vocabulary assessments showed that students in the booster sessions outperformed not only comparable at-risk students who did not participate in the booster sessions but also their average-achieving peers. Again, changes in duration and intensity made a difference.

Coyne, McCoach, and colleagues (2010) investigated the impact of an RTI Tier 2 vocabulary intervention for children in kindergarten. Both the Tier 1 and Tier 2 instruction in the study represented a robust approach. Children identified as at risk were provided whole-class instruction for 30 minutes three times a week. To implement the Tier 2 intervention, Coyne and colleagues doubled the amount of instructional time for half of the vocabulary words. This extra instruction took place in small groups of three or four and included "more explicit instruction with many opportunities for individual responses followed by immediate corrective feedback" (p. 21). Coyne and colleagues found that the children made greater gains for the words that received Tier 2 instruction compared to words that received only the whole-class Tier 1 instruction. Importantly, Coyne and colleagues point out, these at-risk children learned the words given Tier 2 instruction almost as well as their not-at-risk peers who received classroom instruction alone.

The studies by Sobolak (2008, 2011), Puhalla (2011), and Coyne, McCoach, and colleagues (2010) provide examples of RTI interventions for young children. The approaches included a Tier 2 component that provided children with supplemental instruction consisting of additional activities similar to those in the Tier 1 portion of instruction.

Another way to provide more intensive instruction for at-risk students is to bolster initial instruction with modeling and more explicit questioning within activities that require reasoning about words and word relationships.

An important aspect of robust instruction is having students explore relationships among words and between words and the contexts in which they appear. This kind of thinking is a complex mental task, and can be challenging for some students. Yet it is precisely this type of reasoning that will serve students well in reading complex text and encountering unfamiliar words or words used in novel ways.

An example of how support for this type of thinking about words might be implemented is provided in the example below, which is based on the introduction of words as shown in Chapter 7. The example provides increased support that focuses students' attention on specific features of context provided in the RAVE approach. The material in **bold** is what was added to the original example of RAVE in Chapter 7.

RTI Teacher Materials for the Introduction of *expose*

- Preview Context 1:
  - o **Context 1 is about coal mining.**
- Context 1: Some miners work deep underground to dig out coal. Other miners blast off the top of mountains to *expose* layers of coal underneath. They often have to blast away 800 to 1,000 feet of rock before the coal is *exposed* (Goodell, 2006).
- To understand Context 1:
  - o **What are two ways that coal is mined?**
  - o **If needed, support the context even more by offering: One way that coal is mined is by digging deep in the earth. What's the other way that coal is mined?**
- Friendly definition:
  - o If you *expose* something, you let it show or make it known.
- To integrate meaning and Context 1:
  - o **Let's figure out how the meaning of *expose* fits Context 1.**
  - o **We just read the meaning of *expose*. What's the meaning? (response)**
  - o **If needed, have a student read the friendly definition again and go back and reread the part of Context 1 that first uses the word *expose*. Tell students to start with the second sentence—the sentence that begins with "Other" and read aloud with me. "Other miners blast off the top of mountains to expose layers of coal underneath."**
  - o **Now that we've reviewed the meaning of *expose* and checked the context for how *expose* is used, we can combine the two and answer the question "How does the meaning of *expose***

fit Context 1?" by saying something like *"Expose* means to let something show and the context says that miners blast off the top of mountains so the coal will show."
- ○ Actually there is another place that a form of *expose* is used in Context 1. Where is it?
- Preview Context 2:
- ○ **Context 2 is about students being exposed to jazz music.**
- <u>Context 2</u>: Students can be *exposed* to the world of jazz music by attending jazz concerts and by listening to jazz CDs. A new CD, called *Second Set,* exposes students to jazz solos, backgrounds, bass lines, and parts for piano and percussion *(samash.com,* 2010).
- To integrate meaning and Context 2:
- ○ Now let's put the meaning of *expose* and Context 2 together.
- ○ **First, we remind ourselves of the definition of *expose.* What is it? (If needed, go back to the definition and ask the students to read along.) "If you expose something, you let it show or make it known." So what's the first thing to do? (response)**
- ○ **Second, we look at Context 2 to find the first place where *expose* is used. It's in the first sentence. Read the sentence aloud with me. "Students can be *exposed* to the world of jazz music by . . ." What's the second thing we do? (response)**
- ○ **So, to combine the meaning of *expose* and Context 2 we need to mention the meaning of *expose* and how it is used in the context by saying something like "*Exposed* means _____ and Context 2 says that students are being exposed to _____."**
- To integrate meaning across both contexts:
- ○ From the two contexts, what do we know about how the word *expose* can be used?
- ○ ***Expose* can be used to mean showing something, often something that couldn't be seen, like _____, and it can be used to make something known, like _____.**
- Activate vocabulary:
- ○ What kind of music would you like to be exposed to?
- ○ Before children are ready to start school, how can they be exposed to kindergarten?
- ○ How could you expose someone who cheats when playing games?
- ○ How could someone expose what is at the bottom of a muddy pond?

The models in the above example provide the kind of scaffolding and explicit instruction that can support struggling readers in small-group settings recommended for Tier 2 RTI. It is important to note that the examples of the Tier 2 vocabulary instruction in the RTI framework is not *different* instruction but rather *additional* and more *frequent* instruction. Duration and intensity are the key variables. This is in contrast to some recommendations that suggest trying a variety of different approaches or programs.

Compared to the example of standard RAVE in Chapter 7, you can see that in the RTI version the topic of each context is provided before the context is read; "This context is about coal mining," which is not the case in the standard RAVE. The question related to "to understand Context 1" is explicit, in contrast to a more open question in standard RAVE. How "to integrate meaning and Context 1" is modeled and stepped out. Then in Context 2, the one about jazz, the actual steps are provided: "First, we remind ourselves . . ." and "Second, we look at Context 2 to find . . ." Students are asked to say what is done in each step. A response to "to integrate meaning across both contexts" is provided with a little role for the students. In the standard RAVE, the question is more open, that is, "From the two contexts, what do we know about how we can use the word *expose*?"

Of course our goal is that all children be able to respond to open questions, but our experience is that some have a lot of difficulty doing so. We've speculated that some students having difficulty are not really sure of what they are supposed to do. So, we want the procedures to be very clear and practiced, that is, "Now that we've reviewed the meaning of *expose* and checked the context for how *expose* is used, we can combine the two and answer the question." A major motivation for such explicit instruction is that we want teachers to focus students' attention on the content of the friendly definitions and the contexts in direct ways and not present broad cues that are too general or underspecified to focus student thinking in productive ways.

ENGLISH LEARNERS

We use the term *English learner* (EL) to refer to students who speak a language other than English at home and whose English-language proficiency limits their ability to learn grade-level academic material in English. EL students represent the fastest-growing segment of the school-age population, having increased from 6.8% of the total K–12 school population in 1995–1996 to 10.3% just one decade later (Batalova, Fix, & Murray, 2007).

There is evidence that ELs not only know fewer words but also tend to have looser semantic networks between words in their vocabularies

(Verhoeven, 2011) and less developed knowledge about word parts (Carlo et al., 2004; Kieffer & Lesaux, 2012). Consequently, EL students may have more difficulty accessing aspects of word meanings that are relevant to the variety of contexts in which a word might appear. With slower or weaker access to relevant meanings, comprehension may be slowed or prevented.

We've had teachers ask us about a number of issues related to vocabulary instruction and students for whom English is a second language. The two issues that seem most prominent are which words should be the focus of instruction for ELs and what kinds of activities are most effective. We address those two issues in this section.

Considering Which Words to Teach ELs

We begin by underscoring the critical nature of vocabulary knowledge by relaying an experience that Isabel had as a second-language learner—a German language learner (GLL). Isabel writes:

> Many years ago, I went to Germany with my husband, a political scientist, who had gotten a grant to do research at Radio Free Europe in Munich. With my husband's less-than-mediocre German, and the many Germans who spoke at least some English, we managed to get ourselves situated in a small apartment in a residential neighborhood. In the year that I lived in Munich, I went from being a non-German speaker to being a fairly adequate speaker in everyday conversation. I could shop, talk about the weather, ask neighbors about their families, get directions for taking the bus, explain what I was doing in Germany, and the like. Toward the end of my year in Germany, I became friends with two women who lived in the neighborhood, and was invited for coffee (and exquisite pastries) with them several times.
>
> One of my friends, Maria, was a middle school math teacher; the other, Elice, was a photographer. Elice once tried to turn the conversation to current political issues in Europe and the United States, but I was at a loss to engage. At another time, Maria attempted to turn our conversations from small talk to differences in schooling and teaching in Germany and America, but I was not able to understand much of what she said. Moreover, when Elice, who spoke English fluently, translated Maria's questions about teaching in America, I was unable to answer them in German. And there it was, I had hit the lexical bar!
>
> The lexical bar, which we mentioned in Chapter 2, is a concept that characterizes the distinctions between everyday oral language and academic, literate language (Corson, 1985, 1995). Compared to oral language, literate language has a greater variety of words and a greater

density of high-content words, and the words are less concrete and longer. I had become quite familiar with everyday German vocabulary, but not with academic, literate vocabulary. The latter is not common to oral conversation; rather, these are the words that are found in written language.

To provide an example of the distinction between everyday vocabulary and literate vocabulary, I developed the table below showing the kind of German words that I had learned from conversation in contrast to words I would not have known at the time Maria, Elice, and I chatted.

In the first column, I listed a few of the words that I recall learning and using in German. I was able to spark my memory by thinking about situations during my life in Germany, and picturing people and places. For instance:

- I often told folks that "I was *confused* about how to . . ."
- I asked a German–English speaker what the word for *slowly* was as I often wanted to ask folks to speak slowly.
- My memory for learning *other* had to do with seeing people pointing to things behind glass in bakery shops and saying, "*the other*" or "*a different one.*"
- The word *worried* came to my consciousness when a German acquaintance told me that he was worried about being able to go skiing over the weekend because the weather would likely be poor.

I never studied German, my husband and I did not speak it in our home—rather, I learned it from engaging in everyday life. It took me about a year to be moderately adequate in conversational German, which coincides with Cummins's (1994) notion that it takes ELs about a year or two on average to manage everyday English conversation. I was not, however, able to manage academic, literate German as indicated by my inability to converse with Maria and Elice about current events or teaching as I would have with a fellow American teacher.

Everyday words I knew in German	Words in newspapers	Words in academic reading material
confused	*feud*	*proficiency*
slowly	*intensified*	*established*
parking	*administration*	*orientation*

corner	officials	enhances
behind	voluntarily	encounter
different	require	facilitates
other	classified	repertoire
worried	forced	evidence

In the second column of the table, I listed eight words from a 50-word segment of a front-page newspaper article from an American city for which I would not have known an equivalent German word. In the third column, I listed some of the words from the first pages of Chapter 1 from this book for which I would not have known the German equivalent. So, if the newspaper and the book were in German, my lack of academic, literate German vocabulary would limit my access to them.

Much of the problem for ELs lies in the distinction between words in the first column, which are Tier One words, and those in the other two columns, which are Tier Two words. In contrast to the year or two that it takes to learn the kinds of words in the first column and thus be able to manage conversation, Cummins's (1994) work suggests that it takes 5 to 7 years to cross the lexical bar to the meaning system created by academic, literate culture. This makes contact with the findings of Hayes and Ahrens (1988) on the sharp distinctions between the wordstock of informal oral language and that of written language. All students, including ELs, need to cross the lexical bar to achieve any measure of academic success. It is our position that all students need to start crossing early. The question that then arises is What is *early*?

For us, *early* means that when EL students can manage everyday conversation—perhaps to the extent that Isabel could in German—students should receive instruction in Tier Two words. At this point, their native-speaking peers will be unfamiliar with Tier Two words as well. That is, we assume that the answer to questions 3 and 4 below are no. Thus, instruction for EL students can be done along with their native-speaking classmates. To take a deeper look at what we are suggesting, we first ask you to answer the questions on the next page.

---

*We use Spanish speakers as an example of second-language learners, but are fully aware that there are many, many other languages represented in schools. In fact, Kindler (2002) noted that "more than 460 languages were reported to be spoken by limited-English-proficient (LEP) students in the United States" (cited in August & Shanahan, 2006).

1. Is it likely that native English-speaking 5-year-olds know the meanings of these words *in English*?

2. Is it likely that native Spanish*-speaking 5-year-olds know the meanings of these words *in Spanish*?

table

mother

beautiful

sleep

run

---

3. Is it likely that English-speaking 5-year-olds know the meanings of these words *in English*?

4. Is it likely that Spanish-speaking 5-year-olds know the meanings of these words *in Spanish*?

astonished

cherished

devotion

reluctant

triumphant

We assume that your answer to question 1 is yes, thus there is no need to teach English-speaking children the meanings of those words. We also assume that your answer to question 2 is yes, so there is no reason to teach Spanish-speaking children the concepts underlying those words. The instructional issue is that Spanish-speaking children need to learn the English labels for words they know in Spanish. If they understand what the words mean in Spanish, they will understand what the words mean in English when they learn the English labels.

Certainly, native speakers have larger Tier One vocabularies than Isabel had in German, or than ELs who have been here about two years have in English. But if students have enough second-language understanding to "get along on the street," we think it appropriate to start introducing Tier Two words—with one proviso, which is the same for both native- and second-language speakers, that the underlying concept is understood. That is, for example, if children know what *angry* means either in English or Spanish, they can be taught what *livid* means (the word *livid* also exists in Spanish, but it is a very low-frequency word).

It is likely that some instructional time will be needed for Tier One words. But how much time? Keep in mind that Tier One words will continue to be acquired from everyday life, including everyday school life, and that these words are readily learned as they are used frequently in conversation and are highly concrete. In contrast, Tier Two words are more difficult to learn and less likely available from oral conversations. Thus our view is that the majority of direct instructional time should be targeted to Tier Two words. Tier Two words are essential for literacy, and lack of knowledge of such words is at the root of vocabulary and comprehension problems that leave students on the wrong side of the lexical bar, unable to gain facility with higher-status meaning systems of written language.

What Kinds of Instructional Methods Are Needed for ELs?

The key fact here is that there is nothing in the research to suggest that what works with first-language learners does not work with second-language learners. The findings of the National Reading Panel (2000) indicate that research-based strategies used with first-language learners are effective with second-language learners. Furthermore, the most recent intervention studies with ELs have demonstrated that instruction that provides multiple encounters with target words as well as analysis and use of the words is effective at promoting word knowledge (August, Branum-Martin, Cardenas-Hagan, & Francis, 2009; Carlo et al., 2004; Lesaux, Kieffer, Faller, & Kelley, 2010; Proctor et al., 2011; Snow, Lawrence, & White, 2009; Vaughn et al., 2009). There is also evidence that promoting active processing of words has effectively supported depth of word knowledge for EL students (Carlo et al., 2004; Lesaux et al., 2010; Proctor et al., 2011). Carlo and colleagues (2004) noted that the instructional activities for their study of EL vocabulary growth were based on the vocabulary process developed by Beck and colleagues.

What makes the activities that characterize robust instruction effective for any student, whether EL or native-English speaking, is that students meet the words in multiple contexts and have ample opportunities to use and think about the words. The need for students, especially ELs, to develop their vocabulary through using the words in extended talk is emphasized by many language scholars. For example, Corson (1995) asserts that in classrooms for first-language or EL students, word learning takes place when students engage in purposeful talk with others that embeds the target words and displays their uses. Kowal and Swain's (1994) work with second-language students shows the need for conversation and discussion to provide the necessary elaboration to master rules of use of words across contexts. Dutro and Moran (2003) lay out guiding principles for English-language instruction that include creating meaningful contexts for functional use of language and providing opportunities for practice and application.

The kinds of language interactions that characterize robust instructional activities provide the elaborated context availability that ELs need. The focused and extended language input that is provided and output that is prompted by robust instruction benefit the development of language competence for first- and second-language learners.

Special Considerations for ELs

While the methods that make for effective vocabulary instruction are the same for native- and second-language learners, there are some ways to augment instruction to address the unique needs of ELs. Including other strategies is done toward ameliorating the gap between ELs and native speakers. Studies show that both ELs and their native English-speaking peers can increase their vocabulary knowledge at comparable rates. However, interventions are generally not enough to close the gap that usually exists between ELs, who have more limited word knowledge at the outset, and native speakers, whose scores tend to be higher initially. Yet in the face of no intervention, disparities between these groups in both vocabulary knowledge and reading achievement continue to increase over time (Kiefer, 2008; Nakamoto, Lindsey, & Manis, 2007).

Intervention studies that have effectively increased vocabulary knowledge of ELs have incorporated a wide variety of materials and practices to address the specific needs of ELs. Such practices have been of two types. One is strategies that make the language of instruction more supportive, such as providing text previews, often in students' first language (L1) before reading a text in English (Carlo et al., 2004), high-interest texts for EL students (Carlo et al., 2004), and visuals or multimedia texts to support access to text content (August et al., 2009; Proctor et al., 2011; Vaughn et al., 2009). Another type of support is directed at the target words themselves, such as providing translations of the words being taught or drawing attention to cognates—words in two languages that are closely related in meaning and that look and sound alike (Carlo et al., 2004; Proctor et al., 2011). We offer further elaboration of each of these directions below.

Supporting the Language of Instruction

Below we provide a version of the *expose* lesson that incorporates features of instruction that seem to facilitate EL students' learning. We started with the RTI lesson, as we think that EL students also need to be very fluent with procedures, such as what to do when asked to integrate a word's meaning with its use in context. Then we added material in support of EL students. We keep the **bold** to indicate material that was in the RTI lesson and use ***bold italics*** for material that is used only in the EL lesson.

A key question that always arises about instruction for EL students is how much first language and how much second language should be included. Although we concur that translating important words from L2 to L1 is useful (Carlo et al., 2004; Proctor et al., 2011), here we explain in English important words in the text that may be unfamiliar.

EL TEACHER MATERIALS FOR THE INTRODUCTION OF *EXPOSE*

- Preview Context 1:
  - **Context 1 is about *two ways of* coal mining.**
- Teacher reads Context 1:

- Context 1: Some miners work deep underground to dig out coal. Other miners blast off—***blast off* means use dynamite to explode**—the top of mountains to *expose* layers of coal underneath—***underneath* is something under another thing. For example, dirt is underneath grass. (Reread the second sentence.**) Other miners blast off the top of mountains to *expose* layers of coal underneath. They often have to blast away 800 to 1,000 feet of rock before the coal is *exposed* (Goodell, 2006).
- To understand Context 1:
  - **What are the two ways that coal is mined?**
  - **If needed, support the context even more by offering: One way that coal is mined is by digging deep into the earth. What's the other way?**
  - *Why do miners blast off the top of mountains? Try to use the word* ***expose*** *when you answer.*
- Friendly definition:
  - If you *expose* something, you let it show or make it known.
- To integrate meaning and Context 1:
  - **Let's figure out how the meaning of *expose* fits Context 1.**
  - **We just read the meaning of *expose*. What does *expose* mean? (response)**
  - **If needed: direct students back and read the friendly definition again. Ask students to read aloud with you.**
  - **Let's read the part of Context 1 that uses the word *expose*. Start with the second sentence that begins with "Other" and read along with me. "Other miners blast off the top of mountains to expose layers of coal under underneath."**
  - **Now that we've reviewed the meaning of *expose* and checked the context, we can combine the two and answer the question "How does the meaning of *expose* fit Context 1?" by saying something like "The meaning of *expose* is to let it show and the context says that miners blast off the top of mountains so the coal will show."**
- Preview Context 2:
  - *People can be exposed to lots of things. They can be exposed to an illness—like the flu. They can be exposed to a new language. Context 2 is about students being exposed to jazz music. Jazz music started in the black neighborhoods in the southern parts of the United States. Jazz blends black music and popular American music as well as African and European music.*
- Teacher reads Context 2:
- Context 2: Students can be exposed to the world of jazz music by attending jazz concerts and by listening to jazz CDs. A new CD,

called *Second Set*, exposes students to jazz solos—*a <u>solo</u> means that only one musician, maybe a guitar player, a singer, or a drummer is performing by him- or herself. (Reread this sentence from the beginning of the sentence.)* A new CD, called *Second Set*, exposes students to jazz solos, backgrounds, bass lines, and parts for piano and percussion—*examples of percussion instruments are drums, symbols, and gongs*(samash.com, 2010).

- *Teacher rereads Context 2 without explanatory comments.*
- <u>*Context 2*</u>: *Students can be exposed to the world of jazz music by attending jazz concerts and by listening to jazz CDs. A new CD, called Second Set, exposes students to jazz solos, backgrounds, bass lines, and parts for piano and percussion.*
- To integrate meaning and Context 2:
  - **Now let's put the meaning of** *expose* **and Context 2 together.**
  - **First, we remind ourselves of the meaning of** *expose*. **What is it? (If needed, go back and ask the students to read along with you. "If you** *expose* **something, you let it show or make it be known.")**
  - **Second, we look at Context 2 and find the first place where** *expose* **is used. It's in the first sentence. Read the sentence aloud with me. "Students can be** *exposed* **to the world of jazz music by . . ."**
  - **So, we can put the meaning of** *expose* **and Context 2 together by saying something like "***Exposed* **means showing something or making something known and Context 2 talks about making jazz music known to students."**
  - *(Actually there are two places in Context 2 where <u>exposed</u> appears. See if you can find them.)*
- To integrate meaning across both contexts:
  - From the two contexts, what do we know about how the word *expose* can be used?
  - *Expose* can be used to mean showing something, often something that couldn't be seen, like _____, and it can be used to make something known, like _____.
- Activate vocabulary:
  - What kind of music would you like to be exposed to?
  - Before children are ready to start school, how can they be exposed to kindergarten?
  - *How could you expose what is in a piñata?*
  - How could you expose someone who cheats when playing games?
  - *What does it feel like to be exposed to a new language?*

The focused support offered in the above example demonstrates the kind of scaffolding that teachers can provide for ELs. That scaffolding includes providing somewhat more extended background information than for L1 students, presenting cues to direct students' attention to the most important and helpful information in contexts and parenthetically explaining the meanings, in English, of words in text that are important to comprehension.

Incorporating Cognates

When ELs speak Spanish or another Latinate language, cognates are called into play. Cognates are words in two languages that are closely related in meaning and that overlap orthographically and phonologically, such as the English word *adapt* and its Spanish cognate *adaptar*. Some EL students are able to transfer cognate knowledge from their first language to English to infer the meaning of unknown words. But this ability seems to affect comprehension only if students are both adept at recognizing cognate relationships and know the meaning of the word in Spanish. Explicit instruction about cognates can help students become adept at recognizing cognate relationships, which in turn may bolster vocabulary learning and comprehension in English—for those students whose L1 shares cognate relationships with English.

Instructional interventions that use cognates most often simply guide students to recognize how the cognate pair is nearly identical in the target and source languages, providing in essence, a near translation for the words, such as *dictionary* and *diccionario*, and *university* and *universidad*. Use of these "direct cognates" makes sense as a way to support Spanish-speaking students in learning English, as many words students encounter in academic texts do have direct cognates. However, this direct approach is limited to words that have direct cognates and whose L1 word is known by students. A study by Lubliner and Hiebert (2011) illustrates such limitations. They examined words on the AWL and found that 426 of the 570 headwords of the AWL—or 75% of the corpus—shared cognates with Spanish. However, they found that for 62% of the cognate pairs on the AWL, the Spanish words were not high frequency and thus not likely to be accessible enough to support learning of the English word.

Additionally, there is a lack of research on EL students whose L1 is other than Spanish. Although Spanish speakers make up the majority of EL students in the United States, 25% of EL students are speakers of other languages. Insufficient consideration has been given to helping these students with vocabulary learning.

Broadening the Cognate Approach

Along with our colleague Amy Crosson, we have considered whether there may be a way to bolster vocabulary learning for ELs that takes advantage of cross-language relationships but does not rely on direct cognates. Although we have not had the opportunity to try it out, such an approach would teach students about broader morphological relationships among words and how to analyze the meaning constituents of words. The goal would be to help students recognize that words of the same families are related in meaning, and perhaps help them to infer the meaning of an unknown word if its parts are familiar.

The approach would focus on *lexical morphemes*—word roots, such as *min*, which is from a Latin word meaning *small*, and that occurs in *diminish, minute*, and *minimum*. This focus is a departure from most instruction in words parts, which is mostly limited to derivational affixes, such as the relationship between *research* and *research*. Yet the most important constituents of language that carry meaning are not the derivational affixes but the lexical morphemes—the roots. The study of roots could promote students' semantic networks between words related in meaning, and strengthen students' knowledge for each word that shares the root (Snow & Kim, 2007).

Exploiting roots would also allow broader effects than focusing on cognates, because, while many cognates are direct—that is, the Spanish and English words are nearly identical in meaning and appearance—the relationship between the English and Spanish words is much more extensive than that. By definition, words have a cognate relationship because they share a root. In the case of English and Spanish, this is nearly always a Latin root. Typically, this root is shared in not just the cognate pair but also in several other high-frequency words in Spanish, as well as several other academic words in English.

For example, the academic word *innovative* has a Spanish cognate: *inovador*. However, ELs who have not developed advanced literacy in Spanish are not likely to be familiar with this Spanish cognate. Therefore, learning that *innovative* has a cognate in Spanish may not support access to the meaning of the target word. However, the Latin root shared by the cognate pair, *nov*, appears in very high-frequency Spanish words such as *nuevo* and *nueva*. (Granted, the spelling of the root changes as the word moves across languages, which is an aspect that would be attended to in instruction.) The root *nov* is also shared by several other academic words in English, such as *novice, novelty*, and *renovate*. Accessing the related meaning in English and Spanish via the Latin root holds potential for learning several academic words in English. Taking advantage of these common roots would greatly increase the portion of the wordstock that can be supported for students' learning.

The way we see it playing out might include introducing students to concepts about how language developed, specifically that English incorporates words from many other languages. Indeed, it has been said that "if you speak English, you know a little of more than a hundred languages" (Garg, 2011). A specific topic would be the relationship of English to the early language, Latin, and how that relationship ties us to other languages including Spanish, Italian, and French. Instruction around target words would then include introducing the Latin roots of the words along with words in students' L1 that had the same root—thinking here mostly of speakers of Latinate languages. The instruction might focus on a chart that is filled in as lessons move along, as in the following example.

RAVE word	Spanish friend	Latin root and its meaning
convene		
innovative		
utility		
manipulate		
foundation		
incorporate		
diminish		
benefit		

Consider the word *convene*: The friendly definition would be provided as "When people *convene*, they meet together for a purpose." Then the following ideas would be introduced:

- *Convene* has a "Spanish friend": *venir* (We are using the term *Spanish friend* to indicate words that share a Latin root with an English word.)
- The meaning of *venir* is established (to come) and the word written in the "Spanish friend" column on the chart.
- The shared Latin root, *ven*, and its meaning (to come) are introduced and placed on the chart.
- Attention is drawn to *ven* in *venir* and *convene*, and to the relationship in meaning such as "So, *venir* means 'to come' in Spanish, and *convene* means 'to come together for a specific purpose' in English."

After the language relationships are established over the course of several days' lessons, the completed chart would look something like this:

RAVE word	Spanish friend	Latin root and its meaning
convene	*venir*	*ven*—to come
innovative	*nuevo*	*nov*—new
utility	*útil*	*util*—useful
manipulate	*mano*	*man*—hand
foundation	*fondo*	*fundus*—bottom
incorporate	*cuerpo*	*corp*—body
diminish	*menos*	*min*—less/small
benefit	*bueno*	*bene*—good

In using an approach such as that demonstrated above, it would be important to integrate information about language relationships into introducing the words in contexts and other interactive activities, as research about language relationships indicates that its integration within language arts instruction is key to its effects on students' learning (Bowers, Kirby, & Deacon, 2010). The language relationships would also be incorporated into follow-up activities, such as imagining a town where there is not enough room on license plates for full words, so people use Latin roots to personalize their plates.

We think that there might be additional advantages to focusing on broader morphological relationships in that it may offer benefits for EL students beyond Spanish speakers in comparison to a direct cognate translation approach. Learning how Latin roots relate to the meanings of target words may help students remember the meanings, and learning how these roots relate to other words can give students' access to additional words that share the root.

SUMMARY

In this chapter we have considered how to differentiate vocabulary instruction to address the special needs of students who struggle with verbal learning and students for whom English is a second language. In both cases, the most effective instruction for enhancing vocabulary knowledge and affecting comprehension follows the principles of robust instruction, particularly multiple encounters in varied contexts and opportunities to think about, discuss, and apply the words. But students who struggle because of ability or language status may need supplements to instruction in order to achieve near rates of their classroom peers. Such supplements have taken an RTI approach, offering increases in intensity or duration of instruction for struggling readers. For ELs, the most common supplemental instruction involves translation of terms, or for speakers of Latinate language, exploring cognate relationships. We suggested that broader morphological relationships, based on Latin roots of English words, might increase the reach and effectiveness of instruction for ELs.

YOUR TURN

1. Select a set of Tier Two words from a text that your students are reading. Prepare a set of Tier 1 RTI activities to engage students in learning the meanings of the words. Then prepare another set of activities suitable for a small group of students in a Tier 2 RTI setting. Use the Menu of Instructional Activities in the Appendix.

2. Select a set of Tier Two words and explore their Latin roots and find words with those same roots in English and another Latinate language. Good resources for this include the Online Etymology Dictionary at *www.etymonline.com* and *cognates.org*.

CHAPTER 10

Energizing the Verbal Environment

The idea of an energized verbal environment is to have words in play nearly all of the time; perhaps we can think of it as a classroom where words are constantly being noticed, investigated, celebrated, and savored (Kucan, 2012). This means both a frequent use of words that have been taught and taking any and all opportunities to add words to students' surroundings. Even if a teacher can't keep track of all of them, it is valuable to seed the environment generously with the use of interesting and precise words!

The idea of seeding the environment with words may seem in contrast to what we have stressed in earlier chapters: the need for multiple encounters with words for them to truly become known. But here we are talking about an *additional* goal of vocabulary instruction—that of having students become generally alert to words and word use, to become interested in words, and to develop word awareness. We are referring to focusing on words beyond those that are being explicitly taught. It is true that not all of the words that teachers direct attention to will be learned. But, then again, if students do not have the opportunity to encounter new words, there is no possibility of learning them. Exposure will provide students with a chance to pick up and use some words, or an opportunity to recognize other words that they will eventually meet in subsequent experiences.

USING MATURE LANGUAGE

An enormously important orientation is that the classroom verbal environment be one that makes mature language a visible part of everyday practice. Teachers, through their own choice of words, should strive to have students become accustomed to hearing words they do not know, words that are beyond their current knowledge. This helps students stretch their expectations about language. It is important for students to have a glimpse of the language that is still there for them to learn and to come to believe that it is within their reach. Having unfamiliar words in the environment also encourages students to ask what words mean, which is an excellent habit to encourage. Not every use of a new word has to be in a clear, pedagogical context. Sophisticated words should be a natural part of the classroom conversation, as in the following examples:

- Use *industrious* or *diligent* to describe a student who works hard.
- Write *engaging* or *intriguing* to describe well-crafted sentences in a student essay.
- Praise a student response by referring to it as *precise* and *accurate*.
- Comment that a landscape is *bleak* or *desolate*.

An important aspect of developing the verbal environment is that teachers themselves ought to become very sensitive to words. Teachers should strive to bring forth their own curiosity about words, taking time to share with students their "favorite" words. For example, one teacher told her students that she was simply fascinated by etymologies. Her students were intrigued enough to find out what she was talking about. To develop resources for enhancing the verbal environment teachers need to be alert to words and their uses in and out of school. For example, are there words that are used by visiting speakers at school assemblies that can be brought into the classroom?

- *Secure, safeguard* from a police officer
- *Preservation, refuge, regenerate* from an environmentalist
- *Prominent, distinctive, illustrious* from the introduction of local celebrities

What words can be used to describe the school or the classroom?

- *Spacious* hallways
- *Inadequate* locker space
- *Vivid* colors for the newly painted library walls

What words can be used to characterize people and places in the school?

- A *stern* assistant principal
- A music teacher with a *melodious* voice
- A gym teacher who expects *vigorous* exercise
- A *boisterous* lunchroom
- An *astonishing* talent show

Current events, both in the community and across the region and country, are other sources of interesting words. Teachers can bring urbane and sophisticated words into discussions of such events or point out word use by reporters and columnists. Storms that cause *havoc*, peace efforts that overcome seemingly *insurmountable* obstacles, court decisions based on *precedents, suspenseful* moments in a movie—all are grist for a lively verbal environment.

Word Resources

Part of a rich verbal environment are resources that students can use to discover and follow up on interesting words. Various dictionaries provide such a resource. Because dictionaries differ in their styles of defining terms, however, being able to compare across styles can be an eye-opening experience. First, checking more than one dictionary can make for a better start in zeroing in on a word's meaning. Second, seeing the variation in dictionaries can help students understand the openness and flexibility of language—particularly that there is nothing absolute about a dictionary definition.

Of special interest here are "learners' dictionaries." These resources were developed specifically for students learning English as a second language, but they are very well suited to any student of the language. They present definitions in much more accessible language than traditional dictionaries, even dictionaries created for students. A notable one is the *Collins COBUILD English Language Dictionary* (Sinclair, 1987). This dictionary provides discursive explanations rather than traditional definitions. For example, the meaning of *sparse* is presented as follows: "Something that is sparse is small in number or amount and spread out over an area."

Unabridged dictionaries are excellent resources in classrooms for older students. It is often a memorable learning experience to look up a word such as *call* and read all of its rich and varied meanings, which number more than 60!

A thesaurus should also be available for students to consult. Encourage students to use one, but also frame discussions around what they find.

Steer students away from the practice of merely substituting a word with any word they find listed with it in a thesaurus. Explore with students the similarities and differences—both great and subtle—between words that the thesaurus lists as being related. For example, consider the distinctions between the words in these pairs: *grateful* and *obliged, oblivious* and *forgetful,* and *galvanize* and *provoke.*

Other resources that focus on words such as the games Scrabble and Password or crossword puzzles can be made available for rainy day recesses or in centers for independent learning or exploration time. Posters in the computer area of the classroom can alert students to websites such as those listed below, which provide fascinating word information:

- *http://dictionary.reference.com/wordoftheday*
- *http://dictionary.factmonster.com*

If resources related to words are available and if students are given opportunities to use them, then chances are that words will become more of a focus of interest, which is exactly the situation that we hope to create.

Poetry

Reference books are not the only kinds of books to be found in an energized verbal environment. There are numerous wonderful books for students of all ages that celebrate language in fascinating, enthralling, and captivating ways.

Poems are superb sources of interesting and precise words and word combinations. The poem "Fireflies" from the collection *Joyful Noise: Poems for Two Voices* by Paul Fleischman (1988), for example, speaks of "insect calligraphers" whose vanishing messages are "fleeting graffiti." Such mellifluous phrases demonstrate how language can surprise and delight.

The Pig in the Spigot is a book of poems by former poet laureate Richard Wilbur (2000). Wilbur's clever approach is to take a word like *spigot* and draw attention to a word "inside that word," like *pig,* and then present a poem. For example, here's the poem about the pig and the spigot. Notice the sophisticated language used to describe the situation.

When there's a pig inside your spigot, you
Must not cry out, "There's nothing I can do!"
Be sensible, and take the obvious course,
Which is to turn the spigot on full force.
Sufficient water pressure will, I think,
Oblige the pig to flow into the sink.

Poems such as this are ideally suited for performances. Other poems invite students to chime in on memorable refrains, do finger plays, jump rope, bounce balls in rhythmic ways, and sing the lyrics to fiddle tunes and folk songs. Some splendid examples of such poems can be found in the following books:

- *Granny Will Your Dog Bite and Other Mountain Rhymes* by Gerald Milnes (1990)
- *A Rocket in My Pocket: The Rhymes and Chants of Young Americans* compiled by Carl Withers (1948)
- *The Rooster Crows: A Book of American Rhymes and Jingles* by Maud and Miska Petersham (1945)
- *Miss Mary Mack and Other Children's Street Rhymes* by Joanna Cole and Stephanie Calmenson (1990)
- *Play Rhymes* (1987), *Party Rhymes* (1988), *Hand Rhymes* (1993), and *Finger Rhymes* (1996) by Marc Brown

The Shapes of Words

Concrete poems are a delightful way for students to think about the images that words evoke. Simple examples such as those below can be created using Word Art:

More elaborate examples can be found in books such as:

- *A Poke in the I: A Collection of Concrete Poems* selected by Paul Janeczko and illustrated by Chris Raschka (2001)
- *Doodle Dandies: Poems That Take Shape* by J. Patrick Lewis with images by Lisa Desimini (1998)
- *Flicker Flash* by Joan Bransfield Graham, and illustrated by Nancy Davis (1999)

Books about What Words Do

There are some special sets of books that describe words in terms of their part of speech. One set is intriguingly written and extravagantly illustrated by Ruth Heller (e.g., 1987, 1998) and includes eight books that introduce nouns, collective nouns, pronouns, adjectives, verbs, adverbs, prepositions, and interjections and conjunctions. In the book about collective nouns (1987), Heller tells her readers about a *gam* of whales, a *muster* of peacocks, a *kindle* of kittens, and a *parcel* of penguins, among others. In her book about adjectives (1989), she describes how writers can transform nouns and verbs to form adjectives like *famous, remarkable, irresistible,* and *flawless.* Heller's books also provide unforgettable examples of words that might otherwise be considered rather humdrum such as possessive pronouns and comparative adverbs!

A set of books by Brian P. Cleary (e.g., 1999, 2002) also draws attention to words by focusing on their function or use. Cleary's humorous titles, such as *To Root, to Toot, to Parachute: What Is a Verb?* (2001), as well as his child-centered examples and the lighthearted illustrations by Brian Gable and Jenya Prosmitksy, allow student readers to explore many facets of words such as auxiliary verbs and gerunds without the technical language.

Collecting Words

Stories and poems can be a rich source for collecting words. For example, while reading *Catherine, Called Birdy*, historical fiction set in the Middle Ages by Karen Cushman (1994), students can suggest words to put on a bulletin board or poster with pictures or explanations. From the first chapter, students might suggest *abbey, monk, vespers, crusades, solar, privy, shire, minstrel,* and *knight.* After the words have been posted, they can be sorted into categories, such as church words, rooms and places, and people. The display can be referred to as the novel is read, and more words can be added.

But What Do You *Do* with the Words?

Once words have been identified and discussed, what else is there to do? How do you treat words after they have entered the environment? The choices include how explicitly to work with the meaning and whether to keep track of words after they are introduced. Since the focus here is about creating a verbal environment with an abundant variety of words, it is not necessary to explicitly introduce the meaning of every word that you "seed" into that environment. The answer here is to focus on just a few words at a time that are kind of "kept around." A bulletin board display, word wall, or simply a word list on the board is sufficient. These selected words can then be included in other vocabulary activities or Word Wizard-type challenges. And the teacher can look for multiple opportunities to sprinkle them in.

The words that are to become part of the classroom scene for a while can be selected spontaneously. Whether words will stay in the environment or only "visit" temporarily is not something that needs to be planned ahead of time. For example, the teacher may use a word that comes to mind as fitting. For instance, the students may be talking about how lucky a character was that he discovered a way out of a jam. The discovery came as a coincidental event, so the teacher might suggest that the situation was *fortuitous*. Then, suppose later in the day a student bails another out of a jam by lending the student an extra pencil. The teacher could comment that it was quite fortuitous that a student happened to have an extra pencil that day. The two incidents with *fortuitous* might be a trigger to mark that word as one that is going to be returned to in the classroom.

What about developing the meanings of words that the teacher spontaneously uses? It is difficult to come up with a good, clear, appropriate definition. To develop an explanation of a word's meaning, start with a use of the word and then form the explanation around the context in which the word is used. It can help to compare situations in which you would and would not use it, and give further examples. For instance, a definition for the word *receptive* is probably not on the tip of a typical language user's tongue. However, getting across its meaning can be done fairly easily by forming an explanation around a context in which it occurs, such as the following one: "Henry was receptive to the idea of staying with his grandmother." That means that he was open to thinking about staying with his grandmother; he thought it would probably be okay. If you're receptive to something, it means you'll listen to the idea and think about it. I might be receptive to canceling homework for today if everyone gets their work done!

Another way to establish a new word's meaning is to rely on students to *eventually* figure it out. After some new word has been used, put the word on the board and ask if students know it. If not, encourage them to work toward developing a definition, based on what they can figure out about the word from the context in which it was used. Leave the word, any associations students have or clues to its meaning, and the context on the board and see what develops. If students find the word in other contexts, add those, and add to what they know about the word. Or some student might look up the word in the dictionary and the definition can be discussed.

In short, the answer to what to do with words as they enter the verbal environment is to monitor student reactions toward deciding how many words are too many, which words should be kept in play, and which should have meanings explicitly introduced.

EXPLORING WITHIN AND ACROSS WORDS

The teacher can be alert to applying words that have already been introduced, say, for an upcoming story. For example, if *irritate* had been introduced, when a noise disturbs the class, comment on the *irritation*.

Bringing attention to familiar words can also enrich the environment. There are many words that are in students' environment and that they have some passing familiarity with but may not really know much about. This is common, especially if the word is encountered only in stereotypical contexts. Students may understand that context but not really know the word. For example, what is the students' understanding of the word *donate*? Imagine exploring it as follows:

MR. W: We're being asked to donate food to the Food Bank. What does that mean, *donate*?

JANNA: We give it to them.

MR. W: So, *donate* means the same as *give*?

ROB: Give it to hungry people.

MR. W: Can we ever talk about donating something other than food?

CARLO: People donate blood.

SERENA: Or toys at Christmas.

MR. W: So, how can you describe *donate*?

MARVIN: Give things away because someone else needs them.

The benefit of focusing on familiar words has been suggested by research into the depth of word knowledge. Studies have demonstrated that people with more extensive vocabularies not only know more words but also know more about the words that they know (Curtis & Glaser, 1983), and that people with high and lower vocabularies differ as to their depth of knowledge about even fairly common words (Van Daalen-Kapteijns & Elshout-Mohr, 1981).

What is gained from working with familiar words involves relationships among words, a topic we have visited before. Specifically, word knowledge exists not as a list of discrete items but as networks of words clustered into categories. For example, exploring that people donate different kinds of things, but in each case to fulfill a need, makes way for a new word—*recipient*—that students might never have thought about before. So, if that word is introduced, they have not only learned a new vocabulary item but have also developed a broader perspective on *donate*.

Along a similar line, it is also valuable to ask students to consider different uses for words that have likely been learned in particular contexts. For example, upper elementary school students may understand what an *eclipse* is (or may have even experienced one) when that word is encountered in a science text, or perhaps in news coverage of a current eclipse somewhere. But it would be useful to prompt students to think beyond the scientific event. For example: "You know that an eclipse happens when something like the moon comes between us and the sun, blocking the sun's light. So what do you think it would mean if, when we were watching a movie, I said, 'You're eclipsing my view of the screen'?" If students readily understand that usage, then their understanding can be moved a bit further. For example, "What would it mean to say that the performance of the chorus eclipsed that of the band?" It may take some interaction to help students realize that the latter example is no longer a physical "getting-in-the-way" meaning of *eclipse* but a metaphorical meaning of something overshadowing something else in importance or quality.

Another entry point for adding words to the environment is morphological relationships. For example, challenge students to compare *Tyrannosaurus* and *tyrant*, *pedestrian* and *pedal*, and *duplicate* and *duplicity*. It can also be valuable to discuss when relationships seem to exist but do not, as in the case of *gargle* and *garden*. This can help students gain insight into language, such as the fact that the words we use come from many different sources including different languages, or sometimes simply imitate the sound of things, such as the word *gargle*. Including such ideas in discussions of words lets students see language as an open book rather than as mysterious and impenetrable with authority over them. Thus, explorations of words and word relationships can increase their motivation to find out about language, and use it confidently and playfully.

SUMMARY

This chapter has emphasized ways to create a lively verbal environment in classrooms. The teacher who is alert to opportunities for using sophisticated, interesting, and precise language is probably the most important element in such an environment. Teachers who revel in language are those who use words well and are eager to discover new words and word meanings. They play with words, rejoice in word lore, and model a genuine fascination for the feelings and images that words can evoke and create. In the classrooms of such teachers, there are books and bulletin boards, as well as conversations and performances that demonstrate a lively attention to words.

YOUR TURN

We invite you to use what you have learned in this chapter by selecting an activity from those listed below that interests you:

1. Select a poem with phrases that are particularly interesting or noteworthy and decide how you might share it with your students, or have them perform it.

2. Brainstorm a list of words that you might use to enhance the conversation around typical classroom routines and events.

3. Find a group of words that share the same morpheme, or word root, and create a poster for several words that include the root. For example, *tele*, meaning "far or distant," is the Greek word root for *telephone, television, telepathy,* and *telegraph.* Encourage students to create similar posters for other word roots.

APPENDIX

Menu of Instructional Activities

This menu provides examples of instructional activities that you can use to engage students in interacting with the vocabulary words they are learning. We have included seven categories of activities, with from two to five variations within some categories. They are:

- Example/non-example, with five variations
- Word associations, with three variations
- Generating situations, contexts, and examples, with five variations
- Word relationships, with five variations
- Writing, with three variations
- Returning to the story context
- Puzzles, with two variations

In some cases, all the words in a set of vocabulary words can be used within one variation of an activity. In other cases, only some of those words are suited for a particular variation. When that happens, to provide opportunities to work with all the words in a set each day, you may need to include several variations within a category of activities, or you may need to include another category of activity.

In virtually all the activities that follow, each item (question or statement) is really "bait" for students to use language to explain their responses. Most students can answer questions like "Which would make you feel *drowsy*: watching your favorite TV program or eating a big Thanksgiving dinner?" It's what needs to come after—an explanation for their choices—that is the most useful for vocabulary, and indeed, language development. The forced-choice activities and questions are usually designed such that there is an expected response. For example, if we ask "When might you be *reluctant*—going into a dentist's office or going into a toy store?" we expect that students will say "dentist's office." But the most important part is the requirement to explain why: "Because having your teeth worked on is no fun, so you might not want to go in!" However, if a student chooses the less likely response and can justify it—such as choosing toy store "Because I'm trying to save my money and I'm afraid I'd want to buy something"—then, by all means, accept that response. The important point to stress here is *if they can justify it*. It is not acceptable to choose toy store because, for example, "I like toy stores." The justification must relate to the target word.

For the most part, we see the activities as teacher led—that is, we do not advocate regularly converting the activities into workbook pages. Occasionally that can be appropriate if the teacher goes over the work with the class. Also, sometimes activities can be used by assigning students to groups: the students in each group can do the same thing and then come together as a whole class and discuss the similarities and differences between different groups' responses. Or different activities can be assigned to separate groups and then shared with the whole class. Although some activities (e.g., analogies) may be somewhat beyond the capacities of the youngest students, most activities are appropriate for all levels, with the difference being in the words and contexts that are used.

We have arranged the categories of activities in this menu generally from simple to more complex. By that we mean that the categories of activities begin with those that provide the most guidance for student responses and expect the most simple responses from them. From there, the thinking and responding expected becomes more complex—as students are asked to develop contexts, consider relationships between words, respond in writing, and so on.

EXAMPLE/NON-EXAMPLE

Asking students to indicate which statements, descriptions, comments, or the like are instances of a given vocabulary word and which ones are not is a prototypical early interactive activity.

Variation 1

Below is a version we use very often, which presents, one by one, descriptions of situations and asks students to respond to each as to whether or not it illustrates the target word. Students should always be asked "Why?" they responded as they did.

- If I say something that sounds *precarious*, say "Precarious." If not, don't say anything. Students should be asked why they responded as they did.
  - Walking over a rickety bridge that spans a deep canyon.
  - Exploring a new tall school building.
  - Standing on a tall ladder on one foot.

Notice that in this format students are asked to say the target word, which is helpful in getting them to build a strong phonological representation of the words they are learning. That's important for helping to plant the word in students' memories.

Variation 2

A simple variation on the basic example/non-example presented above is to add a little creativity to how students indicate their response. Ask "Why?"

- If any of the things I say are examples of places where it might be *frigid*, say "Brrrr." If not, don't say anything:
    o Antarctica
    o Florida
    o Canada in January
    o Mexico
- If any of the things I say are things that might be *sleek*, say "Smooth, man." If not, don't say anything:
    o A porcupine
    o A duck
    o A leaf
    o A car

Variation 3

Another variation on the example/non-example activity that we use quite often asks students to choose which of two alternatives illustrates the target word. This variation is usually presented as *Which would . . .?* or *Which is . . .?* Ask "Why?"

- Which would be easier to *notice*:
    o A house all alone on a hill or a house crowded in with lots of other buildings
    o A barking dog or a dog sleeping on a porch
    o An ant crawling along the floor or a snake slithering along the floor
- Which would *plod*:
    o Frankenstein in a castle or a ghost in a castle
    o A huge dinosaur or a mountain lion
    o A heavy man or a skinny man
    o A girl who was really tired or a girl in a race
- Which would make a house *festive*: colorful banners hanging outside or turning the lights off?
- Which could make you scream *frantically*: a kitten purring or a snake hissing?
- Which is more *absurd*: a dog wearing glasses or a dog snoring?
- Which is more *versatile*: a heavy fur coat or a coat with a zip-in lining? Why?

Variation 4

Another variation within the example/non-example activity asks students to choose which of two target words represents a situation that is described. This is somewhat more challenging as it asks students to bring to mind meanings of two target words and decide which fits. Several examples follow:

- Would you want the people who cook the school lunch to be *versatile* or *frugal*? Why?
- If you didn't buy a pair of shoes until you wore out the ones you had, would that be *frugal* or *industrious*? Why?
- If you just won the lottery, would you be *jubilant* or *melancholy*? Why?

The format below is a minor variation of the ones above. However, the wording may be helpful when developing activities for some words.

- Which would be something to *resist*:
  - Talking to a stranger or helping a companion? Why?
  - Laughing at someone's joke or laughing at someone's mistake? Why?

Variation 5

Here is a final variation on the example/non-example activity that is useful for drawing attention to the distinguishing features of words that may get confused with each other:

- If you had a very special photograph of a friend who had moved away, would you refer to it as a *memento* or a *talisman*? Why?
- If you had a special keychain, a kind of lucky charm, would you refer to it as a *memento* or as a *talisman*? Why?

WORD ASSOCIATIONS

Word association is another type of activity that gives students something to respond to by relating what is presented with one of the target words. Such activities provide another opportunity for students to make connections between new words and people, happenings, and other things familiar to them. The kind of word association we use differs from the traditional method in which students associate a target word with a definition or synonym. Rather, we up the ante a bit by asking students to associate words with a conversational expression. This method is more challenging because it does not ask for such a direct association as a definition, but requires some interpretation.

Variation 1

With the words *tedious, extravagant,* and *pretentious,* you might ask which of the following comments goes with a target word:

- I spent all my allowance for 6 months on that video.
- I just can't face another minute of this!
- You're so lucky that I am part of your team.

Variation 2

Ask students to come up with an association—it can be a person, a movie, a common experience—to target words, and then explain the connection they see. This activity, as is the case for most of our examples, is meant to be done under teacher guidance. This is especially important in the earlier grades as the teacher can help students express their reasons for the association.

Word	Associations	Reasons/explanation
eloquent	President Kennedy	Kennedy was an excellent speaker. People still talk about his speeches.
pervasive	Computer viruses	Viruses seem to be all over the place and you always have to be on the watch for them.
fidelity	Having the same best friend all your life	You are always faithful to that person.

Variation 3

In this variation—idea substitution—students hear a sentence that has something to do with one of their words, and then indicate which word. They then revise the sentence in a way that includes the word.

- I didn't want to answer his questions so I pretended I didn't hear him. Which new word goes with that sentence? (*evade*) I didn't want to answer his questions so I *evaded* him.
- Milk is something that babies have to have. (*necessity*) Milk is a *necessity* for babies.
- My mother said I had really worked hard when I cleaned the whole house. Which new word goes with that sentence? (*industrious*) My mother said that I was *industrious* when I cleaned the whole house.

GENERATING SITUATIONS, CONTEXTS, AND EXAMPLES

In this next set of activities students are not provided with choices as in the example/non-example and the simple word association activities described above. Rather, students are asked to generate appropriate contexts or situations for statements or questions about their words. Generating language may prompt more elaborated thinking.

Variation 1

The following questions constrain the request for a situation within a specific context: the classroom. In other words, it holds the situation constant and challenges students to find ways to apply different target words to it.

- What would make a teacher say this to the class?:
- What an *industrious* class you are!
- What a *clever* class you are!
- What a *splendid* class you are!
- What a *versatile* class you are!

Variation 2

The questions below require developing situations across various contexts:

- What might a *clever* dog learn to do when its owner comes home?
- What would a *splendid* day for ducks look like?
- Why is eating leftovers a *frugal* thing to do?
- Why might you *examine* an apple you found on the street?

Variation 3

In the following format, we ask students to develop comments that people might make that are associated with target words:

- What might an audience say about a *splendid* musician?
- What might a generous person say to a *miser*?
- What might someone who is *exuberant* say about your new bike?
- What might someone who is *frugal* say when looking at the price tag on a coat?

Variation 4

Variations within this format are good for small-group collaborative work. For example, you might divide the class into four groups and have each group respond to the different portions of the following:

How might a . . . cook . . . a musician . . . a basketball player . . . a teacher show they are:

- *Versatile?*
- *Industrious?*
- *Clever?*
- *Expert?*

Variation 5

Another small-group activity might ask for different groups to develop descriptions of:

- Three things that would be *catastrophic*.
- Three things that would be *preposterous*.
- Three ways that a gymnast is *flexible*.
- Three things a *philanthropist* might do.

Of course, an important part of these activities is discussing the different groups' responses together. You might encourage more creative responses by telling students that they will get points for ideas that are different from another group's.

WORD RELATIONSHIPS

Having students think about and respond to how two words might be related is a strong activity for developing rich word knowledge. Working with two words and how their meanings and features might interact prompts students to explore novel contexts for the words and build new connections. These activities are pretty wide open—you simply need to give the students a pair of words and see what happens! Some possibilities follow:

Variation 1

Ask students to describe how two vocabulary words might be connected or related. For example:

- *Conscientious/haphazard*—A response might be something like "Someone who is *conscientious* would not do things in a *haphazard* way."
- *Compassionate/advocate*—A *compassionate* lawyer might act as an *advocate* for someone who is in need and otherwise could not afford a lawyer.

Variation 2

The activity above can be given more structure by phrasing a question around two words and asking students to respond and then explain their answers. For example:

- Do people with *prestige prosper?*
- What might a *meticulous* person be *vulnerable* to?
- Could someone who is *curious* be a *nuisance?*

Variation 3

Analogies are another form of word relationship. You can develop some, leaving one part for students to fill in. Eventually students can be asked to construct their own—either complete or with a part missing for other students to complete. Here are some examples:

- A *determined* person is someone who is really set on getting something done, while a person who is *wavering* is . . .
- You could describe someone as *morose* who always saw the bad side of things. On the other hand, you could describe someone as *jovial* if . . .

Variation 4

Another way to prompt students to think about relationships between words is to ask them to sort words. Here's where a vocabulary log will come in handy. After students have been introduced to a number of words, encourage them to sort the words into various categories—any categories you can think of will do. The resulting lists could then be used as references when students are writing.

For example, students might group words as follows:

Words that describe people	Words that describe places
determined	*tranquil*
charming	*eerie*
impatient	*monotonous*
meek	*rustic*
eminent	*exotic*

Variation 5

Continuums and other formats for expressing amount or degree are other forms of word relationships. One of our favorites is the word line—because it can be used with any handful of words, and the end points of the continuum can be anything at all!

Ask students to place phrases (by number) on a word line that represents a continuum and to explain their placement. For example:

How surprised would you be if:

- An extremely *fragile* plant survived in an arctic region?
- An *enthusiastic* teacher came to school dressed in a pirate costume?
- A *determined* student gets an excellent grade?

Least surprised ————————————————— Most surprised

The word line format allows you to be as creative as you like! Here is a silly one:

I can handle it ————————————————— Can't handle it!

1. Having to *evade* someone you dislike every day.
2. Everyone in the class thinks your outfit is *appalling*.
3. Being *vulnerable* to a stomach flu.
4. Your best friend is suddenly *reluctant* to talk to you.

Here are just a few word line extremes we have seen teachers use:

pleasing ————————————————— disgusting

easy ————————————————————— hard

calm ————————————————————— scary

lame ————————————————————— cool

There are other simple formats for having students respond about extent or degree of something about their words. For example:

- Clap to show how much (not at all, a little bit, a lot) you would like:
  o To have your project described by the word *preposterous*.
  o Working in a *chaotic* atmosphere to complete your big test.
  o Having your room described as *eerie*.

WRITING

As students move beyond the early primary grades, a goal of a vocabulary program will surely include having them use their words in writing. The following examples are formats that can be used to encourage thoughtful responses and uses of the words as students write.

Variation 1

Provide students with sentence stems, such as the ones below, and ask them to complete them. The value of this format is that students can't just write the obvious ("The King was miserable") from which no one can tell whether a student understands the word. The *because* requires students to explain "Why?":

- The King was *miserable* because . . .
- The Queen was *calm* because . . .
- The child was *perplexed* because . . .

There are many ways that this activity can be implemented in the classroom. For starters, students could complete the sentences individually or in collaborative pairs or groups. Another possibility is assigning several words to groups of students and have them create stems. They then switch papers with another group and complete the stems of their peers.

Variation 2

More extended writing can be generated by formats such as:

- Think of a time when you felt either *diligent, envious*, or *placid*. Write a little bit about what made you feel that way.
- Think of when you might need to *investigate, cooperate*, or be *impressive*. Write a paragraph to tell about it.
- Think of someone you could describe as one of the following: *precocious, meticulous*, or *tenacious*. Tell what that person is like.

Variation 3

You can prompt students to use several of their words in a writing assignment by providing an interesting premise and asking them to use three, four, or five of their vocabulary words in the story. Some of our favorites:

- Going to the mall and all the lights go out.
- Arriving in a new city and people think you are a celebrity.
- Finding a puppy with a bag of money tied around its neck at your door.

RETURNING TO THE STORY CONTEXT

Having students return to the original context in which they met the vocabulary words, the story, is a powerful way to reinforce the connection between understanding vocabulary and understanding story ideas. For example, below are two questions about *The Watsons Go to Birmingham—1963* (Curtis, 1995).

1. When Kenny came to read in Mr. Alums's room, Mr. Alums said to Byron: "If, instead of trying to *intimidate* your young brother, you would *emulate* him and try to use that mind of yours, perhaps you'd find things much easier" (p. 24). What did he mean?
   - Find examples of *intimidation* throughout the novel.
   - Find examples of people that Kenny and Byron try to *emulate*.
2. In his epilogue, Christopher Paul Curtis wrote: "In the Northern, Eastern, and Western states, African Americans often faced *discrimination*, but it was not as extreme and *pervasive* as in the South" (p. 207). What did he mean?
   - Find examples of *discrimination* mentioned in the novel.

PUZZLES

Variation 1

Students always seem to enjoy puzzles that lead them through clues to an answer.

- Provide a series of clues for a vocabulary word. Each clue should narrow the range of possible responses. For example, the following sets of clues lead to the words *spectator, reliable,* and *relinquish.*
1. A lot of people would not actually see this person.
2. It's someone who just watches.
3. The word has nine letters and starts with an *s*_____.

1. Babysitters need to be _____.
2. You can count on people who are _____.
3. The word has eight letters and starts with an *r*_____.

1. It is hard for dogs to do this with a delicious bone.
2. This word means to "give something up."
3. This word has 10 letters and starts with an *r*_____.

Variation 2

When students have some experience with this format, they can create the series of clues.

- Teachers seem to be partial to crossword puzzles, but comment that they take a great deal of time to develop. The website below provides a crossword puzzle generator. Older students can generate them too. In fact, that may be more valuable than completing a puzzle. Provide students with a list of words and after they develop a puzzle, have them exchange it with a partner, so that each student completes a puzzle. *www.edhelper.com/crossword.htm*

References

Adams, M. J. (2009). The challenge of advanced tests: The interdependence of reading and learning. In E. H. Hiebert (Ed.), *Reading more, reading better?* (pp. 163–189). New York: Guilford Press.

Ames, W. S. (1966–1967). The development of a classification scheme of contextual aids. *Reading Research Quarterly, 2,* 57–62.

Anderson, R. C., & Pearson, P. D. (1984). A schema-theoretic view of basic processes in reading comprehension. In P. D. Pearson, R. Barr, M. L. Kamil, & P. Mosenthal (Eds.), *Handbook of reading research* (pp. 255–291). New York: Longman.

Anderson, R. C., Wilson, P. T., & Fielding, L. G. (1988). Growth in reading and how children spend their time outside of school. *Reading Research Quarterly, 23,* 285–303.

Applebee, A. N. (1982). Writing and learning in school settings. In M. Nystrand (Ed.), *What writers know: The language, process, and structure of written discourse* (pp. 365–382). New York: Academic Press.

Artley, A. S. (1943). Teaching word-meaning through context. *Elementary English Review, 20,* 68–74.

August, D., Branum-Martin, L., Cardenas-Hagan, E., & Francis, D. J. (2009). The impact of an instructional intervention on the science and language learning of middle grade English language learners. *Journal of Research on Educational Effectiveness, 2*(4), 345–376.

August, D., & Shanahan, T. (2006). *Developing literacy in second-language learners: Report of the National Literacy Panel on Language-Minority Children and Youth.* New York: Routledge.

Baker, S. K., Simmons, D. C., & Kame'enui, E. J. (1998). Vocabulary acquisition: Research bases. In D. C. Simmons & E. J. Kame'enui (Eds.), *What reading research tells us about children with diverse learning needs: Bases and basics* (pp. 183–217). Mahwah, NJ: Erlbaum.

Batalova, J., Fix M., & Murray, J. (2007). *Measures of change: The demography and literacy of adolescent English learners—A report to Carnegie Corporation of New York.* Washington, DC: Migration Policy Institute.

Beck, I. L., & McKeown, M. G. (2001). Text Talk: Capturing the benefits of read-aloud experiences for young children. *The Reading Teacher, 55*(1), 10–20.

Beck, I. L., & McKeown, M. G. (2004). *Elements of reading: Vocabulary* (Vocabulary supplemental program for kindergarten through grade 5). Austin, TX: Harcourt Achieve.

Beck, I. L., & McKeown, M. G. (2007a). Different ways for different goals, but keep your eye on the higher verbal goals. In R. K. Wagner, A. E. Muse, & K. R. Tannenbaum (Eds.), *Vocabulary acquisition: Implications for reading comprehension* (pp. 182–204). New York: Guilford Press.

Beck, I. L., & McKeown, M. G. (2007b). Increasing young low-income children's oral vocabulary repertoires through rich and focused instruction. *Elementary School Journal, 107*(3), 251–271.

Beck I. L., McKeown, M. G., & Kucan, L. (2002). *Bringing words to life: Robust vocabulary instruction.* New York: Guilford Press.

Beck I. L., McKeown, M. G., & Kucan, L. (2008). *Creating robust vocabulary: Frequently asked questions and extended examples.* New York: Guilford Press.

Beck, I. L., McKeown, M. G., & McCaslin, E. S. (1983). Vocabulary contexts development: All contexts are not created equal. *Elementary School Journal, 83*(3), 177–181.

Beck, I. L., McKeown, M. G., & Omanson, R. C. (1987). The effects and uses of diverse vocabulary instructional techniques. In M. G. McKeown & M. E. Curtis (Eds.), *The nature of vocabulary acquisition* (pp. 147–163). Hillsdale, NJ: Erlbaum.

Beck, I. L., Perfetti, C. A., & McKeown, M. G. (1982). Effects of long-term vocabulary instruction on lexical access and reading comprehension. *Journal of Educational Psychology, 74*(4), 506–521.

Biemiller, A. (2001). Teaching vocabulary: Early, direct, and sequential. *American Educator, 25,* 24–28.

Biemiller, A. (2005). Size and sequence in vocabulary development: Implications for choosing words for primary grade vocabulary instruction. In A. Hiebert & M. Kamil (Eds.), *Teaching and learning vocabulary: Bringing research to practice* (pp. 223–242). Mahwah, NJ: Erlbaum.

Biemiller, A., & Boote, C. (2005). *Selecting useful word meanings for instruction in the primary grades.* Paper presented at the annual meeting of the American Educational Research Association, Montreal.

Biemiller, A., & Slonim, N. (2001). Estimating root word vocabulary growth in normative and advantaged populations: Evidence for a common sequence of vocabulary acquisition. *Journal of Educational Psychology, 93,* 498–520.

Blachowicz, C. L. Z., & Fisher, P. J. (2006). *Teaching vocabulary in all classrooms.* Upper Saddle River, NJ: Pearson Education.

Blachowicz, C. L. Z., Fisher, P. J. L., Ogle, D., & Watts-Taffe, S. (2006). Vocabulary: Questions from the classroom. *Reading Research Quarterly, 41*(4), 524–539.

Bowers, P. N., Kirby, J. R., & Deacon, S. H. (2010). The effects of morphological instruction on literacy skills: A systematic review of the literature. *Review of Educational Research, 80*(2), 144–179.

Bransford, J. D., & McCarrell, N. S. (1974). A sketch of a cognitive approach to comprehension. In W. Weimer & D. Palermo (Eds.), *Cognition and the symbolic processes* (pp. 189–229). Hillsdale, NJ: Erlbaum.

Bronte, E. (1961). *Wuthering heights.* New York: Scholastic. (Original work published 1847)

Brown, M. (1987). *Play rhymes.* New York: Penguin Putnam.

Brown, M. (1988). *Party rhymes.* New York: Dutton.

Brown, M. (1993). *Hand rhymes.* New York: Penguin Putnam.

Brown, M. (1996). *Finger rhymes.* New York: Penguin Putnam.

Carlo, M. S., August, D., McLaughlin, B., Snow, C. E., Dressler, C., Lippman, D. N., et al. (2004). Closing the gap: Addressing the vocabulary needs of English-language learners in bilingual and mainstream classrooms. *Reading Research Quarterly, 39*(2), 188–215.

Carroll, J. B., Davies, P., & Richman, B. (1971). *Word frequency book.* New York: American Heritage.

Christie, A. (1934). In a glass darkly. In L. Mountain, S. Crawley, & E. Fry (Eds.), *Jamestown Heritage Readers, Book H* (pp. 160–167). Providence, RI: Jamestown.

Cleary, B. (1999). *A mink, a fink, a skating rink: What is a noun?* Minneapolis, MN: Carolrhoda Books.

Cleary, B. (2000). *Hairy, scary, ordinary: What is an adjective?* Minneapolis, MN: Carolrhoda Books.

Cleary, B. (2001). *To root, to toot, to parachute: What is a verb?* Minneapolis, MN: Carolrhoda Books.

Cleary, B. (2002). *Under, over, by the clover: What is a preposition?* Minneapolis, MN: Carolrhoda Books.

Cleary, B. (2003). *Dearly, nearly, insincerely: What is an adverb?* Minneapolis, MN: Carolrhoda Books.

Cole, J., & Calmenson, S. (1990). *Miss Mary Mack and other children's street rhymes.* New York: Morrow.

Collins, M. F. (2009). ELL preschoolers' English vocabulary acquisition from storybook reading. *Early Childhood Research Quarterly, 25*(1), 84–97.

Corson, D. J. (1985). *The lexical bar.* Oxford, UK: Pergamon Press.

Corson, D. J. (1995). *Using English words.* Dordrecht, Netherlands: Kluwer Academic Publishers.

Coxhead, A. (1998). *An academic word list* (Occasional Publication No. 18). Wellington, New Zealand: School of Linguistics and Applied Language Studies, Victoria University of Wellington.

Coxhead, A. (2000). A new academic word list. *TESOL Quarterly, 34*(2), 213–238.

Coyne, M. D., Capozzoli, A., Ware, S., & Loftus, S. (2010, spring). Beyond RTI for decoding: Supporting early vocabulary development within a multitier approach to instruction and intervention. *Perspectives on Language and Literacy,* 18–21.

Coyne, M. D., McCoach, D. B., Loftus, S., Zipoli, R., Jr., & Kapp, S. (2009). Direct vocabulary instruction in kindergarten: Teaching for breadth versus depth. *Elementary School Journal, 110*(1), 1–18.

Coyne, M. D., McCoach, D. B., Loftus, S., Zipoli, R., Jr., Ruby, M., Crevecoeur, Y., et al. (2010). Direct and extended vocabulary instruction in kindergarten: Investigating transfer effects. *Journal of Research on Educational Effectiveness, 3*(2), 93–120.

Coyne, M. D., Simmons, D. C., Kame'enui, E. J., & Stoolmiller, M. (2004). Teaching vocabulary during shared storybook readings: An examination of differential effects. *Exceptionality, 12*(3), 145–162.

Culham, R. (2003). *6 + 1 traits of writing.* New York: Scholastic.

Cummins, J. (1994). The acquisition of English as a second language. In K. Spangenberg-Urbschat & R. Pritchard (Eds.), *Kids come in all languages: Reading instruction for ESL students* (pp. 36–62). Newark, DE: International Reading Association.

Cunningham, A. E., & Stanovich, K. E. (1997). Early reading acquisition and its relation to reading experience and ability 10 years later. *Developmental Psychology, 33*(6), 934–945.

Cunningham, A. E., & Stanovich, K. E. (1998). What reading does for the mind. *American Educator, 22*(1–2), 8–15.

Curtis, C. P. (1995). *The Watsons go to Birmingham—1963*. New York: Bantam Doubleday Dell.

Curtis, M. E. (1981). *Word knowledge and verbal aptitude*. Unpublished manuscript.

Curtis, M. E. (1987). Vocabulary testing and instruction. In M. G. McKeown & M. E. Curtis (Eds.), *The nature of vocabulary acquisition* (pp. 37–51). Hillsdale, NJ: Erlbaum.

Curtis, M. E., & Glaser, R. (1983). Reading theory and the assessment of reading achievement. *Journal of Educational Measurement, 20*, 133–147.

Cushman, K. (1994). *Catherine, called Birdy*. New York: HarperTrophy.

Dale, E. (1965). Vocabulary measurement: Techniques and major findings. *Elementary English, 42*, 895–901.

Dale, E., & O'Rourke, J. (1979). *Living word vocabulary*. Boston: Houghton Mifflin.

Davies, M. Corpus of Contemporary American English [Online database]. Retrieved from *http://corpus.byu.edu/coca* or *www.americancorpus.org*.

Delacroix, L., et al. (Eds.). (2007). *Longman advanced American dictionary* (2nd ed.). Edinburgh, UK: Pearson Education.

Duin, A. H., & Graves, M. F. (1987). Intensive vocabulary instruction as a prewriting technique. *Reading Research Quarterly, 22*, 311–330.

Dunn, L. M., & Dunn, D. M. (2007). *Peabody Picture Vocabulary Test—Fourth Edition*. Minneapolis, MN: NCS Pearson.

Dutro, S., & Moran, C. (2003). Rethinking English language instruction: An architectural approach. In G. Garcia (Ed.), *English learners: Reaching the highest level of English literacy* (pp. 227–258). Newark, DE: International Reading Association.

Edwards, A. (2001). My father, the entomologist. *Cricket, 28*(10), 5–9.

Egan, T. (1995). *Chestnut cove*. Boston: Houghton Mifflin.

Farr, R. C., Strickland, D. S., Beck, I. L., Abrahamson, R. F., Ada, A. F., Cullinan, B. E., et al. (2000). *Collections*. Orlando, FL: Harcourt.

Fitzgerald, J., & Shanahan, T. (2000). Reading and writing relations and their development. *Educational Psychologist, 35*(1), 39–50.

Fleischman, P. (1980). *Half-a-Moon Inn*. New York: HarperCollins.

Fleischman, P. (1988). Fireflies. In *Joyful noise: Poems for two voices*. New York: Harper-Trophy.

Fleischman, P. (2004). *Joyful noise: Poems for two voices*. New York: HarperCollins.

Flournoy, V. (1985). *The patchwork quilt*. New York: Dial Books.

Flower, L., & Hayes. J. R. (1981). A cognitive process theory of writing. *College Composition and Communication, 32*(4), 365–387.

Frank, A. (1993). *Anne Frank: The diary of a young girl*. New York: Bantam Books.

Freeman, D. (1978). *A pocket for Corduroy*. New York: Puffin Books.

Gantos, J. (2011). *Dead end in Norvelt*. New York: Farrar, Straus & Giroux.

Gardner, H. (1985). *The mind's new science: A history of the cognitive revolution*. New York: Basic Books.

Garg, A. (2011). A word a day. Available: *http://wordsmith.org*.

Goerss, B. L., Beck, I. L., & McKeown, M. G. (1999). Increasing remedial students' ability to derive word meaning from context. *Reading Psychology, 20*(2), 151–175.

Goodell, J. (2006). Cooking the climate with coal. *Natural History, 115*(4), 36–41.

Graham, J. B. (1999). *Flicker flash*. New York: Houghton Mifflin.

Graves, M. F., Brunetti, G. J., & Slater, W. H. (1982). The reading vocabularies of primary-grade children of varying geographic and social backgrounds. In J. A. Harris & L. A. Harris (Eds.), *New inquiries in reading research and instruction* (pp. 99–104). Rochester, NY: National Reading Conference.

Graves, M. F., & Slater, W. H. (1987). *The development of reading vocabularies in rural disadvantaged students, inner-city disadvantaged students, and middle-class suburban students.* Paper presented at the annual meeting of the American Educational Research Association, Washington, DC.

Hanks, P. (1987). Definitions and explanations. In J. M. Sinclair (Ed.), *Looking up* (pp. 116–136). London: Collins.

Hart, B., & Risley, T. (1995). *Meaningful differences.* Baltimore: Brookes.

Hayes, D. P., & Ahrens, M. (1988). Vocabulary simplification for children: A special case of "motherese." *Journal of Child Language, 15,* 395–410.

Heller, R. (1987). *A cache of jewels and other collective nouns.* New York: Putnam.

Heller, R. (1988). *Kites sail high: A book about verbs.* New York: Putnam.

Heller, R. (1989). *Many luscious lollipops: A book about adjectives.* New York: Putnam.

Heller, R. (1990). *Merry-go-round: A book about nouns.* New York: Putnam.

Heller, R. (1991). *Up, up and away: A book about adverbs.* New York: Putnam.

Heller, R. (1995). *Behind the mask: A book about prepositions.* New York: Putnam.

Heller, R. (1997). *Mine, all mine: A book about pronouns.* New York: Putnam.

Heller, R. (1998). *Fantastic! wow! and unreal! A book about interjections and conjunctions.* New York: Putnam.

Henry, S., Scott, J., Wells, J., Skobel, B., Jones, A., Cross, S., et al. (1999). Linking university and teacher communities: A "think tank" model of professional development. *Teacher Education and Special Education, 22*(4), 251–267.

Hiebert, E. H. (2005). In pursuit of an effective, efficient vocabulary curriculum for elementary students. In E. H. Hiebert & M. L. Kamil (Eds.), *Teaching and learning vocabulary* (pp. 243–263). Mahwah, NJ: Erlbaum.

Hillocks, G., Jr. (1986a). *Research on written composition.* Urbana, IL: National Council of Teachers of English.

Hillocks, G., Jr. (1986b). The writer's knowledge: Theory, research, and implications for practice. In A. Petrosky & D. Bartholomae (Eds.), *The teaching of writing: 85th yearbook of the National Society for the Study of Education* (pp. 71–95). Chicago: National Society for the Study of Education.

Individuals with Disabilities Education Improvement Act of 2004, 20 U.S.C. § 614 *et seq.*

Janeczko, P. B. (2001). *A poke in the I: A collection of concrete poems.* Cambridge, MA: Candlewick Press.

Jenkins, J. R., Pany, D., & Schreck, J. (1978). *Vocabulary and reading comprehension: Instructional effects* (Tech. Rep. No. 100). Urbana: University of Illinois, Center for the Study of Reading. (ERIC Document Reproduction Service No. ED160999)

Johnson, S., & Walker, J. (1828). *A dictionary of the English language.* London: William Pickering Chancery Lane; George Cowie & Co. Poultry Lane.

Juel, C., Biancarosa, G., Coker, D., & Deffes, R. (2003). Walking with Rosie: A cautionary tale of early reading instruction. *Educational Leadership, 60*(7), 12–18.

Kame'enui, E. J., Carnine, D. W., & Freschi, R. (1982). Effects of text construction and instructional procedures for teaching word meanings on comprehension and recall. *Reading Research Quarterly, 17*(3), 367–388.

Kame'enui, E. J., Dixon, D. W., & Carnine, R. C. (1987). Issues in the design of vocabulary instruction. In M. G. McKeown & M. E. Curtis (Eds.), *The nature of vocabulary acquisition* (pp. 129–145). Hillsdale, NJ: Erlbaum.

Kapelner, A. Dictionary squared: Learn more better [Online database]. Retrieved from *www.dictionarysquared.com.*

Kasza, K. (1987). *The wolf's chicken stew.* New York: Putnam & Grosset.

Kieffer, M. J. (2008). Catching poverty up or falling behind?: Initial English proficiency, concentrated poverty, and the reading growth of language minority learners in the United States. *Journal of Educational Psychology, 100*(4), 851–868.

Kieffer, M. J., & Lesaux, N. K. (2012). Effects of academic language on relational and syntactic aspects of morphological awareness for sixth graders from linguistically diverse backgrounds. *Elementary School Journal, 112*(3), 519–545.

Kindler, A. (2002). *Survey of the states' limited English proficient students and available educational programs and services: 2000–2001 summary report.* Washington, DC: National Clearinghouse for English Language Acquisition.

Kohnke, J. M. (2001). The pooka of allihies. *Cricket, 28*(7), 12–16.

Kowal, M., & Swain, M. (1994). Using collaborative language production tasks to promote students' language awareness. *Language Awareness, 3*, 73–93.

Kucan, L. (2012). What is most important to know about vocabulary? *The Reading Teacher, 65*(6), 360–366.

Landau, S. I. (1984). *Dictionaries: The art and craft of lexicography.* New York: Scribner.

Lesaux, N. K., Kieffer, M. J., Faller, E., & Kelley, J. (2010). The effectiveness and ease of implementation of an academic vocabulary intervention for linguistically diverse students in urban middle schools. *Reading Research Quarterly, 45*, 198–230.

Lewis, J. P. (1998). *Doodle dandies: Poems that take shape.* New York: Aladdin.

Lubliner, S., & Hiebert, E. (2011). An analysis of English–Spanish cognates as a source of general academic language. *Bilingual Research Journal, 34*, 76–93.

MacDonald, A. (1999). *Beware of the bears.* Waukesha, WI: Little Tiger Press.

Marulis, L. M., & Neuman, S. B. (2010). The effects of vocabulary intervention on young children's word learning: A meta-analysis. *Review of Educational Research, 80*(3), 300–335.

McCullough, C. (1943). Learning to use context clues. *Elementary English Review, 20*, 140–143.

McCullough, C. M. (1958). Context aids in reading. *The Reading Teacher, 11*, 224–229.

McKean, E. Wordnik [Online database]. Retrieved from *www.wordnik.com.*

McKeown, M. G. (1985). The acquisition of word meaning from context by children of high and low ability. *Reading Research Quarterly, 20*(4), 482–496.

McKeown, M. G. (1991). Learning word meanings from definitions: Problems and potential. In P. Schwanenflugel (Ed.), *The psychology of word meanings* (pp. 137–156). Hillsdale, NJ: Erlbaum.

McKeown, M. G. (1993). Creating effective definitions for young word learners. *Reading Research Quarterly, 28*, 16–31.

McKeown, M. G., & Beck, I. L. (2012). *Effects of vocabulary instruction on measures of language processing.* Manuscript under review.

McKeown, M. G., Beck, I. L., Omanson, R. C., & Perfetti, C. A. (1983). The effects of long-term vocabulary instruction on reading comprehension: A replication. *Journal of Reading Behavior, 15*(1), 3–18.

McKeown, M. G., Beck, I. L., Omanson, R. C., & Pople, M. T. (1985). Some effects of the nature and frequency of vocabulary instruction on the knowledge and use of words. *Reading Research Quarterly, 20*(5), 522–535.

McKeown, M. G., Beck, I. L., Sinatra, G. M., & Loxterman, J. A. (1992). The contribution of prior knowledge and coherent text to comprehension. *Reading Research Quarterly, 27*, 79–93.

Mezynski, K. (1983). Issues concerning the acquisition of knowledge: Effects of vocabulary training on reading comprehension. *Review of Educational Research, 53*(2), 253–279.

Miller, G. A. (1978). Semantic relations among words. In M. Halle, J. Bresnan, & G. A.

Miller (Eds.), *Linguistic theory and psychological reality* (pp. 61–118). Cambridge, MA: MIT Press.

Miller, G. A. (2003). The cognitive revolution: A historical perspective. *Trends in Cognitive Sciences 7*(3), 141–144.

Miller, G. A., & Gildea, P. M. (1985). How to misread a dictionary. *AILA Bulletin,* pp. 13–26.

Milnes, G. (1990). *Granny will your dog bite and other mountain rhymes.* New York: Knopf.

Moore, I. (1991). *Six-dinner Sid.* New York: Aladdin Paperbacks.

Nagy, W. E., & Anderson, R. C. (1984). How many words are there in printed school English? *Reading Research Quarterly, 19,* 304–330.

Nagy, W. E., & Herman, P. A. (1985). Learning words from context. *Reading Research Quarterly, 20*(2), 233–253.

Nagy, W. E., Herman, P. A., & Anderson, R. (1985). Learning words from context. *Reading Research Quarterly, 20,* 233–253.

Nagy, W. E., & Hiebert, E. (2011). Toward a theory of word selection. In M. L. Kamil, P. D. Pearson, E. B. Moje, & P. P. Afflerbach (Eds.), *Handbook of reading research* (Vol. IV, pp. 388–404). New York: Routledge.

Nagy, W. E., & Scott, J. A. (2000). Vocabulary processes. In M. L. Kamil, P. B. Mosenthal, P. D. Pearson, & R. Barr (Eds.), *Handbook of reading research* (Vol. III, pp. 269–284). Mahwah, NJ: Erlbaum.

Nagy, W. E., & Townsend, D. (2012). Words as tools: Learning academic vocabulary as language acquisition. *Reading Research Quarterly, 47*(1), 91–108.

Nakamoto, J., Lindsey, K. A., & Manis, F. R. (2007). A longitudinal analysis of English language learners' word decoding and reading comprehension. *Reading and Writing: An Interdisciplinary Journal, 20*(7), 691–719.

Nation, I. S. P. (2001). *Learning vocabulary in another language.* Cambridge, UK: Cambridge University Press.

National Governors Association Center for Best Practices, Council of Chief State School Officers. (2010). *Common core state standards.* Washington, DC: Author.

National Reading Panel. (2000). *Teaching children to read: An evidence-based assessment of the scientific literature on reading and its implications for reading instruction* (NIH Publication No. 00-4754). Washington, DC: National Institutes of Health.

Nichols, C. N. (2007). *The effects of three methods of introducing vocabulary to elementary students: Traditional, friendly definitions, and parsing.* Unpublished doctoral dissertation, University of Pittsburgh.

Perfetti, C. A. (2007). Reading ability: Lexical quality to comprehension. *Scientific Studies of Reading, 11*(4), 357–383.

Perfetti, C. A. (2011). Reading processes and reading problems: Progress toward a universal reading science. In P. McCardle, B. Miller, J. R. Lee, & O. J. L. Tzeng (Eds.), *Dyslexia across languages: Orthography and the brain–gene–behavior link* (pp. 18–32). Baltimore: Brookes.

Perfetti, C. A., & Adolf, S. M. (2012). Reading comprehension: A conceptual framework from word meaning to text meaning. In J. P. Sabatini, E. R. Alboro, & T. O'Riley (Eds.), *Measuring up: Advances in how to assess reading ability* (pp. 3–20). Lanham, MD: Rowman & Littlefield.

Petersham, M., & Petersham, M. (1945). *The rooster crows: A book of American rhymes and jingles.* New York: Macmillan.

Proctor, C. P., Dalton, B., Uccelli, P., Biancarosa, G., Mo, E., Snow, C., et al. (2011). Improving comprehension online: Effects of deep vocabulary instruction with bilingual and monolingual fifth graders. *Reading and Writing, 24,* 517–544.

Puhalla, E. M. (2011). Enhancing the vocabulary knowledge of first-grade children with supplemental booster instruction. *Remedial and Special Education, 32*(6), 471–481.

Rankin, E. F., & Overholser, B. M. (1969). Reaction of intermediate-grade children to contextual clues. *Journal of Reading Behavior, 1,* 50–73.

Reichle, E. D., & Perfetti, C. A. (2003). Morphology in word identification: A word-experience model that accounts for morpheme frequency effects. *Scientific Studies of Reading, 7*(1), 219–238.

Rey, H. A. (1998). *Curious George goes to a chocolate factory.* Boston: Houghton Mifflin.

Roediger, H. L., & McDermott, K. B. (2000). Tricks of memory. *Current Directions in Psychological Science, 9,* 123–127.

Sachar, L. (2000). *Holes.* New York: Yearling Books.

samash.com. (2010). Adapted from *Dictionary squared.* Original source: Alfred jazz philharmonic second set. Retrieved November 10, 2010, from *http://dictionarysquared. com/?entry=expose&num_written_contexts_per_page=40.*

Scott, J., & Nagy, W. E. (1989, December). *Fourth graders' knowledge of definitions and how they work.* Paper presented at annual meeting of the National Reading Conference, Austin, TX.

Scott, J., & Nagy, W. E. (2004). Developing word consciousness. In J. F. Baumann & E. J. Kame'euni (Eds.), *Vocabulary instruction: Research to practice* (pp. 201–217). New York: Guilford Press.

Scott, J. A., Jamieson, D., & Asselin, M. (1998). *Learning words: Findings from 69 days in 23 intermediate classrooms.* Paper presented at the annual meeting of the American Educational Research Association, San Diego, CA.

Scott, J. A., Skobel, B. J., & Wells, J. W. (2008). *The word-conscious classroom: Building the vocabulary readers and writers need.* New York: Scholastic.

Scott, J. A., Vevea, J. L., & Flinspach, S. L. (2010). *Vocabulary growth in fourth grade classrooms: A quantitative analysis.* Paper presented at the annual meeting of the National Reading Conference/Literacy Research Association, Fort Worth, TX.

Silverman, R. (2007). A comparison of three methods of vocabulary instruction during read-alouds in kindergarten. *Elementary School Journal, 108,*(2), 97–113.

Sinatra, G. M., Beck, I. L., & McKeown, M. G. (1993). How knowledge influenced two interventions designed to improve comprehension. *Reading Psychology, 14,* 141–163.

Sinclair, J. (Ed.). (1987). *Collins COBUILD English language dictionary.* London: Collins.

Smith, M. K. (1941). Measurement of the size of general English vocabulary through the elementary grades and high school. *Genetic Psychological Monographs, 24,* 311–345.

Snow, C. E., & Kim, Y.-S. (2007). Large problem spaces: The challenge of vocabulary for English language learners. In R. K. Wagner, A. E. Muse, & K. R. Tannenbaum (Eds.), *Vocabulary acquisition: Implications for reading comprehension* (pp. 123–139). New York: Guilford Press.

Snow, C. E., Lawrence, J. F., & White, C. (2009). Generating knowledge of academic language among urban middle school students. *Journal of Research on Educational Effectiveness, 2*(4), 325–344.

Sobolak, M. J. (2008). *Effects of amount of vocabulary instruction for low-socioeconomic students.* Unpublished doctoral dissertation, University of Pittsburgh.

Sobolak, M. J. (2011). Modifying robust vocabulary instruction for the benefit of low-socioeconomic students. *Reading Improvement, 48*(1), 14–23.

Spivey, N. J. (1997). *The constructivist metaphor: Reading, writing, and the making of meaning.* San Diego, CA: Academic Press.

Stahl, S. A., & Fairbanks, M. M. (1986). The effects of vocabulary instruction: A model-based meta-analysis. *Review of Educational Research, 56,* 72–110.

Stahl, S. A., & Nagy, W. E. (2006). *Teaching word meanings.* Mahwah, NJ: Erlbaum.

Steig, W. (1982). *Doctor DeSoto.* New York: Farrar, Straus & Giroux.

Swanborn, M. S. L., & de Glopper, K. (1999). Incidental word learning while reading: A meta-analysis. *Review of Educational Research, 69*(3), 261–285.

Thayer, J. (1953). *The popcorn dragon.* New York: Morrow.

Tierney, R. J., & Pearson, P. D. (1983). Toward a composing model of reading. *Language Arts, 60,* 568–680.

Twain, M. (1881, 1992). *The prince and the pauper.* New York: Penguin.

Van Daalen-Kapteijns, M. M., & Elshout-Mohr, M. (1981). The acquisition of word meanings as a cognitive learning process. *Journal of Verbal Learning and Verbal Behavior, 20,* 386–399.

Vaughn, S., Martinez, L. R., Linan-Thompson, S., Reutebuch, C. K., Carlson, C. D., & Francis, D. J. (2009). Enhancing social studies vocabulary and comprehension for seventh-grade English language learners: Findings from two experimental studies. *Journal of Research on Educational Effectiveness, 2*(4), 297–324.

Verhoeven, L. (2011). Second language reading acquisition. In M. L. Kamil, P. D. Pearson, E. B. Moje, & P. P. Afflerbach (Eds.), *Handbook of reading research* (Vol. IV, pp. 661–683). New York: Routledge.

Walsh, K. (2003). Basal readers: The lost opportunity to build the knowledge that propels comprehension. *American Educator, 21*(1), 24–27.

Watts, S. M. (1995). Vocabulary instruction during reading lessons in six classrooms. *Journal of Reading Behavior, 27,* 399–424.

Werner, H., & Kaplan, E. (1952). The acquisition of word meanings: A developmental study. *Monographs of the Society of Research in Child Development, 15*(1, Serial No. 51).

White, E. B. (1952). *Charlotte's web.* New York: Harper & Row.

Wilbur, R. (2000). *The pig in the spigot.* Orlando, FL: Harcourt.

Withers, C. (1948). *A rocket in my pocket: The rhymes and chants of young Americans.* New York: Holt.

Wolf, M. (2007). *Proust and the squid.* New York: HarperCollins.

Yonek, L. M. (2008). *The effects of rich vocabulary instruction on students' expository writing.* Unpublished doctoral dissertation, University of Pittsburgh.

Zeno, S. M., Ivens, S. H., Millard, R. T., & Duvvuri, R. (1995). *The educator's word frequency guide.* New York: Touchstone Applied Science Associates.

Index

Word use
  in high school instructional sequence,
      100–101
  in later grades, 84
  in middle school instructional sequence,
      97–98
  peers' comments about, 77
  RAVE and, 133
  suggestions for, 76–77
  by young children, 67–69
Word Wizard, 16
  for maintaining new words, 111–113
Words
  academic. *See* Academic words
  affective associations of, 15
  differential attention to, 9. *See also* Three-
      tier framework
  enjoyment of, 14
  exploring, 179–180
  high-frequency, 22
  making connections with meanings, 75–78
  orthographic representation of, 12
  phonological representation of, 12
  related, adding to network of, 76
  semantic representation of, 12
  Tier One, 9–10
  Tier Three, 9–10
  Tier Two, 9–10
  See also New words, maintaining; Tier One
      words; Tier Three words; Tier Two
      words
Writing
  background knowledge and, 140
  behaviorist versus cognitive approach to,
      139–140
  enhancing, through vocabulary instruction,
      141–142
  knowledge types involved in, 140–141
  relationship to reading, 139–141
  vocabulary instruction and, 141–143
  vocabulary instruction for improving, 143
Writing activities, 191–192
Writing instruction, vocabulary approaches to,
      144–151
Writing stems exercise, 91

Written contexts, vocabulary learning from, 5
Written language
  domain knowledge and, 141
  linguistic features of, 140
  metaknowledge about, 140
  procedural knowledge about, 140–141
  semantics and, 141
Wuthering Heights (Bronte)
  high school instructional sequence based
      on, 98–102. *See also* High school,
      instructional sequences for
  and maintenance of new vocabulary, 110

Yes/no activity, for young children, 79
Yes/no test items, 107–108
Yonek study, 144–151
  adaptations of, 151–152
  essay analysis in, 150–151
  Michael's essay in, 149–150
  Rolanda's essay in, 148–149
  students' essays in, 146–148
  word-level assessments and results in,
      145–146
Young children
  assessing, 107–108
  context integration with, 58
  and explanations of chosen word choices, 69
  follow-up activities for, 77–80
  interacting with words, 66–67
      by making choices, 67
      with questions, reasons, examples, 66–67
  introducing words to
      additional formats for, 70–75
      components of, 65–67
      format for, 61–65
  production task with, 58–59
  robust instruction with, 56–59
      versus repetition instruction, 57–58
  speaking versus reading/writing
      competence in, 59–60
  vocabulary activities for, 62–75
  vocabulary development in, 59–61
  vocabulary instruction for, 55–81
  vocabulary use by, 67–69
  word selection for, 36–37